Routledge Revivals

The 1992 Single European Market and the Third World

The 1992 Single European Market and the Third World (1992) looks at the impact of the Project 1992 of integrating the member countries of the European Community (EC) into a Single European Market (SEM) on countries of the developing world.

The 1992 Single European Market and the Third World

Edited by
Sandro Sideri and Jayshree Sengupta

Routledge
Taylor & Francis Group

First published in 1992
by Frank Cass & Co. Ltd.

This edition first published in 2026 by Routledge
4 Park Square, Milton Park, Abingdon, Oxon, OX14 4RN

and by Routledge
605 Third Avenue, New York, NY 10017

Routledge is an imprint of the Taylor & Francis Group, an informa business

Publisher's Note
The publisher has gone to great lengths to ensure the quality of this reprint but points out that some imperfections in the original copies may be apparent.

Disclaimer
The publisher has made every effort to trace copyright holders and welcomes correspondence from those they have been unable to contact.

A Library of Congress record exists under LCCN: 92004902

ISBN: 978-1-041-29299-9 (hbk)
ISBN: 978-1-003-76892-0 (ebk)
ISBN: 978-1-041-29301-9 (pbk)

Book DOI 10.4324/9781003768920

THE 1992 SINGLE EUROPEAN MARKET AND THE THIRD WORLD

edited by

SANDRO SIDERI

and

JAYSHREE SENGUPTA

FRANK CASS · LONDON

Published in collaboration with
The European Association of Development Research and
Training Institutes (EADI), Geneva

First published in Great Britain by
FRANK CASS & Co. LTD.
Gainsborough House, 11 Gainsborough Road
London E11 1RS, England
and in the United States of America by
FRANK CASS
c/o International Specialized Book Service Ltd.
5602 N.E. Hassalo Street
Portland, OR 97213-3640

British Library Cataloguing in Publication Data

1992 Single European Market and the Third
World. – (EADI Book Series; v. 13)
I. Sidero, S. II. Sengupta, Jayshree
III. Series
363.88

ISBN 0-7146-3474-3

Library of Congress Cataloguing-in-Publication Data

The 1992 European single market and the Third World /
edited by Sandro Sideri and Jayshree Sengupta.
p. cm. – (EADI – book series; 13)
'Published in collaboration with the European
Association of Development Research and Training
Institutes (EADI) Geneva.'
ISBN 0-7146-3474-3
1. European Economic Community countries –
Commerce – Developing countries. 2. Developing
countries – Commerce – European Economic
Community countries. 3. Europe 1992. I. Sideri, S.,
1934–. II. Sengupta, Jayshree, 1943–. III. European
Association of Development Research and Training
Institutes. IV. Series.
HF3500.5.Z7D442 1992
382'.09401724 – dc20 92-4902
CIP

Printed in Great Britain by
Antony Rowe Ltd, Chippenham

Contents

List of Tables

LIST OF TABLES

Abbreviations

ACP	African, Caribbean and Pacific (countries)
AD	Anti-Dumping
ASEAN	Association of South-East Asian Nations
CAP	Common Agricultural Policy
cif	Cost, insurance and freight
DC	Developed Country
DFI	Direct Foreign Investment
EC	European Community
ecu	European currency unit
EES	European Economic Space
EFTA	European Free Trade Association
EMS	European Monetary System
Eurostat	Statistical Office of the European Communities
GATT	General Agreement on Tariffs and Trade
GDP	Gross Domestic Product
GSP	Generalised System of Preferences
IMF	International Monetary Fund
LDC	Less Developed Country
MFA	Multifibre Arrangement
MFN	Most Favoured Nation
mn	million
MTN	Multilateral Trade Negotiation
NACE	Nomenclature des Activités dans la CEE
NATO	North Atlantic Treaty Organization
NIC	Newly Industrialising Country
NIMEXE	Nomenclature des marchandises pour les statistique du commerce extériur dela Communauté et du commerce entre ses Etats membres
NGO	Non-Governmental Organisation
NTB	Non-Tariff Barrier
ODA	Official Development Assistance
OECD	Organisation for Economic Co-operation and Development
OPEC	Organisation of the Petroleum Exporting Countries
QR	Quantiative Restriction

SITC	Standard International Trade Classification
STABEX	Stabilisation of Export Earnings Scheme
TNC	Transnational Corporation
UK	United Kingdom
UN	United Nations
UNCTAD	United Nations Conference on Trade and Development
US	United States of America
VER	Voluntary Export Restraint

Introduction

SANDRO SIDERI and JAYSHREE SENGUPTA

The collection of nine papers that this volume presents looks at the impact of the Project 1992 of integrating the member countries of the European Community (EC) into a Single European Market (SEM) on the Third World countries.

Five of the papers included in this volume were originally presented at the Sixth European Association of Development Research and Training Institutes' (EADI) Conference held in Oslo in June 1990 in the Working Group led by Sandro Sideri. To complete the Third World perspective of the impact of the SEM, four other papers have been included to cover the economic relations between the EC and almost the entire developing world. During the lengthy process of having the manuscript properly referred and approved by EADI Publications Committee, three of the five original papers have been revised and updated, with the exception of Sideri's and Page's.

The beginning of the Project 1992 can be traced to the White Paper of 1985 which laid down the framework for the SEM. This will mean eliminating the conventional non-tariff barriers between the members of the EC including public procurement regulations, national standards and indirect taxes, all border controls and restrictions on capital and labour movements within the EC. The European Commission has now completed the task of laying before the Council of Ministers all the directives it deems necessary for the completion of the SEM. Taken in its entirety, Project 1992 goes much further than the individual directives seem to indicate, creating expectations like: 'the new Bretton Woods negotiations are in fact now underway – in Brussels.'[1] There are also the fears that the SEM would prompt the emergence of a powerful economic and political block, which will in turn enhance the prospect for the establishment of a similar one in the Americas and in the Pacific.

The SEM was founded on the hope that there will be a quantum leap in the productivity and improvement in the EC's competitiveness vis-a-vis the rest of the world's exporters. If the EC members are able to achieve such a once and for all increase in productivity as predicted by the Cecchini Report then the EC's GDP will increase between 4.5 to seven per cent. As a result, the trade flows between the EC and the rest of the world will alter through trade creation, trade diversion and terms of trade effects. Thus on the positive side, the SEM could lead to an intensified flow of innovations, new processes, new products and to a higher long-term growth rate. If this were to happen, then both trade creation and diversion would increase and as long as trade creation dominates, developing countries could experience a long-term increase in the growth of their exports.

As expected and feared by the Third World countries, the SEM is going to have diverse effects on its exports and investments. Many of the old trading patterns between the members of the EC and their old colonial territories are going to be replaced by new ones which may involve harmonisation of rules, regulations and technical standards. Wider adoption of technical standards presents difficulties for exporters, but they may gain from the certainty that a product when it is acceptable in one country will also be acceptable within the whole EC.

The change in the European scene since the time the SEM was conceived has been due to the opening up of Eastern Europe and the German unification. How this restructuring process will affect the direct foreign investment (DFI) flows from the SEM into the Third World has been discussed in many of the papers. Much of the monetary burden of restructuring Eastern Europe will fall on the countries involved in the formation of the SEM as they are in the same continent, and the possible gains from a restructured Eastern Europe will be numerous for all of them. Not only will it mean a ready market for EC products but Eastern Europe will offer an important cost advantage through a cheaper yet skilled labour force, for EC's manufacturing units that could be located there.

In the first chapter (which was finalised in May 1990 and presents an overview of the *problematique* or issues faced by the Third World with respect to the Project 1992) Sideri observes that the cost of restructuring Eastern Europe and German unification will be heavy and will add to the other negative effects of the SEM on the Third World. For example, the interest rates are likely to go up and this will add to the burden of servicing the Third World's external debt. There is also likely to be a decline in the DFI and aid financing available to the Third World and their difficulties in servicing their debt will also make them less attractive hosts for DFI. The marginalisation of the Third World would then become more acute.

Sideri also discusses the important issue of services and how this sector will be affected by the SEM. The Third World's services sector is concentrated mainly in tourism, construction, shipping, data processing and computer software and offshore financing, all of which is going to be affected by the SEM. The liberalisation of services which may emerge from the Uruguay Round and increased competition in the services market resulting from Project 1992 could certainly benefit the LDCs including the ACP countries which are net importers of services and would enjoy lower prices. Yet there is some fear that the long-term effects of such a liberalisation as well as Project 1992 will negatively influence the establishment of the services industry in the Third World.

In general, the effects of 1992 on the trading systems of the Third World are going to be different as Page points out in the second chapter, because the SEM will be neither a customs union nor a trading bloc. Exploring on how the SEM has evolved could encourage the world trading system to develop a more transparent and more appropriate means of dealing with a variety of different types of trading units which could promote the strengthening of a multilateral trading system. But she warns against the risk of EC increasing in strength and reinforcing the tendency of becoming a major trading power which could bypass the multilateral organisations.

On the positive side, Mori and Fumagalli observe in the last chapter that European countries in general appear to be more open to the manufactured imports from LDCs than Japan and, until recently, the US. But LDCs' exports to the EC have undergone important changes in the past two decades as primary goods (agricultural goods) lost in importance to manufactures. The composition of manufactured exports from LDCs suggests that their main comparative advantage still lies exclusively in natural resource-intensive and unskilled labour-intensive products.

Mori in chapter four also finds that the impact of Project 1992 may be a positive one on raw materials exports from LDCs. She finds that the main obstacle to increasing processed food exports from the LDCs seem to come from the supply side, since there has been a remarkable increase in competition among the countries within Europe in the agro-sector which has resulted in pushing up the quality and technical standards of the products. She proposes that in order to increase the processed food exports to industrial countries, the LDCs should produce competitively stronger products. The best way for LDCs to gain competitiveness is to increase trading between themselves. They will thereby gain in experience and also improve the quality of exports. Thus, 'first sell lower quality products to other developing countries before moving to higher quality varieties for export to industrialised countries'.

Paramithiotti has discussed the effects of Project 1992 on EC's external relations with LDCs. He acknowledges the importance of the GATT Uruguay Round in forecasting EC's external relations after 1992. According to him the EC may reorient its trade policy in some of the more sensitive sectors and implement a strategic trade policy. In order to do so, the EC has already assigned new roles to the Council of Europe and the European Commission. Project 1992 will strengthen the Commission's role as a regulatory agency for resolving any conflict of interests between broadly defined European agents. The adoption of the new majority mechanism in the Council's voting decisions may favour an upsurge in member state coalition, led by the more industrialised countries of Europe who will try to protect precise economic interests. Thus even though in the past, EC's policy instruments such as the European anti-dumping code was just a defensive one, in the future it may become aggressive, supported by the interests of some sort of European economic coalition (industrialists, workers etc.).

The impact of Project 1992 on DFI flows between the EC and the developing countries with special reference to Latin America, has been discussed by Pio. In the case of Latin America he finds that the interest rates and exchange rate fluctuations in Europe had no significant effects on the DFI flows, while GDP growth in the host countries and the net financial flows into the region exerted positive effects. In the case of Asia, the potential for a more rapid expansion of such flows is linked with the growing process of decentralisation of production in Europe as European firms strive for greater efficiency and cost reduction.

The effects of Project 1992 on Africa's exports have been analysed by Davenport. Project 1992 will expand the EC market for raw materials from Africa though the overall balance between trade creation and diversion seems to be negative for African manufacturers. This need not be the case for every country and individual suppliers may find many opportunities in the SEM. But diversion from primary product exports to simple manufacturing will become more difficult on account of certain specific changes in the SEM; expansion into meat and fish products would be more expensive as tighter control on standards is implemented. The degree of effective protection given to African clothing producers by the MFA for example will also be eroded by the SEM. Thus it will be more difficult for African countries to compete with EC's domestic industries in chemicals, fertilisers and textiles.

In the case of Latin American exports to the EC after 1992, Duran finds that the SEM will not make any dramatic alterations to the already extant trade problems between the EC and most Latin American countries. These include the privileged relations between the EC and the ACP countries, which discriminate against Latin American exports and Common Agricultural Policy with its negative impact on Latin American agricultural trade. She emphasises that an overall successful outcome of the Uruguay Round negotiations would result in tariff reductions and improved trading possibilities which would provide Latin American countries and other LDCs better and more reliable access to the EC after 1992. The beneficial or negative effects of the accelerated process of European integration will, in the end, depend on the ability of the Latin American countries to adapt to the new EC rules.

As for the ASEAN countries, the Project 1992 can bring about an important outlet for their exports and is expected to serve as an alternative to the restricted Japanese market and as a substitute to the slower expansion of exports to the US market. Sengupta analyses the past encouraging trends in trade and investment flows between the EC and the ASEAN though she points out that there has been a qualitative change in ASEAN's exports to the EC with a steady growth in the production of manufactured goods. The ASEAN countries have also followed an opening-up process in recent years through a series of liberalisation and export promotion measures. But access to the EC market has not been smooth. ASEAN countries benefit only from GSP and receive no preferential treatment like the ACP and the Mediterranean countries. Many non-tariff barriers have affected the entry of ASEAN exports in the past and, with the SEM, many new barriers may also have to be encountered. If the EC implements policies promoting European sourcing for its manufactures after 1992, then the export-oriented DFI going to ASEAN could weaken. The transnational corporations would then move plants making components located in the ASEAN for sale in the EC to the less industrialised parts of the EC itself even though the ASEAN may be a more suitable location for such investments.

The last chapter also presents an extensive elaboration of useful statistics relative to the trade flows between the EC countries and those of the Third World.

In this volume we have tried to present a varied and, hopefully, a fresh look at the current situation in the Third World and how they are going to be affected by the SEM. We have not tried to suppress the differences in the various contributions, mainly because common positions are much more pronounced than one would expect in such a volume.

We are thankful to the Institute of Social Studies (The Hague) for supporting this endeavour, particularly to Ms Ank van den Berg and Ms Lijske Schweigman for their valuable assistance, thereby enabling us to complete this volume just before the SEM takes final shape. We hope that it does contribute to the current thinking on the SEM and the Third World.

NOTE

1. L.C. Thurow, 1991, 'Europe Will Write the Rules of Trade', *European Affairs*, Vol.5, No.2 (April/May), p.33.

1

European Integration and the Third World

SANDRO SIDERI

I. INTRODUCTION

Project 1992 aims at removing the last obstacles to the free movement of people, services, goods and capital within the EC, hence constituting a substantial contribution to accelerating the process of European integration. It has captured Europe's imagination and has galvanised economic activities and plans, generating a new 'Europtimism', after the stagnation of the 1970s and early 1980s, rightly labelled as the 'Community's dark age' [*Hoffman, 1989: 29*]. During that period business leaders complained about the 'costs of non-Europe', that is, the negative impact of market segmentation on innovations and demonstrated also by European direct foreign investment (DFI) shifting towards the US.

Therefore, Project 1992 was conceived to recreate the EC's dynamism and to counteract growing foreign, particularly Japanese, competition, in most technologically advanced industries. Together with Project 1992, the ecological movement and *Perestroika*, along with the collapse of the regimes of Eastern Europe (EE), have emerged as powerful forces which are contributing to reshaping the future of the Old Continent. The process resulting from the interactions between these three forces is simultaneously both a source of hope and anxiety, the latter reinforced by the rapidly proceeding German unification.

Even though the German unification seems to have contributed towards an acceleration, in the process of integration of the Community it still remains unclear what are the consequences of the massive transfer of resources required for the restructuring of East European (EE) economies. Such a transfer could easily contribute to increased inflationary pressure within the EC, particularly if it is not accompanied by adequate restrictive policies of public and private expenditures, that is, tightening the fiscal screw. The productive relocation in EE that this intervention implies could also aggravate the unemployment problem within the EC, even though it may at the same time contribute to moderate wage pressure, and thereby partly mitigate the inflationary build-up. These developments seem to have started complicating and modifying the direction of the process of European integration: for the EC the stakes have been raised and the apparently simple choice between 'deepening' and 'widening' has acquired many other dimensions.

Most of the measures which make up Project 1992 should have neutral results for the rest of the world, yet the completion of the single market will not fail to have substantial repercussions on the EC's role and its position within the world economy, thus affecting the development efforts of many Third World (TW) countries. Therefore, when the process of European integration is seen within the wider context of the world economy, it also appears that the latter cannot maintain its equilibrium without tackling the following problems:

(i) the management of international indebtedness, which concerns not only the TW, but also the US;
(ii) the economic growth of the TW, which also implies bravely facing the thorny issue of population growth;
(iii) the improvement of the global environment.

Fortunately, international co-operation, crucial for attempting to cope with these problems, is presently strengthened as a result of the lessening of East–West military tensions. Consequently, so are the conflicts within the TW, with the possible reduction of military expenditures and therefore release of the peace dividend for alternative uses,[1] even though the North's arms suppliers which while facing shrinking domestic markets may be tempted to increase deliveries to the South. Essential to tackling these problems is monetary stability, without which the lowering of East–West tensions and the diminished role of the superpowers, may tend to sharpen and exacerbate economic quarrels, as has been illustrated by the worsening of the US–Japanese commercial relations.

II. RESTRUCTURING OF EE'S ECONOMIES

Together with Project 1992, and often in competition with it, two other broader economic schemes are emerging in Europe: the European Economic Space and the wider pan-European scheme implied in

Gorbachev's Common House. The first involves EC with the six countries grouped in EFTA, the second embraces the whole of Europe.[2]

Jacques Delors, the EC Commission president, has attempted to reconcile these various schemes with his theory of the three concentric circles, with the tightly integrated countries of the EC at the centre. With this interpretation Delors, and others, tend to justify the acceleration of the process of deepening within the EC in order better to control and regulate the process of liberalisation taking place in EE. Therefore, they have resisted the call to submerge the Community – that is, its widening – into a broader, less defined and less controllable pan-integration of the whole continent.

Moreover, while the rapid evolution of events in EE is radically modifying the situation of these countries and, consequently, their relationship with Western Europe, it is also becoming increasingly evident that these countries are characterised by economic and environmental disasters that have been left behind by the previous regimes, with their difficult social and political situations, complicated by ethnic tensions. The dramatic situation of many EE countries is forcing the West to look for the means to guarantee their economic growth – which 'has come to a halt virtually everywhere, and in some cases GNP is shrinking' [*Deutsche Bank, 1990: 11*] – and therefore to smooth their transition from socialism to the market economy.

The OECD has underlined, at the beginning of the year, that the transformation taking place in EE 'will probably be beneficial in the longer run', but it has also added that 'the initial impact on the region's financial position . . . has been mainly negative. In 1989 domestic performance worsened and further weakening seems inevitable before changes in economic structure can produce any tangible improvement.' In fact, the current account balance weakened appreciably, while the rate of growth of the region's external debt, already rising since 1985, has further increased. Therefore, net indebtedness has reached $115 billion in 1989 from $71 billion in 1985 ($82 and $56 billion respectively, without the USSR) while its service absorbs 35 per cent of the region's exports: 46 per cent without the USSR.[3]

The Western response to EE's events has consisted of an emergency programme of $1 billion to which the EC has proposed in January 1990 an additional billion. The EC decided to raise its budget by another $3 billion in order to finance the restructuring of EE until the end of 1993. Furthermore, the European Bank for Reconstruction and Development (EBRD) has been rapidly created with a capital base of $12.5 billion, of which the EC has subscribed 51 per cent.

The cost of the reconstruction of EE's economies and the necessary contribution of the West can only be guessed, but, given the order of magnitude involved, it cannot fail to influence the implementation of Project 1992 and the relationship between Europe and the TW. In any case, proposals are being made on how to convert Project 1992 into a pan-European scheme, which would foster commercial interactions among the 800 million people that populate the Old Continent. Among the various proposals so far voiced, one proposal refers to the utilisation of association agreements that are similar to those offered by the EC to the Mediterranean and a group of African, Caribbean and Pacific (ACP) countries. Commissioner Andriessen has declared that the Community was ready to discharge its responsibility towards the rest of Europe by means of 'a series of very extensive "second-generation" association agreements' which include free-trade areas, economic co-operation, aid and joint programmes in the field of environment, nuclear safety and education.[4] East–West trade will be boosted and it is expected to grow faster than world trade, not only with the EC, but also with EFTA, which is expected to benefit from this trade expansion. The commercial position of these two regions 'could be further improved if Eastern European countries were to apply for associate status or membership in these organisations, followed by the elimination of further barriers to European trade' [*Deutsche Bank, 1990: 70*].

Other proposals have been suggested to the countries of EE, which clearly seem to prefer the EC, to join EFTA, which does not require the partial relinquishing of their national sovereignty.

The fact is, however, that the countries of EE must not only abandon central planning for market economics, but also transform themselves from backward, largely rural, economies into modern and internationally competitive ones. East–West trade is actually equivalent to only 40 per cent of OECD trade with the four newly industrialising countries (NICs) of South–East Asia, while some 40 per cent of the former exports to the West are mainly fuels, with USSR accounting for 80 per cent of the total [*Deutsche Bank, 1990: 66–8*]. The costs therefore are substantial for Western Europe, and have many implications for helping these economies to obtain the technology, the managerial capacity, the organisational expertise and the financial means required for overcoming the structural impediments left by the previous regimes.

Aside from opening the common market to EE's products, with clearly negative consequences for producers within the Community and for others outside the EC, the financial resources required by EE can be grouped in the following categories:

(i) grants or loans directed mainly to the building up of EE's foreign exchange reserves to help in stabilising exchange rates and establishing convertible currencies;
(ii) grants or loans to help finance a social safety net for the region;
(iii) cancellation of most of the EE's debt owed to the West;[5]
(iv) long-term financing of development, particularly for the construction or modernisation of the infrastructure and environmental control (the cost of cleaning up the German Democratic Republic (GDR) alone is estimated at deutschemarks (DM) 2 billion) [*The Economist, 3.3. 1990: 68*];
(v) creation of a revolving fund in order to finance the system of direct compensation needed to facilitate commercial interchange among the economies of EE – that is, a clearing union similar to the European Payments Union which proved crucial in the reconstruction of Western Europe after the Second World War. In this context Czechoslovakia's foreign minister has unveiled in a speech delivered on May 1990 at Harvard University, a plan, according to which developed countries (DC) should advance to the EBRD $16 billion over three years. EBRD would credit it to the USSR which could use it to buy industrial products from Poland, Hungary and Czechoslovakia. In turn the latter countries could utilise their revenues to import from the DCs. Like the Marshall Plan, the USSR would match the dollar credits in roubles, thus creating a fund for financing investment in its industry, under EBRD's coordination. The EC Commission's latest estimates are that, excluding USSR, the countries of EE need, before the end of 1993, 15 to 20 billion ecus in order to finance their trade and investment. The EC is already discussing a plan to help EE's six minor economies to break away from barter-based trading and to start using convertible currencies.

In addition to the resources needed for restructuring the EE's economies, there is also the cost of German unification which has been estimated to be between 500 billion to DM 1.1 trillion [*Newsweek, 26.2.1990: 11*]. Concrete measures already taken by West Germany (FRG) include DM 2 billion which is to be extended to DM 6 billion, for concessionary loans, primarily to small and medium-sized businesses, of which DM 1.3 billion would be for setting up businesses in the GDR, DM 2 billion for capital investment in environmental protection and the same amount for plant modernisation, and DM 0,7 billion for tourism.

A further DM 1,5 billion is needed in guarantees for shipments from FRG to GDR. Another DM 300 million would be for environmental protection; and an increase of DM 100 million from 1990 in the flat-rate postal service payment to DM 300 million a year to help expanding GDR's postal and telecommunications systems [*Deutsche Bank, 1990: 35*]. There is then the problem of income compensation, without which 'the majority of the population could not cope with the increase of prices caused by the ending of subsidies', amounting to about DM 44 billion for retail sales estimated at DM 127 billion in 1988 [*Economic Bulletin, 1990: 2*].

According to Deutsche Bank's estimates, FRG's public funds to be transferred annually to GDR would amount to about DM 30 billion, at least in the initial years, while *The Economist* estimates the gross bill for economic and monetary union at DM 60–70 billion for 1991 [*The Economist, 26.5.1990: 73*] [*IHT, 3.3.1990*].

The latest measure announced by FRG in May 1990 is the establishment of the 'German Unity' fund of DM 115 billion, most of which is to be raised, over a period of four to five years, on the domestic capital market, mainly through various certificates and debentures in order to avoid the Bundesbank's control. The adoption of such a procedure for financing the fund is on account of Chancellor Kohl's insistence on excluding the use of fiscal measures which would force the FRG to consume less so as to enable GDR to consume more.[6]

Having excluded the issuing of national bonds and the fiscal squeeze, the growth of the monetary base must necessarily be accompanied by a tight monetary policy in order to contain, within acceptable limits, the inflationary pressure which is bound to increase. On the whole, higher interest rates must then be expected in Germany which, given the role of the DM within the European Monetary System[7] and the world economy, will in turn necessarily force many other countries to follow suit [also *Economic Bulletin, 1990: 2*]. Rather aptly, a top Kohl adviser has stated that 'there is an inflationary push if we do nothing and let millions of East Germans come here, where they will need housing and social benefits. And there will be inflation if we pay to make life acceptable for them in the East.'[8]

Considering all options, the most optimistic estimate of the overall transfer deemed necessary for the restructuring of EE is at least 0.5 per cent of the GDP of the G-7 countries, namely more than $70 billion annually. For the transfer to take place an equivalent surplus must be effected in their current accounts. The total current account of the G-7 shows instead a $66 billion deficit, therefore, the execution of such a transfer implies a rather substantial turnaround in their performance.

GDR's entry into the EC – as it becomes part of the FRG – has consequences also for the Community's budget; the payments related to the structural funds' contribution on their own could easily reach four billion ecus. One way or another, the recent events have altered profoundly the conditions on which Project 1992 was based, namely a moderate but stable rate of economic growth, low inflation and a stable DM. If one includes the eventual continuous increase in the real price of oil considered to be the likely characteristic by the end of this century by various sources,[9] the framework within which Project 1992 is to be implemented becomes rather different. Furthermore, the restructuring of EE is going to absorb the EC's interest, and a large share of its resources, for many years to come, contributing to the future shaping of the European integration process, however possibly increasing further the marginalisation of many parts of the TW.

Yet, the West's growing involvement in EE goes beyond the question of aid and is related to very strong self-interest, particularly for Western Europe's participation in EE's restructuring, which represents the key to its revival and, possibly, its last chance to regain a more central role within the world economic and political system.

III. PROJECT 1992 AND THE THIRD WORLD

Project 1992

The Single Act of 1986 has accelerated what can rightly be considered the most sophisticated example of regional economic integration, causing a profound reorganisation of the member countries' socio-economic structures and requiring a substantial delegation of power to supra-national or federal institutions.

In assessing the overall impact of this process on the TW, one must examine all the possible effects of various and different policies, most of which have not yet been finalised and/or are emerging from discussions and agreements taking place in separate fora, like the Uruguay Round of GATT, the Lomé Convention, the Generalised System of Preferences (GSP) and the Multifibre Agreement [*Sideri, 1990: Ch. 8*].

Since there are few facts to be considered, tendencies, trends and even perceptions must suffice. There is no doubt that less developed countries (LDC), at least affected by the developments taking place within the international scene, are quite worried. Meanwhile, there seems little interest in Europe about the possible effects of Project 1992 on the TW [*Pinder, 1988: 49*], and even less about the implications of the wider integration which may result from EE's evolution. The EC Commission has not felt the need to prepare a white paper on these issues, a fact which may undermine the often defended view of EC's unique relationship with the TW. It however strengthens the opposite view that ACP countries' position *vis-à-vis* the EC is mainly a form of 'collective clientelism' [*Ravenhill, 1985*].

In any case the EC's external dimension, now made more explicit by the attempt to complete the internal market, revolves around the following issues:

(i) marginalisation of or integration with the outside world, an issue which concerns the TW. This relates to the old dispute of whether the EC should pursue a 'global' or a 'regional' approach, a dispute which in turn relates to the implication of the policies towards the TW;[10]

(ii) the EC's reliance on its greater market or on international trade, or, in classical terms, whether the EC integration will be dominated by

 (a) trade diversion, that is, the shrinking of non-EC producers' export and market shares as a result of both more aggressive competition and lower transaction costs in the integrated EC market; or

 (b) trade creation, that is, the growing demand for non-EC countries' exports as a result of greater efficiency and correspondingly higher real income within the EC. This effect is more likely when the integrating market already absorbs a large proportion of imports, as in the case of the EFTA countries, but hardly any from many LDCs. The so-called 'locomotive function' is attributed to the EC for this trade creating effect *vis-à-vis* the world economy. Yet, one must be cautious with interdependence as it can also facilitate the transfer abroad of the burden of the internal adjustment. The third effect connected with integration is

 (c) the spill-over effect in the home markets of the non-EC countries.

This effect can take two forms:

(1) if EC and non-EC markets are less than perfectly segmented, then increased competition within the EC will reduce profit margins in non-EC markets to the advantage of their domestic consumers, but possibly to the detriment of their capital accumulation;

(2) increased competition in export markets may force non-EC firms to abandon some of their products, which certainly is not a gain for the country concerned [*Norman, 1988: 425–6*]. Although the former effect does not seem very relevant for TW countries, or is certainly difficult to detect, it is the latter one that may apply to some LDCs.

To conclude, the EC's greater internal integration impinges on its external commitments and obligations both multilaterally – GATT's bound tariffs and Uruguay Round – and bilaterally – Lomé, therefore leaving open the question of whether it is 'Fortress Europe' that will emerge or whether it will be the officially proclaimed 'Partnership Europe'.

Macroeconomic Effects

In theory, the overall impact of the EC's further integration on third parties, not to speak of Europe as a whole, results from the sum of the opposite effects due to trade diversion and trade creation. Although it is not clear whether which one of the bilateral protection or import guarantees is going to be replaced at the EC level by similar, higher rather than lower measures, the elimination of internal barriers is bound to redirect trade away from traditional suppliers towards EC members, thus transforming some international into internal trade. This substitution is going to affect TW countries' exports of manufactured goods more than that of raw materials.

The impact resulting from an increase in income and, therefore, of the demand for imports that the integration might generate, is going to be felt, instead, more in LDCs' traditional exports than in their actual or potential exports of manufactures. Actually, the latter will have to compete with EC sources, made cheaper by the integration process, and with EE's production. The combination of these two effects – bearing in mind that trade diversion is considered anyway to be the stronger of the two – may tend to reinforce the TW's traditional division of labour because the EC's import market may shrink, even for the manufactures of many Asian NICs.

Furthermore, while trade creation is associated with an increase in the EC's GDP, trade diversion is much more difficult to identify, for it results mainly from dynamic effects, economies of scale, reduction of X-efficiency, etc. [*Baldwin, 1989*]. Even less easily identifiable is the eventual diversion of DFI to the Southern countries in the EC, and the redistribution of exports within the TW, namely, the substitution of exports of one LDC for another's.

The increase in the cost of the TW's exports to the EC may result, not only from the stronger competition from EC sources which may be located in EE, and eventually sustained by EC's DFI, but also from the need to comply with the EC's norms and standards whose harmonisation will tend to take place at the highest level. Information relative to this harmonisation is not cheap and it adds to the cost of TW exports. This is one area where the EC could help by creating an Information Centre for the TW.

TW Trade with EC

EC's trade with the TW amounts to less than one-third of extra-EC trade, but this share, notwithstanding the increase in oil prices during the 1970s, has been declining from almost half at the end of the 1950s. The decline affects both EC exports and imports, the latter more pronouncedly. The distribution of extra-EC imports from most of the TW has evolved as shown in Table 1.

In terms of product categories, the distribution of extra-EC imports from most of the TW, in 1988 is presented in Table 2.

In order to assess the eventual effects of Project 92 on TW exports the different types and categories of products must be distinguished:

(i) primary product exports to the EC will quite certainly increase because of trade creation, which in turn results from volume and price effects. Assuming that the EC's GDP increases by five per cent, the size of the simple trade creation effect (simple because no terms of trade effect is computed, although it should be rather small)[11] with respect to the non-fuel exports of the LDCs recorded in Table 1.2 may vary between −1 and 2.6 billion ecus, according to which estimated income elasticity of demand

TABLE 1
PERCENTAGE DISTRIBUTION OF EXTRA-EC IMPORTS FROM THE THIRD WORLD (1958–88)

	1958	1960	1970	1988
	%	%	%	%
from: ACP	17.2	9.7	8.9	4.5
Med.	7.1	6.6	9.4	7.8
Asean	2.9	3.0	1.6	3.1
OPEC	16.7	14.4	16.3	8.2
LA	10.3	9.7	7.9	5.9
Total	47.2	43.4	44.1	29.4

Source: Eurostat, 1988, *External Trade – Statistical Yearbook 1987*, Luxembourg: EC; Eurostat, 1990, *External Trade, Monthly Bulletin*, Luxumbourg: EC, 5.

for primary commodity imports is utilised.[12] Although tropical products – which make up about 16 per cent of EC imports of raw materials from the TW – present higher income elasticity, and therefore obtain a larger part of the additional agricultural imports generated by the increase in EC's GDP, the overall effect of Project 1992 on tropical products will remain modest.

The TW is divided on the liberalisation of tropical products as the ACP countries fear that they will then lose their preferential access to the EC, something they could accept only if offered, in return, improved access for other agricultural or semi-processed and manufactured products, particularly tobacco, fishery products, oils and oilseeds, processed and unprocessed fruits and vegetables, including soya and olive oils [*Davenport and Stevens, 1990*]. Among the tropical products – about ten per cent of LDCs' exports, but more than 20 per cent from the least developed countries – an interesting case is that of bananas, the future of which is closely linked to the elimination of article 115,[13] imposed by the completion of the single market. Presently half of the EC's imports of bananas come from ACP countries, protected by a 20 per cent ACP tariff preference, and the other half from more competitive producers from Central and South America – the so-called 'dollar bananas'. Although

TABLE 2

GEOGRAPHICAL AND COMMODITY DISTRIBUTION OF EXTRA-EC IMPORTS FROM THE THIRD WORLD (1988)

		ACP	Med.	ASEAN	OPEC	LA	LDCs	TOTAL EC	LDCs/EC
				Billion ecus					%
0.	Foodstuffs	5.1	2.6	2.3	1.3	8.3	19.6	31.9	61
1.	Beverages and tobacco	0.3	0.1	0.1	0.1	0.3	0.9	2.1	43
2.	Raw materials	2.9	1.6	1.6	1.1	4.3	11.5	35.3	33
3,4.	Fuels and fats	4.1	10.8	0.6	24.1	2.3	41.9	48.4	87
5.	Chemicals	0.5	1.6	0.1	0.7	0.6	3.5	24.8	14
6.	Manufacturers	2.8	3.9	1.5	1.2	3.8	13.2	58.4	23
7.	Machinery and transport equipment	0.8	2.2	3.2	1.4	1.5	9.1	105.2	9
8.	Other manufacturers	0.5	5.5	2.3	0.4	0.6	9.3	49.7	19
9.	Other products	0.4	1.4	0.2	1.3	1.0	4.3	27.9	15
	Primary commodities (0,1,2)	8.3	4.3	4.0	2.5	12.9	32.0	69.3	46
	Total	17.2	29.6	12.0	31.6	22.8	113.2	383.7	30

Source: Eurostat, 1988, *External Trade - Statistical Yearbook 1987*, Luxumboourg: EC; Eurostat, 1989, *External Trade, Monthly Bulletin*, Luxembourg: EC, 5.

this preferential margin is already inadequate to protect ACP bananas, the eventual elimination of article 115, by allowing the cheaper and higher-quality 'dollar bananas' to circulate all over the EC, will even more seriously threaten the former. Liberalisation then fosters the exports of 'dollar bananas' to the detriment of other less competitive producers towards which the EC has legally binding obligations resulting from the Lomé Convention.

The completion of the internal market might also improve the prospects for the import of rum from the ACP countries for the national shares of the tariff quota is, according to the Lomé IV Convention, to be phased out, while the new rum protocol provides for a rapid increase in the quota from 1993 and its abolition after 1995. Yet, the exports of other producers in the TW may be negatively affected.[14]

The attempt to harmonise national rates relative to VAT and excise taxes also has an impact on commodity trade. The elimination of the excise tax on coffee could increase the EC's imports by three per cent, world prices by five per cent and LDCs' exports to the EC by about ecu 650 million, while the imports of cocoa could increase by about 50 million ecus as result of the elimination of the excise tax and the harmonisation of VAT on this product. The rate of the excise taxes on tobacco will instead most probably increase, with the consequent reduction of EC's imports of between 10 and 15 per cent and a loss of 50–80 million ecus. To compensate LDC producers, the liberalisation of the EC tobacco regime could bring to an end EC dumping of low-quality tobaccos in the world market. Finally the new standards implemented by the EC will affect mostly the import of meat – beef and veal – products from African countries, while those on fish may concern Asian exports of shellfish. Meat's import elasticity is not too small, but as meat exports of some ACP countries result mainly from EC preferential quotas (which represent about two days of European consumption),[15] the removal of the latter while increasing international beef prices will also reduce the domestic prices in these privileged countries, thus lowering their production and, most likely, also their exports. Yet, liberalisation may increase 'the EC's import needs for beef . . . somewhat more than estimated by several studies' [*Van Berkum and Rutter, 1990: 23 and 42*].

In general, and not only for bananas, the positive effects resulting from the elimination of article 115 could be reduced or fully erased by a more frequent use of anti-dumping tariffs, already imposed on steel imported from Brazil and Mexico, on

South Korean video cassettes and on some Chinese minor trinkets. Of the anti-dumping actions initiated by the EC during the period 1980–88, 21 per cent concerned LDCs – plus seven per cent only Yugoslavia – covering an annual average volume of exports of 133 billion ecus and 'causing' them, on average, an annual reduction of 11 per cent [*Weidman, 1990: 33*]. Furthermore, it has been demonstrated that given the effectiveness of anti-dumping measures in protecting import-competing industries, the EC countries, as well as other DCs, may prefer such measures over the voluntary exports restraints (VER), 'despite the "procartel" bias of anti-dumping procedures and the corresponding cost for the country imposing' them [*Messerlin, 1989: 264*]. Although recently 'the demand for protectionism has increased both in the European Community and in the United States, . . . for European firms, the Community market remains more protected than major export markets, even in sectors where demand is strong' [*European Economy, 1989: 32 and 46*].[16] The problem, therefore, is whether anti-dumping actions will increase after 1992 and whether the closer ties that the EC may establish with EE – presently the area most hit by these actions – will make the TW the main target of any anti-dumping tariffs.

Mutual recognition may not apply to many LDCs and the certification of tests and other requirements constitute not only extra costs for TW but also act as an instrument that a determined bureaucracy can easily transform into protectionist measures. Commodity prices, in general, should remain unstable, with a possible downward trend in real terms.

(ii) Lowering the level of EC's protection of temperate products – such as grains, meat and dairy products – whether as a result of GATT multilateral trade negotiations or of EC unilateral action, will certainly affect the interests of the TW as the likely increase in world market prices of temperate products[17] which it is widely expected to cause, should also:[18]

(a) improve the welfare of LDCs' exporters, while lowering that of LDCs' importers as terms of trade will move in favour of the first and against the latter;
(b) affect other markets like those of tropical products and so benefit LDCs' exporters of such products;
(c) divert resources to agriculture with resulting increased efficiency of this sector to the possible detriment of other sectors;
(d) stimulate agricultural production in many LDCs, particularly that

of grains, like wheat, rice and maize. Whether or not these LDCs can expand their exports by moving into the processing of products such as citrus fruits and horticultural crops will depend on the tariffs and non-tariff barriers (NTB) applied by DCs and therefore by the outcome of the Uruguay Round and the terms of Lomé IV [*Faber, Stevens and van Vijfeiken, 1990: 4*].

The net effect will then vary for each and every LDC and its assessment becomes even more difficult when one tries to take into account the impact of price changes on income and its distribution. Furthermore, it seems unlikely that LDCs will be able to take advantage of higher world market prices and increase their supply without 'additional supportive measures in different economic fields', such as cushioning their own consumers from the price shock and the provision of the necessary financial instruments to increase output.[19] So, while the two benefits of liberalisation do not easily materialise, there will be its higher import costs plus the income losses arising from the dismantling of preferences; thus the net effect of EC's agricultural liberalisation on the TW, particularly on the ACP countries, is not necessarily positive without the concrete support of the Community.

(iii) Manufactured exports from LDCs are relatively small and it is not likely that their trade creation effects will be much larger than those from trade diversion. Assuming, as in the Cecchini Report [*Cecchini, 1988*], that the reduction in the imports of manufactures is no less than ten per cent and the import elasticity three per cent, then the income increase must be higher than three per cent for trade creation to surpass trade diversion.

One of the most important manufactures exported by the TW are textiles and clothing, which alone represent about ten per cent of TW's exports or about $177 billion in 1988, half of which is strictly regulated by the Multifibre Agreement (MFA).[20] The EC MFA is particularly complex with its 368 quotas, covering 17 LDCs and five 'socialist' economies, each subdivided into member quotas. The abolition of the latter as a result of Project 1992 implementation would lead to some liberalisation but, aside from the fact that no final decision has yet been reached, the retention of EC quotas may extend them to exporting countries not yet covered. As for the ACP, since their clothing exports are concentrated in a small number of EC countries and the most protected ones, they 'will have to increase their marketing activities in order to preserve their existing market share in the EC' [*Faber, Stevens and van*

Vijfeiken, 1990: 6]. EC quotas may also replace national bilateral quotas (sometimes established at the industry-to-industry level without government involvement) on footwear and electronics extending the protection of these products.

Furthermore, in most manufacturing sectors the effect of EE's competition may be quite strong. The access to the EC market that the countries in EE demand – and that the EC cannot easily deny if it is seriously interested in their economic restructuring and their political stability – should worsen the balance of payments of the TW and, hence, make its industrialisation difficult. Yet many countries of the TW need even more than before to diversify away from dependence on commodities. A recent UNCTAD study shows that for the period 1967–86, of 86 LDCs examined, only one-third achieved a significant decrease in dependence on commodities for export-earnings, while half of the remaining witnessed an increase in dependence.

The new tighter standards being agreed upon will certainly have an impact on manufactures imported by the EC. One of their effects is to penalise old producers and favour new ones who will find it less costly to comply with them. The redistribution of production that is so promoted could be used to establish invidious distinctions between LDCs, and also to obtain better conditions for the eventual DFI that the new producers might need. Furthermore, the harmonisation of standards might also give an advantage to the countries in EE, whose systems and methods of production lack the necessary flexibility to generate many goods and satisfy differentiated demands, while they are better off in the large-scale production of few products. The completion of the single market, together with the standardisation of the EC's technical measures, however, should, stimulate ACP countries to diversify their pattern of trade, which is still heavily concentrated on the their respective former colonial powers, a fact that underscores the colonial roots of the 'Eurafrica' concept on which rest largely any justification of the Lomé Conventions [*Hewitt, 1989: 285–7*].

The combination of a trade diversion effect which is larger than the trade creation effect and EE's access to the EC market seem:

(a) to take away a large share of the EC market from the manufactures of many LDCs, even including the Asian NICs;
(b) to consequently reinforce the TW's traditional division of labour.

This conclusion is underlined by the eventual diversion of DFI, European and otherwise, towards the South of the EC and EE.

(iv) TW's trade in services is limited and LDCs, as a whole, show deficits in this trade.[21] Whereas DCs remain highly competitive also in the world market of non-factor services, the LDCs' service sectors – which contribute about 20 per cent of their external transactions – are concentrated mainly in tourism, construction, shipping, data processing and computer software and off-shore finance sectors which cannot escape, and will be affected by the completion of the single market.

The EC relationship with its trading partners, including the TW, will be shaped by how the reciprocity vs. national treatment issue will be dealt with and the kind of standards it will adopt. The first issue refers to the EC demand that to share in the benefits of the single market the other countries must either reciprocate by carrying on an equivalent liberalisation of this sector, or simply extend to the EC interests abroad, the same treatment reserved for the domestic ones. Even more potentially restrictive of trade is the setting and harmonisation of technical standards. The utilisation by the LDCs, particularly by ACP countries, of their competitive advantage in some labour-intensive services – such as construction, shipping, some types of air transportation and some professional services – will depend largely on the extent to which labour movements across frontiers will be allowed, and on the concessions that EC will be willing to make in areas left unregulated by GATT.

The liberalisation of services which may emerge from the Uruguay Round and the increased competition in service markets resulting from the implementation of Project 1992, both much feared by the more advanced LDCs, would certainly benefit the less developed ones, including the ACP countries which, being net importers, could then enjoy lower prices. Yet, the fear comes from the realisation that the long-term effects of such a liberalisation as well as of Project 1992 cannot fail to influence negatively the establishment of the services industry in the TW, while also reducing 'substantially the effectiveness of any possible preferential treatment that ACP countries could receive from the EC'.

As for manufacturing, the technical and social standards being elaborated by the EC, particularly if a social clause is introduced into preferential trade agreements, will not prompt the emergence of competitive service sectors in many countries of the TW [*Nicolaides, 1990: 130–31*].

Trade Policy

Introduction: Although 'the Community repeatedly claims to adhere "scrupulously" to GATT rules . . . its commercial policy measures have a complex preferential (i.e. discriminatory) bias', for the EC has a tradition of discrimination, itself still being essentially a preferential trading arrangement [*Pelkmans, 1987: 15*]. The most cumbersome system of discrimination is the one built by the EC with respect to the TW,[22] the so-called 'pyramid of privileges' which distinguishes, in order of privileges offered: Mediterranean; ACP; GSP; ASEAN; Andean Pact; some Latin American countries; and some other LDCs.

The EC differentiates between LDCs in many ways, the main instruments utilised being:

(i) tariffs: the average common customs tariff being low, almost negligible for LDCs, but there are exceptions. Then there is the common agricultural policy (CAP) by which rates can jump easily to 200 and 300 per cent. Furthermore the EC actual tariff rates applying to LDC exports may be higher than those applied to DCs' exports, since there still is in the EC tariff schedule an important escalation from primary products to intermediate goods; and
(ii) a series of non-tariff instruments, some utilised at both the national and the Community level.[23]

EC trade policy also includes rules of origin and product coverage, particularly for its GSP, and it cannot be properly assessed without considering its close links with the Community's industrial policy.

Of the above listed instruments the particularly relevant ones for the TW are: VERs, which includes the bilateral agreements made within the MFA's framework; quotas; surveillance; and dumping. How Project 1992 is going to affect the utilisation of these measures is still unclear. The implementation, within the GSP, of graduating the most successful competitors without introducing more liberal measures for the remaining supplying countries, the increasing discrimination against NICs in recent years and Lomé IV (see following section on Lomé Convention) are not very encouraging. From the point of view of LDCs 'serious criticism can be levelled at the discrepancy between lofty objectives and numerous impediments to free trade and security of access to the Community's market' [*Pelkmans, 1987: 38*].

The reasons for continuing with protectionism and discrimination are:

(i) the burden of internal restructuring and adjustment;

(ii) the increasing importance of Eastern Europe;
(iii) the growing environmental preoccupations; and
(iv) the reciprocity issue.

Considering its preferential agreements with EFTA, ACP and the Mediterranean countries, including the VERs applied to them, only 25 per cent of the EC's total trade is conducted on a most-favoured-nation basis, against almost 90 per cent of the USA's.

A very rough guesstimate indicates that Project 1992 will certainly affect negatively the Mediterranean – particularly as result of DFI diversion – and the ACP countries, while it may benefit the Asian NICs.

Uruguay Round: The most debated issue in this Round of multilateral negotiations is the high and costly protection that the major DCs offer their agricultural sector. The most fiercely fought against is the EC's CAP, the effect of which is particularly important. Given the dominance of agriculture in many LDCs [*Cooper, 1990*], CAP's main effects on these countries are the following:

(i) the increased world supply and, hence, reduced prices, of some temperate commodities, mainly cereals, imported by many LDCs. The importers' gains have been paid by the profound crisis, most evident in Africa, affecting their agriculture, a crisis which has further eroded their self-reliance in food while the widened productivity gap with DCs has become insurmountable for many of them;
(ii) the increased instability of world prices;
(iii) the negative effect of low agricultural prices on LDCs' exports of tropical agricultural products and on their imports of manufactures;
(iv) the distorted EC investment as a result of which non-agricultural output has grown less than otherwise expected, and food-importing LDCs have lost on non-agricultural imports what they gained on agricultural imports.

The EC has made it clear that it is not going to accept the dismantling of its CAP, although it has already frozen the support prices of many agricultural products.

The Community's proposals to the mid-term review of the Uruguay Round in December 1988 fell short of TW expectations even as to tropical products. In fact its limited coverage excludes all products regulated by CAP, namely, oilseeds and vegetable oils, tobacco, rice and cassava, while ACP sugar and bananas receive special treatment under the Lomé Convention which, according to the EC, should be included instead in the global agricultural negotiations. The EC proposes to reduce or eliminate tariffs on some 140 products (in terms of the eight digit Combined Nomenclature) to reduce GSP rates on two, and to eliminate quotas on 21. Although ACP countries have complained that the proposal – which in any case improves their access to non-EC countries – threatens to reduce the value of their trade preferences, its 'potential direct impact appears to be modest', for 'even a much more thoroughgoing liberalisation in certain important commodities, including coffee and cocoa, would have relatively modest implications for the ACP market'. Even worse is that the ACP countries 'are the only group of developing countries unlikely to benefit' from such a liberalisation [*Davenport and Stevens, 1990: 62, 64 and 77*].

Still under discussion is the future of the MFA with the eventual re-establishment of GATT rules on this type of international trade. In February 1990 the US proposed a ten-year phase-out, restructuring DCs' textiles and clothing industry, starting at the beginning of 1992. Japan has proposed instead that the present MFA-4 be ended in 1991 and that, therefore, all restrictions based on it be eliminated. If necessary, the Japanese proposal envisages a transitional period which could run until the end of 1999. The EC, however, appears to insist that any weakening of the MFA must be reciprocated by LDCs' own liberalisation. In any case the elimination of individual country quotas and of article 115, that must accompany the completion of the internal market, cannot fail to affect seriously the MFA which may follow the present agreement after 1991. In addition to the risk of reducing EC quotas to the level of the most protectionist members, the setting of quotas at EC level by the Commission 'may mean a considerable reallocation of trade to the (member) countries that are at present most restrictive'. This removal of national quotas should also affect intra-EC trade, as a result of the freeing of supplies, which, given the elasticity of substitution and the elasticities of demand, will displace some in favour of others. The implementation of Project 1992 should further contribute to the lowering of production and distribution costs within the EC, thus fostering EC competitiveness *vis-à-vis* foreign producers. In any case 'anti-dumping might become the substitute instrument if MFA liberalisation went "too far" for the EC' [*Page, 1990: 99 and 105*].

Another heated discussion concerns the problem of services, for the first time on the agenda of such a multilateral trade negotiation, due to the strong opposition of some of the larger and more advanced LDCs. Their objection derives primarily:

(i) from the DCs' resistance until now to liberalise even sectors such as textiles and steel, in which the LDCs have a comparative advantage; and
(ii) from the LDCs' desire to retain the option to develop their own non-traditional service sectors.

The increasing share of this sector to about one-third of TW's total production, also underlines the importance it is assuming for many LDCs [*UNCTAD, 1986*]. Furthermore, it is recognised that services provide an increasingly essential input for many other production activities, thus the importance, firstly, of their availability and, secondly, of their procurement at the lowest possible price so as to reduce the cost of production of the final goods produced with their help. Assuring this availability may justify the national production of services, to improve the competitiveness of final goods in international markets, otherwise it demands their importation whenever they are cheaper than those domestically produced. Given these considerations, liberalisation[24] should be acceptable, especially if simultaneous plans are made in order to apply to the service sector an import substitution strategy in the not too distant future.

The need to protect intellectual property rights must be balanced by LDCs' public interest, development and technological objectives. Clearly these objective are not easily reconcilable. Given the relatively modest or incipient stage services are in many LDCs, they can hardly liberalise them and even less likely, offer reciprocity. The EC's insistence on this, therefore, should not include LDCs, at least, not all of them.

Recently the US and the EC have expressed their willingness to grant concessions on their merchandise imports in exchange for more liberal conditions for their exports of services to LDCs, that is, to link concessions on merchandise trade to those on services. LDCs oppose such a link and insist that DCs should resolve the problems of merchandise trade by means of standstill and roll-back arrangements under existing GATT obligations, which they have not wholly fulfilled yet.

Following US success with bilateral negotiations in order to obtain protection for its industrial and intellectual property rights (patents, trade marks, copyrights, all made even more relevant by the information technology revolution and the bio-revolution), the EC has begun to demand equivalent treatment, threatening to remove preferential market access as an 'inducement' to co-operation, the first example of such an action being the withdrawal of GSP access to South Korean exports.

Lomé Convention: Although considered the linchpin of the EC's 'pyramid of privileges', 25 years of preferential treatment for the ACP countries have not enabled a single one of them to climb into the league of the NICs. Furthermore, not only has the ACP share of EC imports not increased since the first Convention, but it has actually declined from 7.3 per cent in 1975 to 4.5 per cent in 1988, as has the ACP's share of EC imports from TW countries decreased, namely, from 21 to 16 per cent, during the same period [*Eurostat, 1988; Eurostat, 1989*]. Even in relation to primary commodities, which constitute more than four-fifths of ACP exports to the EC, the ACP countries in the 1980s 'have performed relatively less well compared to other developing countries', most notably in the products where they have a margin of tariff preference over the latter [*McQueen and Yannopoulos, 1989*].[25]

Although Lomé preferences do not seem to have a distinctively positive effect on ACP countries, they fear that the Uruguay Round of negotiations and the coming review of the EC's GSP in 1991 might further erode even that margin of preference that they still have. These fears are compounded by the possible impact that both the completion of the single market and, more recently, the EE's economic restructuring may have on them.

The 4th Lomé Convention signed on 15 December 1989 – effective from 1 February 1990 and now grouping 69 countries from Africa, the Caribbean and the Pacific areas – does not auger well in terms of EC's future interest in the TW.

Of the ACP's demands the ones only accepted by the EC are:

(i) extension of the time coverage of the Convention from five to ten years, contributing to more stable co-operation;
(ii) admission of three new states: Haiti, the Dominican Republic and Namibia;
(iii) discontinuation of mandatory reimbursement of Stabex transfers;
(iv) addition of gold and uranium to the Sysmin (or Minex) list;
(v) some small improvement to trade provisions, such as allowing requests for a derogation from the rules of origin and thus reducing to 45 per cent the threshold for minimum local value-added.

By insisting that an ACP product undergoes a minimum – 40–50 per cent – amount of transformation to avoid trade deflection, EC regulations actually constitute a serious obstacle to the exports of manufactures by the APC countries. The criteria specified by the rules also present the following problems, the solutions to which cannot be expected from the few derogations allowed [*McQueen and Yannopoulos, 1989; McQueen and Stevens, 1989: 253–5*]:

(i) the exclusion of 'simple assembly; which penalises small, less developed economies, while allowing EC 'screwdriver' plants to be established there, since EC inputs are considered as ACP originating products (cumulation principle);

(ii) the setting of a maximum outside content for manufactured ACP goods at 40–50 per cent of the price of the finished product when it leaves the factory. Coping with such a rule enables ACP products to benefit from total free access, further defined by a complex set of regulations, while requiring an integrated industrial structure that only a few ACP countries may possess already;

(iii) the requirement for textiles and clothing that the starting material should be yarn, which forces ACP countries to develop a substantial transformation well beyond what is required for avoiding trade deflection;

(iv) the qualification that fishery products should be caught in vessels at least 50 per cent ACP or EC owned, with further restrictions applying to the nationality of the captain and the crew when, clearly, ACP countries rarely own deep sea fishing fleets. The fisheries agreements – that is, the instruments by which the EC fleets gain licensed access to ACP waters in return for financial compensation as well as concessions covering employment and training of ACP nationals, transfer of technology, research, on-board observers and use of by-catches – 'have not been particularly successful beyond satisfying the strictly commercial needs of the ship owners', for ACP signatories do not have the means to control the correct execution of these agreements [*Lomé Briefing, 2.10.1989*].

The ACP countries' bargaining position was not strengthened by their difficulty in finding a united stance, which in turn contributed to their not obtaining the New Convention they wanted, and hence forced them to accept even a much smaller volume of financial aid than they had proposed, that is, from 15.5 billion ecus for five years to 12 billion: the 7th European Development Fund allocated 10.8 billion ecus for programmable and non-programmable aid (including 825 million ecus for risk capital), and the European Investment Bank 1.2 billion ecus for loans. On the whole this amounted to merely 4.4 ecus per capita annually. A small six per cent decline of ACP exports to the EC (for the period 1986–88 averaging 17.8 million ecus, against 23.8 for 1981–85) an more than wipe out a year's aid provided by Lomé III, namely, 958 million ecus. Considering the rate of inflation, the growth of population and the accession of the three new countries, this new amount is much higher than the 8.5 billion ecus provided by the previous Convention.

Officially presented as Lomé IV's most important innovation is 'the new system of support for economic rationalisation (structural adjustment) policies' [*Marin, 1990: 13*]. The system consists of the allocation of 1.15 million ecus, to which a limited part of the resources of each country's indicative programme can be added, for assisting ACP countries undergoing structural adjustment programmes, that is, mainly balance of payments support, or, more simply, paying out money for imports or technical assistance. This allows the EC to continue increasing its control over the allocation of resources, a control already introduced by the 'policy dialogues'. Meanwhile, by further strengthening the coordination of its aid with that of the World Bank and the IMF, the Community accepts implicitly their criteria for the allocation of resources, including conditionality, viewed by the EC as a 'necessary extension of dialogue to the macro-policy level'. Yet, by institutionalising the practice of using Lomé credits not only for development, but also to support adjustment policies, the new system seriously risks having 'development . . . sacrificed to financial discipline', an outcome 'unacceptable' even to former Commissioner Pisani who is responsible for the introduction of the 'policy dialogues' [*Pisani, 1988*]. Besides directly absorbing more Lomé aid, the balance of payments support provided by the structural adjustment programmes, particularly those influenced by the Bretton Woods institutions with their emphasis on the demand for the reduction or elimination of tariff protection, may contribute indirectly to scaring away DFI, thus further reducing the availability of resources for the longer-term development priorities of the ACP countries [*Page, 1990: 209*].

Access to the EC market for agricultural products, which is restricted by the CAP, has been improved by Lomé IV by a modest increase in the quantities eligible, and a slight reduction in levies or customs duties for the few products that have already been receiving preferential treatment and extended to some 40 more products, such as sorghum, millet, yams, rice, molasses, strawberries, tomatoes, citrus fruit, the imports of which are still mostly restricted both in terms of marketing timetables and quantities benefiting from preferential access [*Vander Stichele, 1991*].

Regarding rum and bananas, the Lomé IV protocol increases the quantities of rum which may be imported free of customs duties, and plans for the abolition of this tariff quota in 1995. As for sugar, the impact of the subsidising 'is substantial . . . on the sugar exports of ACP countries, thus helping to contain the economic risk to which the sugar producing sector is subjected'. Such subsidisation 'does not foster development . . . nor is [it] employed to adjust to the keener competition on the world market'. Moreover, the admission of the Dominican Republic and Haiti may even worsen the situation of the other ACP countries [*Koch, 1989*], whereas CAP liberalisation would necessarily reduce EC's sugar price, and hence ACP's.

The implementation of the EC food strategy in Africa does not easily square with the price depressing effects of the CAP's cereal dumping, a fact that underlines 'the interaction of the CAP with precisely those domestic policies identified as obstacles to the recovery of smallholder production' in Africa, as well as in other parts of the TW [*Watkins, 1989*]. Given the DCs' high and growing productivity, relaunching African agriculture cannot be conceived without some regional harmonisation or a certain amount of protection for this sector. It is necessary to take into account the complementary nature of this sector and its transformation. The regional approach in production is made difficult by the country-by-country approach of the structural adjustment programmes. Moreover, being oriented mainly to the international market, structural adjustment programmes cannot foster the creation of regional markets for indigenous agricultural products [*Tubiana, 1989*].

While Stabex 'transfers' will no longer be repaid, the EC's control over the use of the money has increased noticeably and newly processed products will not be covered by the stabilisation scheme. Further, little progress has been made on the easing of the fruit and vegetable regime. The proposal by the ACP countries to help them to support the efforts to alleviate the considerable supply-side problems facing them, by means of a programme for the processing, marketing, distributing and transporting of their export commodities (PMDT), has not found the necessary financial backing.

In addition, new measures on promotion, protection, financing and support for foreign and local investment are unlikely to reverse effectively capital outflow and divestment, which in turn will affect the possibility of ACP countries reducing their overwhelming dependence on unprocessed primary commodities – a dependence often resulting from the interacting CAP and Lomé measures. A clear example is the high prices of Lomé's Sugar Protocol which have certainly contributed to preventing the allocation of production factors to more efficient sectors of the ACP economies. Furthermore, as little effort has been made to utilise the extra resources so obtained even for restructuring their sugar sectors, the ACP countries have remained almost exclusively exporters of raw sugar [*Koch, 1989: 296*].

In any case, as recently as 1987 the 'new' products, that is, the non-traditional ones, exported by ACP countries to the EC had only reached 800 million ecus, thereby representing less than seven per cent of these countries' total non-fuel exports. Although they may no longer be considered insignificant [*McQueen ans Stevens, 1989*], raw material processing clearly has not advanced sufficiently in many ACP countries.

The sector of services has remained a rather neglected topic in the Lomé Conventions. For the ACP countries, which are unable to export much and, therefore are largely net importers in this sector, the problem is not one of trading arrangements, but one concerning the development of their domestic and regional capacity for producing services, particularly in the traditional non-factor, labour-intensive sectors, such as tourism or travel, other transportation and shipping [*Thiais, 1990: 138–42*]. Such a development cannot be achieved by an indiscriminate liberalisation of trade in services as among the DCs, and without substantial financial and technical assistance from the EC, the latter clearly not yet available. Instead, the completion of the single market, while enabling the ACP countries to obtain cheaper services from the EC, is also likely to contribute to the worsening of their comparative disadvantage in services, 'since their productive system does not yet appear flexible enough to benefit from the forthcoming opportunities' [*Thiais, 1990: 143*].

Finally, there is the disappointing level of implementation and the poor results of the previous Conventions, as also indicated by the fact that at the end of 1988, only ten per cent of the funds of Lomé III had been disbursed.

Generalised system of preferences: The EC has been the first to implement in 1971 a GSP, that is, a scheme of sub-most favoured nation (MFN) preferential tariffs on industrial imports from the LDCs, covering $9.3 billion in 1980 trade, almost twice as much as that covered by the US. Yet, after more than a decade in operation, there is not much evidence of benefits from the overall scheme, the EC's or the GSP of most other DCs [*Brown, 1989: 759; Langhammer and Sapir, 1987: 69*].

Duty reduction or suspension concerns primarily industrial products, the preferential treatment of agricultural products being limited to small tariff reductions on selected products, a measure made necessary for preserving preferences granted to Mediterranean and ACP countries. Eligibility is limited by quotas so that MFN tariff rates are applied to imports exceeding these quotas. The countries admitted to the GSP must also make sure that they respect the 'individual country amounts', established to limit preferential imports from particular LDCs and the rules of origin. Thus it is not surprising that a large volume of trade between the eligible countries does not actually receive preferential treatment. Therefore, if one adds to the products forthrightly excluded – such as agricultural and metal products, iron and steel those receiving special treatment – such as textiles and clothing, it becomes apparent that 'the products of greatest immediate interest to the less developed countries have not been the object of significant reductions in tariffs and NTBs' [*Brown, 1989: 756*]. Meanwhile, the uncertainties surrounding the GSP treatment are difficult to take into account in pricing decisions by exporters and importers, as well as in investment decisions related to the products that are GSP-eligible.

The most recent estimate of the impact of the EC's and EFTA's GSPs together show a trade-creating effect of $130 million based on 1976 trade, inclusive of the improvement in the beneficiaries' terms of trade. The trade-diversion effect of $57 million, concerns mainly the imports from the USA and Japan, at not very large cost to both these countries. The GSP has also caused a decline in the EC countries' welfare, most notably for the FRG – $45 million – and a reduction in employment, albeit modest, compensated by production and employment increases in the major export sectors [*Brown, 1989*].[26]

Given 'the overall tendency in international trade policy to discriminate against successful individual suppliers', the actual EC' GSP, like that of the US', aims 'at controlling the amount and allocation of benefits among the beneficiaries', well reflecting 'a 'rationale protectionist's view of preference'. Its reform should therefore aim not so much at providing larger preference margins, but 'more transparency, a longer time horizon and the removal of limitations which cause uncertainty and reluctance to invest'. However, the future evolution of the GSP might depend even more on the implementation of all trade liberalising measures already agreed by the DCs [*Langhammer and Sapir, 1987: 79 and 74–5*], an eventuality which appears politically not very feasible.

Thus, the GSP has remained a relatively minor issue in North–South trade policy discussions and it is even arguable that an unrestricted GSP would really make a major difference. Yet, the simulation of the impact on world prices and EC trade flows of the liberalisation, that is, extending of the GSP to zero tariffs, of Community imports of six important tropical products, namely, coffee, cocoa, tobacco, rice, cassava and tropical vegetable oils, shows that the effects 'are very significant to the GSP-eligible countries' [*Davenport and Stevens, 1990: 65*]. Such a liberalisation appears to be all the more necessary since the prices of tropical products, the LDCs' output of which continues to expand while world demand remains sluggish, present a rather gloomy long-term outlook [*World Bank, 1988*].

Capital Flows

EC countries remain an important source of foreign investment in certain LDCs, their share of DFI in the TW being 38 per cent in 1970–71, 33 per cent in 1979–81 and 40 per cent in 1982–84. The direction of EC's DFI cannot fail to be affected by changes in EE, particularly considering that the FRG has until now been the main source of DFI to the TW.

Given the advantages of producing within the unified EC market, Project 1992 will also tend to attract DFI both from within and from without, hence contributing to limit further LDC's access to capital and, with it, to technology, and hence their capacity to compete in the international market. Under these conditions the call within the Uruguay Round for LDCs' trade liberalisation appears irrelevant or even dangerous. If for other DCs it is possible to invest in the EC to enhance their presence there, and hence reap the benefits of the growing competitiveness of the latter, the same strategy is not available to LDCs (except some NICs, such as South Korea, which is expanding DFI in Europe). The only alternative left to most LDCs is that of joint ventures, within the reduced capital available for investment in many parts of the TW.

The negative impact of the expected stagnation in investment, aid and technical assistance flowing to the TW in the near future is compounded by the unlikelihood of a substantial improvement in the prices of most primary products, with the notable exception of oil. It becomes, therefore, even more relevant for many LDCs, including the ACP countries, to have an improved, that is, preferential, access to their traditional markets, and the promotion of their international competitiveness whereby the latter can be achieved without excessive foreign assistance. It is clear, however, that any such action will tend to reinforce the traditional international division of labour.

European Monetary Union

The ecu, a basket currency which has become the symbol of the EC monetary integration process, has official recognition in transactions among the European central banks and among the governments of the Community member countries. Its use has also experienced a considerable development in international financial markets, although more modest in commercial transactions.[27] The success of this innovation is due both to the EC's increasing relevance and to the stability that this monetary instrument has demonstrated, especially when compared with the high volatility and unpredictability of exchange rates, particularly against the US dollar, which have characterised financial markets during the 1980s. This area of exchange rate stability resulting from the establishment of the European Monetary System (EMS) has greatly reduced the exchange rate risk in intra-Community trade. Given its low transaction costs and its relative stability, the utilisation of the ecu could be very useful, too, in extra-Community trading, for both European and non-European operators, because it would tend to:

(i) stabilise export revenues of raw material suppliers by delinking them from the fluctuations of the US dollar;
(ii) simplify currency management for non-European operators trading with several EC partners;
(iii) facilitate access to Community financing; and finally,
(iv) stabilise the value and the burden of the external debt of the TW [*SDA-ISLA, 1989: 28*], as well as of EE [*Bartha, 1989: 28*].

To these advantages which TW countries may derive from the reduction of the level of 'dollarisation' that characterises international transactions, one should also add the possible contribution that the ecu could make to some of the integration processes taking place in the TW.

In order to facilitate the introduction of the ecu, the countries that opt for currency diversification should fix their exchange rates on the basis of a basket of currencies, which also includes it and should increase its share in their reserves. The Community should instead denominate its foreign aid in ecus and any other intervention directed to these countries, establish a compensatory facility to stabilise the effects of exchange variations on the ecu-denominated debt, and contribute to the creation of ecu-denominated regional monetary instruments – somewhat similar to the Andean peso utilised by the Andean Reserve Fund for compensating net balances arising among its member countries [*SDA-ISLA, 1989: 43*]. Interesting in this respect, aside from the Andean Pact, is Africa's experience, particularly the Franc Zone created half a century ago, has provided some 15 LDCs with a level of monetary stability unlikely to have been achieved otherwise [*Saclier, 1988: 85*].[28] In any case, the EC's eventual monetary union also means that it will have to 'effectively adopt the monetary burden (and benefits) of the Franc Zone', which could be absorbed into a larger ecu-based zone [*Hewitt, 1989: 297*].[29]

The intrinsic stability of ecu and the fact that it is not the currency of a single country, makes it very appealing as an exchange currency, thus the discussion in the second half of the 1980s about the eventual creation of an ecu-based monetary zone with countries of the Middle East, Latin America, that is, some of the most significant parts of the TW, and some of EE.

Similarly, the absence of a structure for North–South monetary relations makes more difficult among other things, the management of international debt, while the expansion of the EMS could contribute to the promotion of such co-operation. However, restructuring EE's economies and the German unification will not only absorb most of EC's resources, but may also jeopardise the DM's stability and therefore the ecu's. Any complications arising from the EC's monetary unification will also thwart further expansion in the use of the ecu and prevent the establishment of any such ecu-based area in the TW.

Development Co-operation

'One of the most prominent features of the EC's development co-operation policy has been its regionalist approach in the geographical allocation of its development assistance' [*Tsoutsoplides, 1989: 2*]. This statement does not refer to member countries' bilateral aid, but to the Community's, which amounts to no more than ten per cent of the financial assistance given by the whole EC, although the bilateral aid is even more discriminatory.

The EC transfers resources to the TW in many ways:

(i) disbursements by the European Development Fund and concessionary loans to ACP and Mediterranean countries by the European Investment Bank;
(ii) emergency aid to non-associates, coming directly from EC budget;
(iii) contributions to EC and LDC non-governmental organisations (NGO); and, more indirectly,
(iv) Stabex and Sysmin, as far as the transfers granted by these stabilisation schemes involve a significant grant element; and
(v) tariff preferences to LDCs, although the identification and measurement of their aid component have proved impossible.

To this one must add trade financing via export credit insurance, which is practised by each EC member country according to national schemes, and which appears not be replaced by a single Community agency. However, against this transfer to the TW, there are the welfare losses suffered as a result of EC protectionism, losses that, following recent general equilibrium studies relative to overall TW–DC relationship, seem to outweigh the positive impact of aid received by the TW.

Furthermore, about 70 per cent of bilateral aid from the EC countries – that is, more than $12 billion out of the total $17.6 provided in 1987–88[30] – is estimated to be partially or entirely tied. Shifting from national tying to Community tying, that is, allowing LDCs to buy from the cheapest Community source, may increase the value of the same aid to recipient countries by about 20 per cent [*Jepma, 1988: 797 and 804*], generating a gain of $2.5 billion. This is equivalent to the most optimistic estimates, considered above, relative to the impact of Project 1992 on TW's commodity exports. The untying could be further enhanced by:

(i) reducing disparities in aid-volume performance between EC member states;
(ii) co-ordinating co-operation at Community level, a process which will eventually transfer execution to Brussels, and which in turn can be facilitated by
(iii) harmonising national procedures.

Although untying bilateral aid implies that the remaining special bilateral relationships between EC countries and their former colonies will be further dismantled, a large transfer of bilateral assistance for disbursement through the Community may be even more useful for the TW. Such a possibility appears to be conditioned by the answers to the following questions:

(i) will the implementation of Project 1992 make such a transfer of resources to the Community more feasible than it has been until now?
(ii) will the priority of such a Community remain the same or will there be a shift in its interests?

If the diversion of development resources towards EE is not yet apparent at the Community level, it is already taking place at the national level. The argument on which this reduction of aid is being built centres around the assumption that, after all, the restructuring of Eastern Europe should also be made advantageous to the TW. Even though this may be done only in the long run, the very long run, or even more distant future, it tends, however, to make the situation more serious for many countries in the TW facing the immediate problem of survival.

IV. CONCLUSIONS

The proposition that, on the whole, the effect of Project 1992 on the TW will be positive, even if modestly so, has become even more questionable since the dramatic changes in EE. Taking into account the cost of restructuring EE and the German unification, the more likely negative effects of European integration on the TW could be:

(i) the increased burden of servicing its external debt, as the level of interest rates is most likely to go up; and
(ii) the decline in DFI and aid financing available to it. Also, as the difficulty to service debt increases, the attraction for DFI to go to the TW will decrease;
(iii) the growing competition that TW manufactured exports would have to face in the European market.

The impact of 1992 on the raw materials sector of the TW may be mixed and possibly positive, although not excessively large. However, the process of restructuring European economies may further generate innovations intended to replace many raw materials by less bulky, lighter and cheaper substitutes.

The TW situation could be made even worse if the predicted increase in the price of oil takes place during the 1990s. In fact, such an increase would have negative effects, directly, on oil-importing LDCs, and indirectly, on most TW countries. This would result from: first, the squeeze on their exports caused, as in the 1970s, by the tight monetary policies pursued by DCs to fight the inflation induced by growing oil prices; and secondly, the deterioration of their terms of trade due to an increase in the price of their manufactured imports.

In any case, the problems of EE and its integration into the world economy will tend to absorb not only the entire attention of the EC, but also most of its resources for many years to come. Even though the end of the East–West rivalry and the EE's re-entry into the fold may not necessarily cause Europe's disengagement from the TW, there should be no doubt that the North–South dialogue has lost any immediacy and has hence moved to the back-burner.

NOTES

1. According to G. De Michelis, Italian minister of foreign affairs, disarmament should liberate at least 0.8 per cent of Western Europe's GDP, *International Herald Tribune* (*IHT*), 25.3.1990.
2. From the perspective of the TW, Gorbachev's Common European House becomes, according to Professor Manning Marable of the University of Colorado, 'a new manifestation of Eurocentrism', as elements of the Soviet bloc unite with the West to control TW markets, raw materials and a cheap labour force, *IHT*, 13.6.1990.
3. OECD, *Financial Market Trends*, 45 (Paris: OECD, 1990), p. 11; Table 4, p.20; Table 9, p.26. Total net debt is estimated at over $120 billion by the Deutsche Bank [*Deutsche Bank, 1990: 56*], of which $13 billion that of GDR. However, more recent data show that GDR's debt reaches more than $23 billion or approximately DM 40 billion.

4. *Newsweek*, 12.3.1990, p.9. On April 28 the Community said it was ready to start a second stage of economic relations with EE, namely, talks for association accords that also cover political consultations. Meanwhile, the EC signed in May 1990 a new trade and co-operation agreement with Czechoslovakia which, apart from replacing the agreement relative to industrial products signed in December 1988, is seen by the Czech authorities as the stepping stone to an association agreement, and thence to their request for admission to the EC. Also in May 1990 Bulgaria and GDR signed a similar agreement with the EC, but the latter will be changed once the two Germanys create an economic and monetary union. The ten-year accords with the EE countries provide for economic co-operation in many sectors, including farming, the environment and research projects, easing curbs on imports of EE's goods and raising two-way trade, presently about $50 billion, of which half is between the USSR and the EC.
5. At the Washington meeting of the Bretton Woods Committee in May 1991 the US Senator B. Bradley and the Italian Minister of foreign affairs G. De Michelis suggested a substantial forgiveness of some of the $100 billion in government-to-government debt owned by EE.
6. Also according to U. Cartellieri, member of the Deutsche Bank's board, FRG can do its share in developing the RDT without either raising taxes or jarring capital markets with higher interest rates, *IHT*, 30.3.1990. On this point see also *The Economist*, 26.5.1990, p.73.
7. 'In the EMS the exchange rate commitment has led to an implicit agreement giving the role of fixing the system-wide money stock to the German Bundesbank' [*De Grauwe, 1989: 203*]
8. *IHT*, 23.2.1990. As the supply of housing in FRG is unlikely to keep pace with the vertical rise in demand, sharper increases in construction prices and rents can be expected in the next few years.
9. See the declarations of BP's Chairman, Cambridge Energy Research Associate of Massachusetts, executive vice-president of Chase Manhattan, Energy Information Association of the US, in *Newsweek*, 12.3.1990.
10. While some saw the EC's privileged relation with the TW largely as exploitative and fostering its fragmentation and dependency (Galtung), others concluded that liberal and multilateral trading could serve much better TW's interests (Pomfret) [*Featherstone, 1989: 186*]
11. According to Matthews' calculations [*Matthews, 1989: 5*] the terms of trade effect relative to African non-fuel exports could be worth around 1/2 billion ecus.
12. Estimated increase in the value of most LDCs' primary commodity exports to an EC's GDP growing by five per cent:

If one uses the GATT's estimates of apparent income elasticities (see also *European Economy* [1989: Table 4, 14]), the following picture emerges:

	EC's Imports from LDCs Bil.ecu	Income Elasticity Balassa- Bond		Billion ecu Balassa- Bond	
Food stuff	19.6	0.6	1.20	.59	1.18
Beverages and tobacco	0.9	0.6	0.65	.03	.03
Raw materials:	11.5				
agricultural*	6.0	0.3	0.56	.09	.17
mineral*	5.5	0.7	2.16	.19	.59
				-----	-----
				0.90	1.97

*Estimated distribution of these two categories.

Source: Balassa [*1988*]; Bond [*1987*].

	EC's imports from LDCs Bil ecu	Elasticity average 1985–86 (a)	(b)	Billion ecu 1980–86 (a)	(b)
Agric. materials and food stuff	26.5	.76	.4	1.01	.53
Minerals and energy products	47.4	.68	−.7	1.61	−1.66
				------	------
				2.62	−1.13

The apparently much higher estimates reached by *ODI Briefing Paper* [*1989*], namely, 4.6 billion ecus, is due to the inclusion of imports of fuels, which alone amounts to another 35 billion ecus, plus textiles and shoes, and which, with the impact of Project 1992, is estimates at about 850 million ecus and 260, respectively. As for oil, given the EC's objective of reducing its imports, extra-EC oil suppliers cannot be expected to gain much from Project 1992.

13. To avoid trade deflection, more protectionist member countries could extend these measures to include imports from more liberal member countries.
14. The estimates of the impact of Project 1992 on various products utilised in the next two paragraphs come from *ODI Briefing Paper* [*1989*].
15. With the Lomé IV protocol on meat the overall annual quantity of this product's imports covered by a preferential treatment has been raised from 30 to 39.1 thousand tons, while the ACP exporters are no longer required to levy an export tax in exchange for the 90 per cent reduction in levies accorded by the Community.
16. According to Koopman and Scharrer [*1989: 208*] 'about one-quarter of all export restraint arrangements registered by the GATT secretariat, ranging from voluntary self-restraints via orderly marketing arrangements to market-sharing accords between industry associations, involve EC members as the importing countries seeking protection'. The same authors report that during the period 1978–87, the Community resorted to the GATT safeguard clause 12 times; also see Kelly [*1988: 137*].
17. See, for instance, the 1984 EC decision to curtail the production of diary products, as a result of which the international price of cheese and skimmed milk has already almost doubled while other dairy products have also shown steady price increases [*Van Berkum and Rutten, 1990: 39*].
18. Other important effects, less relevant in this context, attributed to the liberalisation of agriculture are the decrease in its production in countries where this sector is highly protected; the increase in the volume of agricultural products internationally traded; and the lowering of its price fluctuations.
19. For a calculation of the welfare gains and losses of EC liberalisation to several groups of LDCs, see Matthews [*1985: 142 and 145*] and also Van Berkum and Rutten [*1990: 24–33, and 36*]. The latter also rightly quote Matthews' assertion that 'it is not axiomatic that a country which is a net exporter after the world price increase must be a net gainer' [*Matthews, 1985: 251*].
20. This is a 51-nation accord which since 1974 (it has been extended three times already) allows DCs to protect their textile industry from cheaper imports through individual pacts – VERs – limiting foreign deliveries. The VERs identified by GATT as active in the period 1986–87 totalled 137, 68 of which protect the EC market. Three-quarters of the 137 VERs deal with six products in the following order: steel, agricultural products, autos and transport equipment, textiles (not yet included in the MFA), electronic products and shoes.
21. World trade in 'invisibles', one half of which is constituted by commercial services, and the other mainly by investment income and then unrequited transfers, represent roughly one-third of that in merchandise and it is growing very fast, namely, at an annual average of 13 per cent for the period 1970–87 [*GATT, 1989: Vol. I, Table*

20 and 21, 30]. Difficult to establish TW share in this trade, estimated at less than one-fourth of the total [*UNCTAD, 1988: 150–51*]. See also Secchi [*1988: 150*].

22. According to Weiss [*1987: 464*] 'European trade policy . . . discriminate[s] . . . also against the less developed countries'. Not only do the tariff structures of DCs tend to discriminate against LDCs, but the EC presents a relevant tariff escalation from primary products to intermediate goods; Siebeke [*1989: 300*] quotes some German studies as well as, naturally, Cairncross [*1982: paragraphs 3.51 and 3.52*].
23. An incomplete list of NTBs includes the following measures: safeguards (article 19 GATT); VERs, that is, formal or informal bilateral agreements; countermeasures under the New Trade Policy Instrument (NTPI) for dealing with 'unlawful trading practices', that is suspension or cancellation of concessions agreed during trade policy negotiations, increase in existing tariff rates, introduction of quantitative restrictions; anti-dumping, which can also be imposed on products assembled within the Community if imports of these products are already subject to such an anti-dumping tariff and the proportion of parts supplied by the country concerned is at least 60 per cent of the total component value; countervailing duties; technical regulations and certification; public procurement; EC surveillance, that is, accelerated processing of statistical information on selected products so as to establish the basis for eventual action to limit their importation; minimum prices; quotas.
24. While the EC's emphasis is on individual liberalisation measures, that of the US is on the right of establishment and on the national treatment.
25. However, others [*Davenport and Stevens, 1990: 60–61*] hold the view that for tropical products 'as a group there has been little difference between the average rate of growth of Community imports from the third world and that from the ACP states', even though the growth of the latter 'has been considerably in excess' of the former exactly 'where ACP preference margins are substantial' as for coffee, tobacco and palm oil.
26. Brown's adoption of a general equilibrium computational approach explains that the resulting estimates are substantially smaller than those obtained with partial equilibrium analysis by Baldwin and Murray [*1977*], Karsenty and Laird [*1987*] and Langhammer [*1983*], because 'general equilibrium changes in exchange rate and prices were found to offset a substantial portion of the impact effect of the GSP on trade' [*Brown, 1989: 774*].
27. Among the several reasons for the ECU's difficult take-off as a commercial currency, some 'lie at the institutional level (the lack of a European central bank and the negative attitude *vis-à-vis* the ECU by certain monetary authorities), while others are traceable to market characteristics and, at a micro-level, to the treasury management practices followed by individual companies' [*Ecu Newsletter, 1990: 16*].
28. For the positive impact of the discipline imposed by monetary union participation on the relative growth performance of the countries of the Franc Zone, see Guillaumont [1988].
29. For the African countries' reactions to such a development of the Franc Zone, see South [1989].
30. Figures at 1987 prices and exchange rates, excluding France's DOMTOM [*Wheeler, 1989: Table 1. 204–5*].

REFERENCES

Balassa,B., 1988, *The Adding Up Problem*, Washington: World Bank Working Paper WPS30.

Baldwin, R.E. and T. Murray, 1977, 'MFN Tariff Reductions and Developing Countries', *Economic Journal*, 87, March.

Baldwin, R., 1989, 'The Growth Effect of 1992', *Economic Policy*, 9, Oct.

Bartha, F., 1989, 'The Ecu and Implications for East–West Monetary Relations', *ECU Newsletter*, Tourin: Istituto Bancario San Paolo, 29, July.

Bond, M.E., 1987, 'An Econometric Study of Primary Commodity Exports from Developing Country Regions of the World', *IMF Staff Papers*, Vol. 34, No. 2.

Brown, D.K., 1989, 'Trade and Welfare Effects of the European Schemes of Generalized System of Preferences', *Economic Development and Cultural Change*, Vol. 37, No. 4, July.

Cairncross, A.. *et al.*, 1982, *Protectionism: The Impact on Developing Countries*, Report by a group of experts to the Commonwealth Secretariat, London: Commonwealth Secretariat.

Cecchini, P., 1988, *The European Challenge: 1992*, Aldershot: Gower.

Cooper, A.F., 1990, 'Exporters versus Importers: LDCs, Agricultural Trade, and the Uruguay Round', *Intereconomics*, 25, Jan.–Feb.

Davenport M. and C. Stevens, 1990, 'The Outlook for Tropical Products', in Stevens and Faber [1990].

Davenport M. and C. Stevens, 1990, 'The Outlook for Tropical Products', in Stevens and Faber [1990].

De Grauwe, P., 1989, *International Money, Post-War Trends and Theories*, Oxford: Clarendon Press.

Deutsche Bank, 1990, *Special Eastern Europe*, Frankfurt: Deutsche Bank, Economics Department, Feb.

Economic Bulletin, 1990, 'The East German Economy at the Start of 1990', Deutsches Institut für Wirtschaftsforschung, 27, 2, April. *The Economist*, various issues.

Ecu Newsletter, 1990, 'The Commercial Use of the Ecu: Invoicing and Import–Export Practices', Tourin: Istituto Bancario San Paolo, 31, Jan.

European Economy, 1988, 'The Economics of 1992', 35, March.

European Economy, 1989, 'International Trade of the European Community', 39, March.

Eurostat, 1988, *External Trade – Statistical Yearbook 1987*, Luxembourg:

Eurostat, 1989, *External Trade Monthly Statistics*, Luxembourg, EC, 5.

Faber, D.C., C. Stevens and T.M. van Vijfeijken 1990, 'Introduction', in Stevens and Faber [1989].

Featherstone, K., 1989, 'The Mediterranean Challenge: cohesion and external preferences', in Lodge [1989].

GATT, 1989, *International Trade 88–89*. Geneva: GATT.

Guillaumont, P., Guillaumont, S., and P. Plane, 1988, 'Participating in African Monetary Unions: An Alternative Evaluation', *World Development*, Vol. 16, No. 5.

Hewitt, A. 1989, 'ACP and the Developing World', in Lodge [*1989*].

Hoffmann, S., 1989, 'The European Community and 1992', *Foreign Affairs*, Vol. 68, No. 4. *International Herald Tribune* (IHT), various issues.

Jepma, C.P., 1988, 'The Impact of Untying Aid of the European Community Countries', *World Development*, Vol. 16, No. 7.

Karsenty, G. and S. Laird, 1987, 'The GSP, Policy Options and the New Round', *Weltwirtschaftliches Archiv*, 123.

Kelly M. *et al.*, 1988, *Issues and Developments in International Trade Policy*, Washington: IMF (IMF Occasional Paper No. 63), Dec.

Koch, T., 1989, 'The Sugar Protocol: an Appraisal', *Intereconomics*, Vol. 24, No. 6, Nov.–Dec.

Koopman G. and H. Eckart Scharrer, 1989, 'EC Trade Policy Beyond 1992', *Intereconomics*, Vol. 24, No. 5, Sept.–Oct.

Langhammer, R.J., 1983, *Ten Years of EEC's Generalized System of Preferences for Developing Countries: Success or Failure?*, Working Paper No. 183, Kiel University.

Langhammer R.J. and A. Sapir, 1987, *Economic Impact of Generalized Tariff Preferences*, Aldershot: Gower.

Lodge, J.(ed.), 1989, *The European Community and the Challenge of the Future*, London: Pinter Publishers.
Lomé Briefing, 1989, 'Fisheries and the Lomé Convention, 8, April.
Marin, M. 1990, 'Lomé IV – The Scope of a New Convention', *The Courier*, 120, March–April.
Matthews, A., 1989, 'African Primary Product Exports to the European Community: Prospects Post 1992', unpublished paper presented to the Senior Policy Seminar of the World Bank and HEDCO on Africa and Europe After 1992; Dublin, 27–30 Nov.
Matthews, A. 1985, *The Common Agricultural Policy and the Less Developed Countries*, Dublin: Macmillan.
McQueen, M. and G. Yannopoulos, 1989, 'ACP Trade: An Urgent Need for an Imaginative and Generous response by the EC', *Lomé Briefing*, 11, Oct.
McQueen, M. and C. Stevens, 1989, 'Trade Preferences and Lomé IV: Non-traditional ACP Exports to the EC', *Development Policy Review*, Vol. 7, No. 3.
Messerlin, P.A., 1989, 'The EC Antidumping Regulations: A First Economic Appraisal, 1980–85', *Weltwirtschaftliches Archiv*, 125, 3.
Newsweek, various issues.
Nicolaides, P., 1990, 'Trade Policies for Services: Options for the ACP Countries', in Stevens and Faber [*1990*].
Norman, V., 1988, 'EFTA and the International European Market', *Economic Policy*, Oct.
ODI Briefing Paper, 1989, London: ODI, Nov.
OECD, 1990, *Financial Market Trends*, Paris: OECD, 45.
Page, S., 1990, 'The Outlook for Textiles and Clothing', in Stevens and Faber [*1990*].
Pelkmans, J., 1987, 'The European Community's Trade Policy Towards Developing Countries', in Stevens and van Themaat [*1987*].
Pinder, J. 1988, 'Enhancing the Community's Economic and Political Capacity: Some Consequences of Completing the Common Market', in R. Bieber *et al.*, *1992: One European Market?*, Baden-Baden: Nomos Verlagsgesellschaft.
Pisani, E., 1988, 'Warning', *Lomé Briefing*, 2, Sept.
Ravenhill, J., 1985, *Collective Clientelism: the Lomé Convention and North–South Relations*. New York: Columbia University Press.
Saclier, P., 1988, 'A North–South, ECU-Based Monetary Zone?', *The Courier*, 110, July–Aug.
SDA-ISLA, 1989, *The Use of the Ecu in International Transactions: The Case of Latin American Countries*, preliminary draft of the Summary Report, Milan: SDA-ISLA Bocconi University, Feb.
Secchi, C. 1988, *L'Italia e il commercio internazionale di servizi*, Milano: Franco Angeli.
Sideri, S., 1990, *La Comunità europea nell'interdipendenza mondiale*, Milan: Edizioni Unicopli.
Siebeke, R., 1989, 'Is the GSP Antiquated?', *Intereconomics*, Vol. 24, No. 6.
South, 1989, 'Frisson in the Franc Zone', Sept.
Stevens C. and D.C. Faber (eds.), 1990, *The Uruguay Round and Europe 1992; Implications for Future ACP/EC Cooperation*, Maastricht: ECDPM Occasional Paper.
Stevens C. and J. Verloren van Themaat (eds.), 1987, *Europe and the International Division of Labour, Survey 6*, London: Hodder & Stoughton. *The Economist*, various issues.
Thiais, P., 1990, 'Trade in Services: the position of the ACP States', in Stevens and Faber [*1990*].
Tsoutsoplides, C., 1989, 'The Determinants of the Geographical Allocation of EC Aid to the Developing Countries', Graduate School of European and International Studies, University of Reading, Discussion Papers in European and International Social Science Research No. 30, March.
Tubiana, L., 1989, 'The GATT Negotiations: Danger for ACP Countries', *Lomé Briefing*, 5–6, Jan.–Feb.

UNCTAD, 1988, *Trade and Development Report, 1988*, New York: UN.
UNCTAD, 1986, *Services in the Third World*, TD/B/1100, Geneva: UNCTAD.
UNCTAD, 1985, *Services and the Development Process*, TD/B/1008, rev. 1, Geneva: UNCTAD.
Van Berkum S. and H. Rutten, 'Liberalisation of Temperate Agriculture', in Stevens and Faber [*1990*].
Vander Stichele, M., 1990, 'The Lost Spirit of Lomé', *Lomé Briefing*, 14, Jan.–Feb.
Watkins, K., 1989, 'Towards a Coherent Agricultural Policy for the ACP and the EC?', *Lomé Briefing*, 5–6, Jan.–Feb.
Weidman, R., 1990, 'The Anti-Dumping Policy of the European Communities', *Intereconomics*, 25, Jan.–Feb.
Weiss, F.D., 1987, 'A Political Economy of European Community Trade Policy Against the Less Developed Countries?', *European Economic Review*. 31.
Wheeler, J.C., 1989, *Development Co-operation in the 1990s: 1989 Report*, Paris: OECD.
World Bank, 1988, Revision of Commodity Price Forecasts and Quarterly Review of *Commodity Markets*, Washington, DC: World Bank, Sept.

2

Why is Project 1992 Different?

SHEILA PAGE

I. INTRODUCTION

It is inevitable that a major restructuring by one of the principal traders and investors in the world economy will have significant effects on other countries. These can be divided into two economic types and two more that are difficult to classify. The economic are:

(i) the sectoral effects arising from actual changes in the EC's controls on trade;
(ii) the macroeconomic effects of completion of the SEM, trade diversion and creation (the only ones considered, although inadequately, in the original EC reports).

These are explored in other chapters in this volume and elsewhere (see references). The others are the subject of this chapter:

(i) the results of the various legal, administrative and other intermediate steps required as part of the process;
(ii) the effect of the reorientation of the EC and its members to a more collective and formal relationship to other countries and to multilateral organisations.

In principle the conventional questions could be asked and answered about the formation of a common market, using the methodology of measuring trade creation and diversion effects, extended in very reasonable ways to 'investment creation' and 'investment diversion'

This chapter has already been published in *The European Journal of Development Research*, Vol. 2, No. 2 (1990).

by analogy. This extension, however, breaks down when it is extended to labour, because increased imports of labour are unlikely to be as acceptable as those of capital or even goods. But there are more serious limitations to analysing the impact of the changes following from 1992, by policy change, by country, or by economic sector, one-by-one. The objective of 1992 (in contrast to those of the Treaty of Rome) is not just to remove obstacles, but quite deliberately to create a new type of market and ensure its efficient operation. To discuss its effects in conventional terms risks underestimating both the case-by-case results and the broader impact of the process.

This chapter will attempt to define the differences which are important for the trading system between the Single European Market (SEM) and a common market or free trade area, and why the process of its formation is likely in itself to have an impact on the international system. Project 1992 will affect the way in which the GATT negotiations are carried on, the trading system that emerges from them, and could influence patterns of trade more generally. Many of these effects will be particularly strong for developing countries.

II. THE NATURE AND COVERAGE OF THE SEM

In goods, the trade diversion and creation effects do not, with minor exceptions, stem from the lowering of traditional tariff barriers to trade. This immediately differentiates it from the North American free trade area, EFTA, and from most developing country groupings. (The Andean Pact was an exception at its foundation, but has drawn back from its more interventionist stance; it, Central America and Southern Africa have limited regional payments mechanisms.) In the EC, the tariff elimination effects have already happened (except for some remaining transitional arrangements for Spain, Portugal, and Greece).

The SEM effects go beyond these. First, they include some conventional *non-tariff barriers*: it is now well accepted that measures of their 'tariff equivalents' do not in any useful sense measure their effect as they are not equivalent to tariffs. Removing them will change incentives and perceptions, and remove distortions, as well as the tariff-effect of reducing the costs. Removal of those with external effects could be particularly beneficial to developing countries (in aggregate) because they have faced most non-tariff barriers.

The second difference goes beyond trade, to encompass agreements on mutual recognition of *standards*, and national-economy-type regulation of disparities among *taxes* and of cartels or mergers. The spread in the number of goods and services for which there are standards, the increase in the strictness that is occurring in some, and simply the greater frequency with which they are being adopted create serious informational problems even for the most advanced suppliers to the EC.[1] Developing countries, particularly small or poor ones for whom the fixed informational costs are higher relative to the actual or potential trade flow, will suffer most. New entrants will also suffer because the act of setting standards increases the barriers to entry. Developing countries will also suffer more than proportionately because many of the products to be regulated are among their exports: toys, fireworks, plants, fruit and vegetables, fish and shellfish, and meat.

The third change is one whose effects were probably underestimated by the EC's own studies: removal of *all controls at borders*. This is not simply a mechanical consequence of the others: it depends on them, because until all goods are free of barriers, every shipment must be checked if only to ensure that it does not come under one of the remaining controls, but this is what industry or commercial commentators invariably list first as Project 1992 effect. The freedom from delays and bureaucratic 'hassle' for any shipment is not important 'only' for small firms (as the EC's estimates of 1992 effects suggested). Studies of firms' behaviour suggest that improvements of administrative procedures have a significant effect, and this probably removes an important barrier to entry (in the traditional, not the trade sense).

This reform is an essential tool for the SEM's purpose of increasing internal trade, and therefore potentially has large trade diversion effects. It will help outside suppliers as well, but principally those large enough to be supplying several EC countries, and therefore regularly involved in transshipments. The benefits to developing countries may, therefore, be less than to non-member industrial countries, and the diversion damage may be greater: it is likely to be lower value goods which have been more constrained by high costs of transit.

Fourth, goods which have up to now largely escaped GATT trade negotiations (and which are frequently excluded from other free trade areas) are included: not only temperate agriculture, but also those subject to special regulations or taxes like alcohol, *coffee and tobacco*. Regarding coffee, this may favour developing countries; in the case of tobacco, taxes may rise, damaging them.

One of the central purposes of the SEM is to extend the freeing of trade in goods to *services*. This is a 'new area' in the negotiations, and one not covered in most other regional trade agreements. Because of the nature of services, they are more likely to be government-regulated than (most) goods. More services require 'prudential' or health regulation. An efficient market, without regulation, is more difficult because the provision and consumption of services are time-specific, introducing potentially large discontinuities in supply and demand; they are often supplied over a period of time, making fully informed decisions at the outset difficult, and requiring additional information, or creating additional risks, about the company providing them and about changes in the market. The reconciliation of markets and regulations is difficult at the national level; it requires the nature of negotiations at the international level to change, within the EC but also with the rest of the world. Trade diversion and creation effects are potentially larger, therefore, than on goods, because the starting point is so far behind, but there will also be a potential systemic effect because so many are trade-related. If the efficiency effects are significant, the cost of trade, within and outside the EC, will fall, possibly precipitating a step increase in its relationship to income or production.

The sixth difference again brings us to the international institutional system. Free trade areas (including the North American) do not imply a *common external policy*, and even other common markets or pacts do not carry this as far as the EC. The EC is the competent negotiator in the GATT. Bringing more areas into EC competence for internal purposes through the SEM means that the role of unified EC policy, not simply those of its members, must increase in these areas, although, as will be discussed below, there are still unresolved issues here. Common policies on such issues as rules of origin and the administration of trade negotiations with individual non-member countries mean that trading partners must be aware of the complications of member country-Commission relations. Where a unified policy does exist, it brings consequential effects: the EC is increasingly, and self-consciously, a new strong economic bloc. The SEM goes beyond product markets to *factors of production*. It has required removal of formal internal restrictions on mobility of labour and capital, and efforts are now directed at relaxing domestic regulations or standards that obstruct this movement. The EC is also moving towards monetary coordination and/or union. This should have the effect of reinforcing all the other improvements in market functioning (it is ultimately justified by and based on such effects). As in trade-related services, these changes could lower the cost of all trade, if the removal of capital controls and monetary union do promote more efficient financial and other markets.

All these changes are moving the EC into a status which falls between a common market and a country, and which is difficult to accommodate, in theory or in practice, in an international system which is formally equipped only to encompass one or the other, and which in practice has had difficulty even with common markets. The common external policy and monetary union should also affect the EC's role in the international monetary and payments system; the roles of the EC and its members in the international institutions and in relationships like the Franc Zone constitute one of the ambiguities of the current situation.

The use of the terminology and methodology of labour and capital movement 'creation' and 'diversion' implicitly requires that the assumption that the efficiency and welfare effects of these are well understood, which is uncertain, and that they correspond to national policy: only where foreign investment is wanted can its 'diversion' be a loss to non-EC members. 'Creation' of demand for non-EC labour may not fit EC political priorities.

III. THE COMPLICATIONS OF THE TRANSITION

Some are inevitable (seen from an EC point of view) as various international policy arrangements are moved from national to EC level, but all (seen from outside the EC) involve technical, and potentially damaging, inconsistencies. What would be for other countries national concessions and controls on trade which are outside the GATT, against the GATT, or involve derogations from the GATT, are at present divided between the members and the EC, and moving from one to the other. The Generalised System of Preferences (GSP) is now almost entirely at EC level, but the level of income per capita in individual member countries is still treated as a legitimate criterion for granting eligibility to supplying countries. This permits it to exclude some higher income developing countries. Multifibre Arrangement (MFA) restrictions and special entry guarantees for traditional suppliers of bananas or rum are bilateral, and how to move these to EC level or find alternative ways of enforcing country differentiation remains an unresolved issue.

Most of the quotas, VERs, industrial arrangements and other contrary-to-GATT controls are at country level. Some, however, are acknowledged at EC level, and enforced under the article 115 provisions which allow restriction on intra-EC trade to enforce extra-EC controls. It is, however, the EC which is responsible to GATT for the Uruguay Round commitment to roll-back and standstill on such measures, and whose trade policy will be examined under the new powers given to the Secretariat. The quotas which are allowed by GATT because they predate GATT rules (Italy on Japanese cars, for example) are for GATT purposes country-specific, and also depend on article 115.

On the new areas where there is little or no tradition of international negotiation, the EC can take the initiative from the beginning. On those where there are existing bodies (non-GATT organisations regulating shipping, air services, intellectual property, for example), the situation remains uncertain. The clearest complications arise in capital flows, money, and exchange rates. The EC countries are individual (and as seen over reallocation of IMF quotas in 1990 not always harmonious ones) members of international bodies, and individual donors of aid or regulators of banking systems, but the existence of intra-EC capital mobility, non-discrimination on government procurement, and coordinated, if not common, exchange rate policy makes it difficult to treat them as totally independent.

The coincidence of the SEM transition with the GATT Uruguay Round, the growing participation of developing countries in international trade and trade negotiations, and the formation of new free trade areas or other regional links poses special dangers. Preoccupation with 1992 nearly prevented the EC from supporting the holding of the Uruguay Round, and it still means that both officials and economic groups in the EC countries are much less concerned with its outcome than is true, for example, in the US. From the beginning, the EC has given the impression of not having any very strong objectives for the outcome (as the US had for services or agriculture, and many developing countries have for agriculture, tropical products, or textiles and clothing). It has defensive ones (concessions on intellectual property or access to developing country markets in exchange for any changes on MFA), but GATT is clearly not the most important international trade forum for EC policy in the early 1990s. The effects of this timing may, however, have been more favourable in the opposite direction: one of the motives for the Round was to help the US government to constrain US protectionism; it may be having a similar effect on the EC instinct to pass on any costs to producers of greater economic union to outside suppliers.

The areas where progress is being made in the GATT round may also affect the nature of the SEM: if textiles and clothing trade is put on a transition path to a non-MFA system, then it is not administratively worth the effort to find a substitute for article 115 to separate national markets for these sectors for seven to eight years. If the only remaining beneficiaries of preserving national markets are a few minor banana exporters, then *ad hoc* measures, whose breakdown would not be regarded as serious, may suffice.

The 'diversion of negotiators' interest' (not just to Project 1992, but now to Eastern Europe (EE) as well) is important, however, not just because it may limit the outcome of the Uruguay Round. Treating multilateral negotiations as secondary does not encourage developing countries, many of which are new, or newly active, GATT members to consider them a strong part of the international trading system, or, by extension, to treat multilateral trade opening as a useful policy to pursue. The EC has been relatively backward in debt and other capital flow initiatives for developing countries in recent years.

IV. EFFECTS ON THE URUGUAY ROUND

An important positive effect has been what the experience of negotiating Project 1992 can offer. The EC already has, and continues to gain, much more experience than others in introducing new areas into trade negotiations; in encouraging countries to accept that previously 'purely national' parts of the economy, services, investment incentives, subsidies with international effects, government procurement . . ., are now legitimate areas for international concern. It knows how to find ways to broaden the competence of international negotiations. The Commission's experience in increasing its own areas of competence as new issues are introduced may have been an example to GATT: its new examinations, if not yet supervision, of member countries' trade policies; its more active and public role in seeking agreement in this Round. The GATT negotiations in turn reinforce the Commission's own position: bringing new areas under GATT, where the Commission is recognised as competent, implies, if it does not require, a stronger EC role relative to national governments. The EC also has the practical knowledge of where difficulties can arise from combining different national systems, as well as different national interests. The new subjects which have been introduced into the Uruguay Round are in many cases those which are also Project 1992 subjects, and therefore they are more familiar to Community negotiators. This could help explain why progress in some of these areas, notably services, has been faster than had been expected.

It has also meant an increased ability and willingness to identify the protective effect of other countries' arrangements. On agriculture, other countries have led, but in steel and engineering goods, and probably also on phyto-sanitary regulation, the EC can use its experience with its own members to examine other countries' actions. This may facilitate the type of close examination of countries' trading systems embodied in the new GATT supervisory provisions.

But on the other side, the EC's experience in looking beyond trade to domestic trade-affecting measures can be used to extend the boundaries of protection as well as those of trade negotiations. Setting rules of origin or national composition to restrict the benefits of trade concessions to developing countries (a problem for ACP (African, Caribbean and Pacific countries of the Lomé Conventions) and GSP beneficiaries) or to extend the coverage of quotas (the proposal to include products of Japanese car companies' operations abroad in quotas for Japanese cars) could become more important risks for the trading system. All this experience of trying to define the trade effects of national policies and then apply EC rules to them directly, not through GATT agreement, may make it hard for the EC to challenge credibly the legitimacy of the US Super-301 'crowbar', or the strategic impediments initiative against Japan.

The EC needs, and is finding, fewer, but more precisely targeted, forms of trade intervention to use after 1992. This incentive to develop new weapons of protection (which other countries, developed and developing, have not been slow to adopt) helped to refine and increase use of anti-dumping actions. These are in turn made more effective by experience gained from intra-EC disputes of close examination of countries' subsidies and taxes on individual sectors, or regions, which can offer 'unfair' advantages in trade. Efforts to define a Social Charter within the EC have been accompanied by growing EC acceptance (and indeed pressure from industrial and union interests) for a social clause in trade with developing countries, although not with other industrial countries. The continuous moving, and blurring, of the border between 'international' and 'domestic' policies is inevitable within the evolving EC, but is also related to the growing importance of trade within all countries, discussed later in this chapter.

In one respect, the EC approach to trade is the antithesis of the multilateral, and this would be a danger to a faltering or unsuccessful GATT Round. All major countries face the choice between bilateral and multilateral. But the EC, much more than the US or Japan, has always divided the rest of the world into clearly ranked groups in its trade policy: its own members, EFTA, the Mediterranean countries, Maghreb, ACP, GSP countries (with further subdivisions) . . . Its first reaction to EE has been to assign it a step on this pyramid (between EFTA and the Mediterranean) and to package it, with new trade concessions and capital arrangements: the European Bank for Reconstruction and Development (BERD). (A new ambiguity: the US assigned 'responsibility' for EE to the EC, but both the ISL and the individual countries are members of the Bank.) Project 1992 has probably not actually increased this tendency, although it has reinforced it, through requiring more formal definitions of trading relations with traditional partners. In a few cases (notably

EFTA and the ACP), it may have provided further encouragement to its trading partners to adapt their own trade policies more to this, and to seek new, more special, arrangements.

V. EFFECTS ON THE GATT SYSTEM

There are three areas to be examined: the possible shift to a rule-based system compared to a discretionary one; the shift in balance resulting from substituting a third very large country for 12 of assorted sizes; the pyramidical compared to the equitable approach to other countries. These interact, and all also influence the more basic issue of the choice between bilateral and multilateral interventions.

On *rules*, the practical effect on the world's trade regime of more Community quotas, more Community standards or mutual recognition of standards, and more use of anti-dumping by the EC will depend on the overall nature of the outcome of the Uruguay Round, and also on the economic climate of the next few years. In their immediate effects, they increase protection. EC and non-EC countries that did not participate before will be covered by quotas. As described above, the setting of standards has a protective effect, and the standards themselves may do so: particularly on goods which are not produced with the EC (including many horticultural and fish products of interest to developing countries), the absence of EC producers and the presence of those who produce substitutes may lead to health and safety standards being set in forms which pay minimal regard to cost or feasibility. The use of anti-dumping has been seriously and deliberately protectionist, and it is seen as the substitute for the MFA. But it could also be a weapon for the developing countries to adopt, to mitigate any reduction in their barriers required in the Uruguay round. It seems increasingly likely, for example, that opening their markets to imports of textiles and clothing products will be part of any agreement to phase out the MFA.

For the trading system in the medium term, however, it is significant that quotas and standards, when applied by an international organisation and administered by national authorities, and anti-dumping, under all circumstances, require detailed, legally verifiable, criteria and procedures. They are therefore subject to examination and challenge. They are replacing national measures which were in many cases completely matters of administrative discretion, or even managed by industry cartel, as in cars.

One of the most damaging changes to the trading system after 1974 was the growth of uncontrolled, semi-official, 'grey area' trade interventions, outside not only GATT but countries' own normal procedures for government accountability. This created a climate of uncertainty about future (sometimes even actual) protection which reinforced the damaging effect of the actual protectionist actions. This breakdown in international observance of rules extended also to interest and exchange rate management, where again experience in the EC is moving back to a more regulated if not fixed system. If the need to define national measures to make them enforceable at EC level reinforces the bringing of the 'new areas' of agriculture, services, etc., into GATT and the restoration of the derogated areas, like the MFA, the international system that emerges could move trade back towards the rule-based path followed from the formation of the GATT to the early 1970s.[2] The most extreme signs that the international climate is changing are the calls for GATT finally to become the International Trading Organisation that was originally intended, with a more formal continuing role of monitoring, regulating, and enforcing trading rules. These are led by an EC member country (Italy). Small, economically weak, countries, especially those not members of any regional group, categories which would include many of the developing, would gain from these changes.

On the whole, breakdowns in international economic order have been damaging in the past (the 1930s as well as the 1970s) and restorations, as with the founding of GATT itself, favourable. They do carry the same short-run danger that stems from the EC's growing use of common standards: that more regulation requires a more experienced or more professional approach to trade, perhaps favouring large countries or companies. It has been argued that this would increase the gap between successful countries and the poorest. This is probably not correct, as the risks from the present erratic system are probably at least as great, even if they are harder to see. An unregulated system with unpredictable government intervention and management is unlikely to offer efficient markets.

If, however, the SEM does produce something more like a country than a collection of countries, it could increase the risk that the international trading system is dominated by co-operation among a group (in industrial language: controlled by market-fixing within a cartel) of three participants, as has already happened on exchange rates. However benign such co-operation may seem to the participants, economic theory does not suggest that it will necessarily benefit the rest of the world. It does not have the advantages of either market or regulated economic relationships. It is always difficult to distinguish (non-subjectively) between intervention to improve markets and interference in them.

One effect of Project 1992 is to make the EC more conscious of an ability to use US-type economic power, illustrated by its issuing of lists of US malpractices in trade in reply to those published by the US.

The outcome of these two conflicting influences, the move to rules and the abuse of size, on the nature of the trading system is not yet clear. The still different commercial interests of the EC members, the fact that they do not act as a unit in other international organisations, and perhaps even the lack of strong EC interests in the Uruguay Round may encourage the return to rules.

Within the GATT negotiations, the EC's pyramid approach is in fact modified to make use of a variety of different allies in different groups, and the fact that EE has seen its 'step' moved up in the last six months confirms that 'pyramid' gives too hard an image. Interpreted as simply a differentiated approach, it may still seem unpleasant at a bilateral level, but it is reconcilable with a multilateral approach.

VI. THE SEM AND OTHER NEW ISSUES FOR THE INTERNATIONAL SYSTEM

In other areas, the formation or the existence of the SEM alters the international framework, but the implications for the rest of the world are unclear.

The GATT system assumes that there is trade and there are domestic policies; there are countries and trading areas; and there are advanced and developing countries. The present structure of the international economy, of policy-setting, and of participants in the GATT system is much more complicated, and the SEM introduce new problems of definition.

The growing weight of trade in national economies and therefore of the size and range of its potential effects, as supplier or competitor for national consumers and companies, makes it harder to treat it as an undifferentiated macro-economic force for which governments need consider initially only the total impact (normally good provided the appropriate policies are followed), with any distributive problems manageable at national level in the second round. It is now necessary to take account of countries with very different organisation of their trading systems, assistance to individual sectors, and national industrial and trade objectives. These affect more than the 'national economy' of their trading partners. The behaviour of foreign firms or policy-makers can determine not only the success of individual units, but also the success of particular behaviour in terms of market-seeking, innovation, even old-fashioned employment preservation, which governments may wish to encourage or discourage. A perception that a system is 'unfair', even if it increases national income, cannot be ignored.

Three current issues may illustrate this. On both, the traditional international economist's answer is clear, but taking account of the broader implications for the national economic ambience could give a different answer. In macroeconomic terms a country will gain by opening its own borders to textile and clothing products regardless of whether its suppliers do the same. But domestic producers asked to compete without policy assistance on their home ground but against foreign producers who do receive assistance on their ground will consider the system 'unfair'. From a country's point of view, to receive an import as cheaply as possible (at best, dumped below cost) is a benefit (excluding special strategic cases). For a producer, or farmer damaged by subsidised EC exports, who has a (non-economic) pride in his ability to produce that good efficiently or to high quality, a system which forces him out of business is 'unfair'. A special case of this, particularly relevant for developing country exporters, is if the good from abroad is not dumped, but simply produced with lower cost labour. If such imports actually lower the relative income of unskilled labour to skilled in an industrial country importer (see, for example, Wood [*1990*]), this may seem an 'unfair' distribution of the benefits and costs of trade.

The same forces that lead to the inclusion of new areas in the negotiations, and extension of negotiations on 'trade subsidies' to negotiations on 'subsidies with trade effects', inevitably lead to countries' interest in other aspects of their suppliers' or competitors' behaviour. The forces which have given rise within the EC to the perceived need to progress towards a Community policy on mergers, taxation, and product and labour standards affect relationships among other countries as well. It is too early to expect this degree of international 'interference' to be acceptable at GATT level, but it is influencing negotiating positions. It has important implications for developing countries operating or considering industrial strategies which include export promotion or import substitution policies, particularly if they use subsidies, price controls, or other instruments open to trade complaints.

The fact that the EC is in a transition from a point already beyond a Customs Area to one still short of country status brings out issues of negotiations between countries with different internal political structures and different degrees of political intervention in trade. This has always been a problem perceived by the EC in trade with the US, and bringing services, particularly banking and other financial services, into GATT makes the role of US state governments even more a complicating factor. Membership of some EE countries in GATT, and applications from others and from China, will bring new types of economic structure, and of price–cost relationships. In the case of both the USSR and China, these may complicate their position in international agreements at the same time as they resolve their own problems of regional control and reorganisation. GATT does not have obvious mechanisms for dealing with this: the Secretariat's studies of members' trading systems may contribute to understanding. But how the effects of the reorganisation of the EC are handled will set important precedents.

At present, GATT recognises only two income levels for countries, developed and developing. There is growing recognition in trade and other international relations that the procedure of graduation between these should be less *ad hoc* and discretionary than it is now, but also that more levels need to be distinguished. One clear tendency in the current round (already embodied in working papers in areas like services and textiles and clothing) is to define a lower, least developed, group. This would, however, be less restrictive than the UN's very poor, least developed category. What is not yet clear is how far these countries will get additional privileges and how far the existing privileges, special and differential treatment now to all 'developing', will in future be restricted to these 'least developed'.

What has not been even recognised is the more complicated problem that for most countries (including those in the 'developed' class) it is more sensible to talk of some developed sectors and other less developed than of completely or not-at-all developed economies. The newly industrialising countries (NICs) are the obvious cases of countries with widely varying degrees of development among sectors, but examples can be found above and below them (Japanese agriculture? or Indian software?). The much more sectoral approach that becomes necessary as trade's importance grows (symbolised by the 15 negotiating groups of the Uruguay Round) brings these out. The groups have seen very different dividing lines. (The Cairns group in agriculture is only the most well known of the mixed developed and developing alliances.)

The interaction of trade with other matters of economic policy is starting to acquire formal GATT recognition. Consultations with the IMF and the World Bank have become regular, although not formal. But the use of balance of payments requirements as a criterion for when certain derogations from GATT are permissible, and the growing use of implied or actual conditions on trade policy by the IMF and the World Bank suggest that the system will have to evolve more formal exchanges of information, on how conditions are set, even if not coordination. One issue which has already arisen, which is very relevant to the EC, is the treatment of common markets in the context of programmes of national trade liberalisation. While GATT does recognise that special derogations with regard to most favoured nation and other GATT obligations can apply to them, with, at least in principle, established procedures for compensating other trading partners if necessary, the other international organisations do not. A clear contrast is provided by the treatment of the Central American Common Market, an obstacle to complete trade liberalisation from the World Bank's point of view; a reason for favourable trade treatment for the US or the EC.

More generally, the other international agencies and *ad hoc* groups like the Group of 7 (or 5 or 3) do not seem to have accepted that the long-established principle of compensation of non-members for any ill effects from a customs area now needs to be extended to groups with non-trade agreements. In the 'new areas', any special arrangements on services, capital movements, exchange rates, interest rates . . . need a form of international review and protection for non-members analogous to that for trade.

Unilateral, member country against member country, controls on trade in beef in June 1990 illustrated that even the EC has not yet found a way of preventing, or ending, national interventions to control intra-EC trade in total contravention of EC rules and procedures. This suggests that the efforts for GATT to do so will not succeed at least in this Round, although faster and more certain legal procedures may be devised. It is arguable that it also indicates that a system may tolerate occasional completely illegal actions more comfortably than the persistent efforts under GATT to devise rules which would explicitly allow discriminatory intervention. Breaking rules only in response to unforeseen events is perhaps less damaging than identifying foreseeable events, and then providing for an unsatisfactory unilateral response rather than a more regulatory one.

VII. REGIONALISM

Fears that the world is dividing into blocs did not start with the move to SEM, but they have increased much more than might seem justified from the relatively minor direct effects on third countries which can be identified by either macro or sector-by-sector approaches. But what is relevant for this chapter is whether either the SEM or the fears which it has inspired have led to a more regional policy towards trading, not its effects on actual flows. Division into fixed and regional negotiating blocs in the Uruguay Round would be an obvious example: this has not happened. Outside it, the advantages which the EC expected to gain through becoming a stronger economic power, and those which others fear that it will gain from greater protectionism, have led other areas to look for potential regional trading groups. Both the African and Asian Development Banks have suggested that these offer advantages for their members. Smaller areas, such as the Caribbean Economic Community, and larger ones, like the 'Pacific Rim', are also showing renewed interest. Most of these are envisaged only as trading areas, so that it appears that it is the threat from European economic power, rather than the example of internal benefits from the SEM, that is the motive. The North American moves, including the new proposals for Mexico, and ultimately all of Latin America, do appear to stem from regional interests there (the same forces that brought the original formation of the EC), but again, and like the US–Canada agreement, limited to trade not a general economic strategy.

The moves to an SEM do not seem to have changed other countries' trade policies, although they may have altered their hopes for success. In particular, areas like Latin America which are trying to diversify their trade towards the EC may fear that Project 1992 will raise obstacles to this, but do not treat this as a signal that the strategy itself is misdirected, and that it is better to turn to deals with traditional trading partners. This is the same reaction as that of other developed countries: the US and Japan are watching EC provisions on access to markets precisely because they do expect to continue to enter them. The traditional GATT (and trade theory) view of traditional common markets, that they are steps toward, not away from, more efficient world allocation of resources seems to be implicitly accepted (except among some economic commentators). The evidence for developing countries in the last 20 years certainly would not support a regional approach: one very clear trend as any developing country moves up the NIC ladder is away from a high share of exports to its traditional industrial country market and towards important shares for the other two. This has been true for countries previously associated with the EC (the moves by Jamaica and India to the US) and those which a regional approach would assign to the US or Japan (Latin America and South East Asia). It is the EC's weakest trading partners that maintain their dependence on it (the ACP). The counter-example could be policy-makers in the EC itself: but even the pyramid is not a regional one, and, as EE has shown, its stones are movable.

VIII. THE EFFECTS ON DEVELOPING COUNTRIES

The effects from the specifically economic consequences of 1992, including those on the 'new areas', are best examined point-by-point, and the conclusions will vary for countries with different types of product and different trading relationships with the EC. This is also true of some of the specific SEM formation effects discussed in the first part of this chapter.

If the optimistic view is taken of the transparency and return to legal order effects of Project 1992, these offer benefits to all the EC's trading partners. Developing countries would benefit more because they have more difficulty in an uncertain, poorly informed system. But if Project 1992 accelerates the move of international regulation into new areas and new controls on old ones, this could bring developing countries under constraints on the types of policies they can pursue and the instruments which they can use at a stage in their development much earlier than such constraints were imposed on the present developed countries. While the least developed may be protected from this, those above this classification will be even less protected than at present and facing even more extensive international regulation. There is no clear indication from theory whether this will benefit them. The benefits from more open trade must be measured against the dynamic costs of constraints on industrial strategy. On new areas, such as the regulation of services or the appropriate weight to give to property rights in intellectual property, it is by no means clear whether countries which are still large scale importers of these will gain from regulations which have evolved to suit exporters, and which the present developed countries did not accept when they were net importers.

If Project 1992 leads to decreased multilateral decision-making and a clear shift to a three-party oligopoly, the probability is that developing countries (together with smaller industrial) will lose (at least in aggregate). If the complications introduced by the SEM and by the reintegration of EE and other countries with different economic systems into the trading system lead to a rethinking of what trade relations are appropriate among different types of national or regional units, this could encourage a more appropriate response to incorporating different levels of developing country, including the 'semi-developed', into the system.

NOTES

1. These are frequently the potentially harmful Project 1992 effect first cited by US suppliers. The problems are: access to the standard-setting process; timely information about new decisions; recognition of non-EC testing or safety procedures; the potential for inconsistent enforcement at different EC borders and/or failure of customs officials in one country to accept proof of acceptance by those of

another. These are all, of course, precise parallels of EC complaints about Japanese impediments to trade.

2. Some of the swing in sentiment probably stemmed from recognition of the high costs and complexity of the 1970s and 1980s regulation of trade, where literally pages of documentation became necessary to define a particular article of clothing under the MFA.

REFERENCES

Clercq, de, W., 1988, '1992: The Impact on the Outside World', speech, 29 Aug.

Commission of the European Communities, 1988, *Research on the 'Cost of Non-Europe', Basic Findings, Basic Studies: Executive Summaries*, Vol. 1, Brussels: EC.

Commission of the European Communities, 1988, *Studies on the Economics of Integration*, Vol. 2, Brussels: EC.

European Economy, 1988, 'The Economics of 1992', 35, March.

Croner, 1990, *Croner's Europe*, London.

Davenport, M. and S. Page, 1990, 'The Effects of 1992 on the Developing Countries', unpublished paper, London: Overseas Development Institute.

Davenport, M. and S. Page, 1991, *Europe – 1992 and the Developing World*, London: Overseas Development Institute, Aug.

Frisch, D., 1988, '1992: the Internal Market and the Developing Countries', speech, 25 Oct.

Hiemenz, U., Agarwal, J.P., Langhammer, R.L., Schnader, J.-V., Spinanger, D. and V. Stuven, 1990, 'European Trade Policies Towards Developing Countries', report prepared for Institute of Developing Economies, Tokyo.

Hoekman, B.M., 1989, 'Services-related Production, Employment, Trade, and Foreign Direct Investment: A Global Perspective', unpublished, Geneva.

Kelly, M., Kirmani, N., Xafa, M., Boonekamp, C. and P. Winglee, 1988, *Issues and Developments in International Trade Policy*, International Monetary Fund, Occasional Paper 63, Washington, DC: IMF, Dec.

McAllister, E.J., 1989, 'US Views on the EC Single Market Exercise', Washington, DC: United States Department of State, Bureau of Public Affairs.

National Association of Manufacturers, 1990, 'Manufacturing Creates America's Strength', Testimony before the Committee on Ways and Means, United States House of Representatives, Jan.

O'Cléireacáin, S., 1990, 'Europe 1992 and Gaps in the EC's Common Commercial Policy', *Journal of Common Market Studies*, March.

Page, S., 1989, *Europe 1992: A Handmaiden to GATT? Comment*, prepared for Erenstein Colloquium, organised by the European Institute of Public Administration.

Stenven, C. and D. Faber (eds.), 1990, *The Uruguay Round and Europe 1992: Implications for future ACP/EC cooperation*, Maastricht, European Centre for Development Policy Management.

Wood, A., 1990, 'How Much Does Trade With the South Affect Workers in the North?', *World Bank Research Observer*.

3

Is Project 1992 the First Step Towards European Protectionism?

GIANNI PARAMITHIOTTI

I. INTRODUCTION

It is widely acknowledged that the EC's external relations with third countries is one of the main areas where the effects of the Single European Market (SEM) of 1992 will be most striking. The intense debate on the SEM testifies to the subject's importance, the argument being whether the EC's external policy from the 1 January 1993 will be more or less protectionist. On one side there are the official or semi-official fears, mainly from the Americans and the Japanese who believe that the post-1992 Europe will be a 'Fortress Europe', while on the other side, there is the European Commission's official position which is directed towards a more fruitful co-operation among Europe's major trading partners in the future. Hence 'Not Fortress Europe, but Partnership Europe'.

Whether these effects will be positive or negative in terms of welfare is still unknown and very difficult to forecast since it depends not only on EC's behaviour towards the future evolution of the principles and rules governing the world trading system (that is, the conclusion of the GATT Uruguay Round), but also on its efforts to protect its own and its exporters' interests.

The aim of this chapter is to show that although the future evolution

The author wishes to thank Professors Carlo Secchi and Sandro Sideri and all the participants in the discussions of the Working Group 'World Trade and Commodity Policies' held during the 6th EADI General Conference (Oslo, 27–30 June 1990) for their useful comments on an earlier version of this paper. The usual disclaimer applies. This paper is part of the research poject 'Progetto Finalizzato Internazionalizzazione', Sottoprogetto 3, Tema 5, Unità Operativa 3.5, directed by Professor Sergio Alessandrini, funded by Consiglio Nazionale delle Ricerche.

of the EC's external trade policy will not be towards strict protectionism, different elements combine to implement an active European trade policy, or a strategic trade policy (STRAP), especially in those sectors still not related to GATT. The internal market completion process represents a sort of prerequisite for the conduct of such an active policy, since it is the first step towards the strengthening of European industry especially in the most technologically advanced sectors.[1,2]

Several circumstances provide the rationale for the implementation of an active trade policy in the post-1992 environment by the Community. First, the new procedures set up by the Single Act in different areas such as the external policy concerning the majority rule within the Council, leads to a collusive behaviour towards foreign competitors by the European industries in some of the major EC member states.

Second, as pointed out by some authors [*Padoa-Schioppa, 1987*], the internal market will not be a zero sum game; internal losers and gainers will show up so that European efforts to secure for its members the most profitable industries could determine those who are likely to lose in the internal efficiency game. This hypothesis is associated with the Single Act's effect of strengthening the Commission's role as a regulatory agency, which has pursued the objective of concentrating in its hands all powers concerning the external trade policy. This has been facilitated by some recent pronouncements of the European Court of Justice.

To these two basic economic circumstances, some psychological effects must be added. The move from several segmented markets to a single one may offer the European economic agents the opportunity to a tougher behaviour in the international environment, which in the language of economic models means abandoning the small country behaviour for the big country one.[3] The Cecchini report also considers various opportunities for a more intensive exploitation of scale economies in those industries which are still excluded by the existence of non-tariff barriers (NTB).

All the conclusions drafted so far are mainly speculative. Since Economics does not still possess a valid method of forecasting future behaviour of economic agents, the perceptions of this chapter are supported by the analysis of the EC's past use of protectionist tools in pursuing a sort of pre-1992 (that is, before the 1992 programme was launched) STRAP.

Analysing the past, it seems that the extensive use of NTBs by the Community, especially anti-dumping (AD) measures, seems to have served well as an active trade policy. In fact, as will be shown, the AD measures have constituted an excellent and very powerful means of protection for some very selected European industrial interests. Moreover, the advertisement quoted in the conclusion seems a very good example of the different social parties' joint claims, which may be a prelude to their explicit demand for protection.

II. THE NEW SINGLE ACT'S DECISION MECHANISM, COUNCIL ACTIVITY AND STRAP

One of the Single Act's major achievement is the introduction of the decision mechanism based on the majority vote. According to article 18 in conjunction with article 10, the Council can now decide on almost all matters, including external policy, by a special majority vote. Only tax harmonisation measures and legislation concerning the functioning of labour markets require a unanimous vote.

The new majority mechanism may in future give way to an upsurge in member states' voting in coalition, within the Council.[4] Given that the total number of weighted votes in the Council sums up to 76 (Germany, France, Italy and the UK possess ten votes each, Spain eight, Netherlands, Belgium, Greece and Portugal five, Denmark and Ireland three and Luxembourg two) and the minimum votes required for any decision are 54, this implies that any decision can be blocked by a coalition of three large countries or by two large countries in co-operation with any of the medium-small ones, excluding Luxembourg.[5]

This means that the external policy interests of the leading and the more industrialised European countries will be well protected within the Council's activity. An example may be the post-1992 Japanese car import regime, which may soon become a subject of the Council decision. Its sudden liberalisation is strongly opposed by some big EC members and auto producers, such as Italy, France and Germany to some extent, while it is supported by some of the small EC members like Greece, which does not posses a domestic car industry. Until now, however, no official decision has been taken. It seems that the institution of a transitory regime, lasting for at least a three-year period beyond 1992, is a probable solution. This regime, while protecting the European car industry from Japanese competition for a longer period enables EC authorities to trade the liberalisation of this important sector for Japanese concessions in other sectors which are of great European interest.

III. PROJECT 1992 AND THE EVOLUTION OF THE COMMISSION'S ROLE IN DEFINING EXTERNAL TRADE POLICY

The Single Act has affected not only the Council's decision rules, but also the Commission's task since it has strengthened its role as an administrative regulatory agency tackling the conflict of interests which will arise in the future among member states, regions, industries and other European economic agents.[6]

Differences in development trends between various European regions may in fact arise in the future because of the effect of Project 1992 itself. This difference may lead to a further conflict of interests among European economic agents themselves which the Commission will be asked to settle. As is well known, the abolition of internal barriers to trade by 31 December 1992, which is one of the major aims, will result in an increase in competition among European firms and will prove beneficial to European consumers since they will experience a price reduction. European firms will reinforce their capacity to withstand international competition through price reduction of inputs and better exploitation of economies of scale, leading to international specialisation.

The other side of the coin consists of the fact that entire industrial sectors belonging to different European countries which have up to now survived, thanks to the protection granted by each country's NTBs, will find themselves in a very critical situation. Thus it is possible that in the near future, European firms belonging to sectors negatively hit by the effects of 1992 will increase their demand for protection from internal competition by claiming more state subsidies, although national authorities may also increase subsidies for protecting national champions.

However, an increase of national subsidies to declining industrial sectors is nothing new, since this has already been suggested by some authors, although for different reasons.[7] According to them, the use of subsidies by member governments should replace their loss in controlling normal policy instruments, such as monetary and fiscal policies, which with the completion of the integration process will be concentrated in the Community.

This solution to the problem seems inappropriate for two main reasons. First, it contradicts recent pronouncements concerning increased competition as suggested by the Internal Market General Directorate and implemented by the Commission.[8] Second, this practice would be dangerous for the Community as a whole since its members, in protecting national champions, could end up in an expensive subsidy war. For these two reasons, Community efforts will be directed towards the strict control both of the national subsidies given by member states and of subsidies demanded by the negatively hit national industries, especially as a result of 1992.

But this strict control of internal subsidies may lead the Commission to raise protection in some industrial sectors, particularly during the transition period lasting for a few years beyond 1992, in order to compensate for the decrease in the member states' internal protectionist barriers. In other words those industries, negatively hit by the effects of 1992, may be induced to collude internally in order to obtain an increased level of protection which will permit members to survive in a dramatically changed environment. Examples of such behaviour are still lacking, since up to now no sector has shown such a real need, but public procurement industries may fit this working hypothesis soon in the future. The television industry may also be included, although European standards for this industry have been defined independently for Project 1992.

A more straightforward approach by some authors to the problem of the post-1992 EC's external relations also leads to the same conclusions, that is, implementation of an active (protectionistic) trade policy. According to those authors, the restructuring of European industry brought about by 1992, especially in sectors where economies of scale increase market concentration and hence plant closing, will justify a protectionist conduct in order to permit them to reach the minimum efficient technical scale of operation in these sectors [*Dornbush, 1989*].

It is quite obvious that such a policy exchange between internal and external protection will drive the Community's external policy towards, at least, an active trade policy in favour of those sectors needing a new and higher level of external protection. Thus it would be very easy for this policy, at a later stage, to turn itself into a policy directed towards the objective of capturing firms generating extra profit (STRAP).

Increased specialisation among European partners following 1992 may also enhance the Commission's role as a regulatory agency. The enlarged Community includes countries structurally very different in factor endowments and in development levels. The internal market completion process may deepen these structural differences, enabling the structurally similar and more advanced original members to specialise in the technological capital-intensive production under STRAP, while leaving its less developed members with the labour-intensive ones. Thus these countries will suffer international competition from low-wage countries, especially NICs. Such a situation, excluding labour-intensive members from partaking of STRAP advantages, may increase their demand for an active trade policy that would defend their interests in labour-intensive sectors. The textile and apparel sector seems to be a good example where these predictions have been realised: a coalition of the sector's industrialists and unions has presented to the Commission some guidelines regarding the EC's external policy which negate the free trade principle (see Annex I and the chapter's conclusions).

All the possibilities examined concerning what may influence the future of the European trade policy could become effective well before January 1993. As is well known, a common commercial policy is one of the central features of the Treaty of Rome, although in this Treaty article 115 was inserted to prevent trade deflection.[9] Thanks to this article, the overall quantitative restrictions on imports are negotiated by the Commission, but quotas are defined for and administered by individual nations, thus leaving room for bilateral agreements between an EC member and a foreign country.

Abolition of article 115 is included in the White Paper's programme for the removal of internal physical barriers to trade. This will remove the instrument permitting each member state to conduct its own trade policy to safeguard its specific industrial interests, while also contributing to the concentration of powers in the hands of the Commission regarding external trade relations. But two recent sentences by the European Court of Justice have declared the existence of national quotas in contrast with the spirit of the Treaty of Rome, and will accelerate this process. Foreign trade decisions will thus be concentrated with the Commission which will be responsible for the solution of all problems concerning protection, granted by article 115 until recently.

IV. THE EC ANTI-DUMPING CODE: A LEGITIMATE OR A PROTECTIONIS 'STRATEGIC' TOOL?

So far the possible evolution of the nature of the EC's external relations after 1992, due to the different roles of the Council and the Commission and to the different national economic agents' behaviour, has been examined. We can now look at the use of a very particular external policy instrument, that is, the anti-dumping code which has demonstrated itself as a very powerful tool in controlling selected foreign targets. Anti-dumping codes are designed to protect domestic markets from the unfair actions of foreign business enterprises. The economic rationale for anti-dumping rests on the principle that injurious dumping is to be condemned, since it is based on an artificial rather than a true comparative advantage resulting from cost efficiency. Moreover, more often than not, the mechanism which permits dumping is market isolation in the exporting country, due primarily to such factors as high tariffs or NTB and anti-competitive practices. This usually prevents the importing country's producers from competing with the foreign supplier on his own ground, while allowing him to attack their domestic market by sales which are often made at a loss, or are financed from the profits made from the sale of the same or different products in a protected domestic market.

If the above argument can be the economic rationale for anti-dumping, it is important to investigate whether AD codes have always been applied in response to an unfair trade practice, or have been used as a STRAP instrument to support strategic domestic industries in achieving industrial policy objectives. Whatever the interpretation, a fair judgement of the case is extremely difficult since it is open to contrasting interpretations. Taking the Community's case, obviously the Commission's support is for the former interpretation of its conduct in the matter, while dumpers consider the latter to be true.[10]

The EC anti-dumping regulation is consistent with GATT article VI (and probably this is one of the reasons why AD provisions are most invoked by European firms, as will be seen later), which requires a positive finding of injury for the imposition of an anti-dumping duty. It came into effect in 1984 (Regulation 2176/84), broadening the scope of the existing rules. Two years later, the EC extended the concept of 'unfair' trade practices to a service industry – shipping, which is not yet covered by GATT rules.[11] This EC legislation allows the Commission to intervene against shipping lines practising 'predatory' pricing. In June 1987, the concept of anti-dumping was extended to the so-called 'screwdriver plants' established by non-EC producers in the Community to prevent circumvention of anti-dumping duties on finished products.

Under the EC procedures, dumping's definition is based on the price prevailing in the exporters' domestic market. If market imperfections make the price not representative of costs, the AD investigation is based on estimated production costs, which assume average cost pricing and may be subject to considerable margin of error because a similar country may be selected as a representative of the productive environment of the dumper's country of origin.

The brief outline of the mechanism on which EC's anti-dumping procedure is based on is sufficient to point out how much room there is for the Eurocrats' discretion. These include the definition of the correct price prevailing in the exporter's domestic market inclusive of profit margin, the estimation of production costs, and the selection of a similar country in cases where cost estimation is impossible due to a lack of data, which are all issues subject to Eurocrats' judgements. The suspicion is that these judgements might not be neutral with respect to the interests of the European industries, and this may be one of the reasons explaining European industrial associations' preference towards AD complaints as compared to other trade instruments (that is, the anti-subsidy code and the New Policy Instrument).

The number of anti-dumping cases initiated by the EC in the 1980–88 period totalled 349. It soared during the first half of this period while the US dollar exchange rate was overvalued, due to the high level of American interest rates which suddenly decreased in 1986 and rose again in 1987 and 1988 (see Table 1).

TABLE 1
AD CASES INITIATED BY EC AGAINST ALL COUNTRIES (1980–88)

1980	1981	1982	1983	1984	1985	1986	1987	1988	Total
25	47	55	36	48	36	24	39	39	349

Source: EC Commission (1990), Annex 0.

During the first half of the 1980s, the number of AD investigations that ended with an injury finding and thus resulted in the imposition of restrictions increased, while the no-injury findings increased in the second half of the 1980s (see Table 2).

TABLE 2
AD CASES CONCLUDED BY THE APPLICATION OF AD MEASURES (1st row) AND WITHOUT MEASURES APPLIED (2nd row) (1980–88)

1980	1981	1982	1983	1984	1985	1986	1987	1988	Total
53	16	42	46	31	12	29	17	18	264
12	14	9	10	10	19	18	4	8	104

Source: EC Commission (1990), Annex 0.

The geographical origin of products sanctioned with this kind of administrative measure is shown in Table 3. The LDCs, and among those the NICs, are the countries most affected. In the NICs group Korea, Taiwan, Singapore and Hong Kong have been the ones most affected. The main sectors whose exports to the EC have been hit by the imposition of an AD duty are: textiles, chemicals including fertilisers, iron and steel, mechanical engineering goods and wood and paper products.

TABLE 3
EC's AD ACTIONS: PERCENTAGE GEOGRAPHICAL DISTRIBUTION (1980–87 average)

USA	Japan	LDCs	NICs	NMC (a)
8.7	9.5	11.9	32.5	37.4

Note: (a) NMC = Non-Market Countries
Source: EC Official Journal, various issues.

These data support the analysis outlined in the previous paragraphs about the quality of European protectionism: it has been mostly directed against countries which are newcomers in the world trade and are therefore weaker in defending their interests in international organisations. The aim of European protectionism has been to protect its labour-intensive sectors or sectors like mechanical engineering, where the EC industry is lagging behind in product or process innovations with respect to industries belonging to the NICs.

So far EC anti-dumping actions have been addressed in very general terms, but they differ in the conclusions that have been reached. In fact anti-dumping measures can be split into five main categories: *ad valorem* duties, 'other' duties, undertakings, mixed measures and 'possibly' protective measures. 'Other' duties refer to specific or variable duties, both based on reference prices.

Undertakings are unilateral commitments offered by exporting firms to the EC Commission with respect to minimum import price or maximum export quantities. These commitments are private agreements regarding price or quantity between foreign and EC firms, which most of the time lead to anti-dumping actions. During the 1980–88 period, the EC Commission accepted undertakings in 178 cases, whereas only 86 investigations ended with the imposition of definitive duties on all exporters affected. Undertakings may aim at eliminating either the margin of dumping;[12] or the margin of injury.[13]

Mixed measures correspond to cases where a mixture of measures are applied to economic agents involved in AD action. Finally 'possibly' protective measures correspond to investigations of cases that have either led to dumping, minimum dumping, or no injury. Table 4 illustrates AD measures divided in the five categories just indicated.

The striking features of Table 4 is the high percentage of price-fixing mechanisms: undertaking with 'other' duties amount to a 44.3 per cent of all measures taken. This figure should be compared with the scarce use of *ad valorem* duties, which represent less than six per cent of all measures taken.[14]

TABLE 4

EC's AD MEASURES: PERCENTAGE OF DIFFERENT CATEGORIES OF REACHED CONCLUSIONS (cases initiated between 1980 and 1985)

Ad valorem duties	Other duties	Undertakings	Mixed measures	Possibly protective measures
5.8	4.2	40.1	19.4	30.5

Sources: EC Official Journal, various issues and Messerlin [*1989*].

The frequent use of undertakings as a settlement of AD disputes lends itself to contrasting interpretations. On one side there is the Commission's official position, expressed by its former Commissioner in charge of External Relations who claimed that the high percentage of price undertakings was the evidence that would substantiate the statement that the EC's anti-dumping policy 'is incontestably by far the most liberal' of all jurisdictions [*de Clerq, 1988*]. In the Commissioner's view, the Commission's acceptance of an undertaking is a manifestation of a liberal behaviour since it is adopted as an alternative to the imposition of an anti-dumping duty which generally requires a higher import price with respect to an undertaking.

Moreover, according to the Commission, not only has AD not been selective, that is, concentrating on imports from a particular country or geographical region, but also the European authorities have opened AD investigations

> . . . on receipt of a satisfactory complaint on behalf of a Community industry, and never on its own initiative. Therefore any allegation that the Community's AD policy is being used as a tool in the construction of a 'Fortress Europe' must be regarded as a pure figment of the imagination, the reality being rather that it is applied impartially to protect the Community industries against isolated instances of injurious dumping, a practice which is condemned by the GATT [*Commissione, 1990: 19–20*].

The efficacy of AD measures not only for constructing a 'Fortress Europe', but also for protecting the European industries from unfair competition has been questioned by the European Confederation of different industrial associations. According to this Confederation the implementation of the European AD policy is very difficult not only because at least a 15- to 18-month period elapsed from the complaint presentation to the case conclusion, but also because of other technical impediments that usually delay the conclusion of the case.

On the other hand, others argue that special 'undertakings' are in fact government-sponsored cartels with all the negative welfare consequences that a cartel imposes upon economic agents. The origin of this second view of the real nature of EC anti-dumping rules lies in the fact that AD proceedings are initiated at the request of a small number of domestic complaints, and are aimed at a small number of known foreign exporters. Thus the structure of the relevant market for an AD action tends to be oligopolistic, and, according to economic theory, oligopolistic firms try to collude when given the opportunity to exploit their collective market power.

Evidence collected by some authors about this issue demonstrates not only that a high percentage of all AD actions in the Community is initiated by the coalitions of up to eight European firms, but also that there is an inverse relation between the number of firms and the success of the complaints. This can be measured by the difference between the requested and the granted margin of dumping, that is, the smaller the number of firms the higher the margin on the export price imposed by the Commission.[15]

There is no public evidence that the Commission's procedures for the negotiation and enforcement of price undertakings in AD suits offers opportunities for firms to organise collusion. 'What is known is that those agreements, with authorities' approval, have been used "creatively" to restrict international competition in ways that couldn't have been achieved by the direct imposition of AD duties.'[16]

Moreover, in some specific situations price undertaking might have been used to circumvent internal anti-trust legislation because, according to some authors, in some circumstances a price undertaking agreement concluded under AD regulation would have been prosecuted under anti-trust legislation [*Stegeman, 1989*].

Thus, if the interpretation suggested about 'undertakings' favouring the exercise of economic power by exporters is accepted, then European complainants and other economic interests have been instrumental in their adoption. First of all, they have demonstrated themselves to be very efficient in hitting the expected target, since they have always proved efficient in reducing import quantities. The decline of imported quantities of goods subject to EC anti-dumping actions was sharp: five years after a protective measure had been taken, EC import quantities have been reduced by one-half on average. However, what is more important in this respect is the fact that the mere threat of initiating an AD action has also had some effect: imports declined by five per cent on average between the year before the initiation and the year of the initiation.

Secondly, the measures taken are severe, with an average *ad valorem* tariff equivalent of roughly 23 per cent that is, (five times the average post-Tokyo most favoured nation tariffs) [*Messerlin, 1989: 70*]. This criticism regarding the magnitude of EC anti-dumping measures is challenged by the Commission on the ground that comparing similar cases under US and EC procedures, US tariffs have resulted in much higher margins [*de Clerq, 1988*].

Finally, and most importantly, as was already outlined in the chapter, the EC anti-dumping code is consistent with GATT, while VERs are not. This leaves room both for the calculation of the dumping margin and its final imposition by the Commission's intervention which may well be influenced by European cartels.

V. CONCLUSIONS

The impact of the project of completing the internal European market by the end of the year 1992 on EC's external relations must be recognised as one of the utmost importance, but with unknown effects. Although the overall effect will be measured *ex-post* by the calculation of the sum of the trade-creation and trade-diversion effects, the *ex-ante* forecasts about the EC's future behaviour towards foreign partners are very difficult to formulate, since they are influenced by several often contrasting factors. The conclusion of the GATT Uruguay Round is an important factor since, for example, it might or might not include an agreement on services, thus binding EC's behaviour on this delicate sector of international trade.

The analysis conducted reveals that different elements of Project 1992 constitute a sort of prerequisite for a reorientation of the European trade policy by the Community's authorities. This in turn may anticipate the implementation of STRAP, at least in some of the more sensitive European industrial sectors. The origin of this new approach to foreign trade policy problems could be found in the roles assigned by the Single Act to the Council and to the Commission. The adoption of the new majority mechanism in the Council's voting decisions may in fact favour an upsurge in member state coalitions, led by the more industrialised countries, protecting precise economic interests.

Project 1992 will also affect the Commission's role of strengthening its capacity as an administrative regulatory agency for resolving conflicts of interest which will arise between broadly defined European economic agents. This new role of the Commission may start well in advance before 1993 due to some recent sentences by the European Court of Justice that have contributed to a concentration of power concerning foreign trade policy in the hands of the Commission.

My own perception on this important issue is that the Commission, due to the possible rise of internal conflicts amongst its members about the protection of economic sectors, which have hardly been hit by the consequences of Project 1992, and in order to avoid a subsidy war to sustain those sectors, may be forced to raise the level of protection for those and other economic sectors as a trade-off for the progress of Project 92. This trade-off may also be supported by lobbying activities within the Council. The new role of the Commission, especially its consequences on the domestic economic policy of member states, has already been understood by some European politicians.

The past use of the EC's policy instruments, such as the European anti-dumping code, supports my perception. The supposed difference between the past and the future situation is that, before Project 1992, trade policy has been just a defensive policy, promoted by some European producers' associations hit by unfair foreign competition, while the future policy action may become aggressive, and be supported by the interests of some European economic coalitions (industrialists, workers, etc.).

Again, the possible shift of European trade policy towards a more active one through greater use of correct policy instruments, such as the threat of AD actions, may be checked by an increase of press propaganda. Disposable cigarette lighters from Taiwan, car stereos from Korea, clothes and garments from the LDCs and the NICs and oceanic fishing by Polish ships are examples of economic activities for which AD suits have been announced by European economic (oligopolistic) coalitions.

Moreover, the proof that European economic coalitions of industrialists and workers are consciously moving from the request of a defensive trade policy towards STRAP is contained in Annex I. This document not only articulates the worries of employers and trade unions of the major European textile and clothing firms about the future of this very important sector of the European industry, but also precisely dictates the guidelines that should orientate the Commission's future actions. Among these, the priority for integrating the Eastern European countries rather than opening up internal markets to Asian countries, and the banning of LDCs to practise social dumping, must be underlined. This public announcement may also support the opinions of those who believe that the new voting mechanism within the Council's activity will favour the coalitions' upsurge. It therefore seems that the European Authorities' task of preventing European trade policy shifting towards aggressive protectionism in the near future may prove difficult to activate.

In conclusion, leaving room for a positive expectation about this important issue, it must be remembered that the EC has depended heavily in the past, and will do so in the future, on external trade for its growth. Its degree of openness is in fact more than 50 per cent, which is high compared to 14 per cent for the US and eight per cent for Japan. These figures, while reducing the weight of the chapter's perceptions, are useful in confirming the view that the EC's external trade policy can be prevented from shifting towards strict protectionism as has been feared by many foreign trade partners of Europe and, therefore, easing the task of the European Authorities.

NOTES

1. According to Katseli [*1989: 15*], STRAP's origin must be indicated in the Single Act itself. In fact article 24 of the Single European Act states that the goal of the European Community is to strengthen the scientific and technological foundations of European industry and to facilitate the promotion of international competitivness. This interpretation seems to go a little beyond the spirit of the Single Act.
2. To avoid any confusion about the terms used, protectionism is defined as any state policy action which is adopted for the purpose of improving the competitive position of local economic agents, just because they are local, *vis-à-vis* their foreign competitors and it is analogous in form to the traditional instruments of protectionism (see Regan [*1986*]). A STRAP is any state policy action that by itself is not desirable, but that alter the behaviour of others in ways that work to the strategic players' advantage (see Helpman and Krugman [*1989: 83*]). Such actions are directed towards capturing the rents belonging to oligopolistic industries reaping economies of scale and thus capable of generating extra-profit so as to increase its market share in the world economy at the expense of others, while gaining protection from international competition.
3. For a similar opinion about the effects of Project 1992, see Page [*1990*].
4. This hypothesis has been particularly suggested by Katseli [*1989*].
5. Any decision may be also supported by a coalition of the four large countries in cooperation with at least three medium ones.
6. The increase in the administrative power of the Commission is fostered by different articles of the Single Act, which has vested it with an important executive function of supervising Council activity (article 10), of developing a social dialogue among partners (article 22), and of coordinating the activities of the different financial funds and of the European Investement Bank. The exercise of all these powers would permit the Commission in some ways to overtake the single European governements in deciding the destination of funds for development programs directed to their own region.
7. See Padoa-Schioppa [*1987*], for supporting this opinion, while see Winters [*1988*], for a very skeptical one.
8. These pronouncements have concerned subsidies granted by different national governements to important local industries, for example, Italy's Enimont and Alfa Romeo, and France's Renault.
9. Actually the most vigorous use of article 115 has been in the defence of the Multi-Fibre Agreement. Other goods subject to controls include vehicles from Japan, footwear from China and various electronic and sporting goods from East Asia.
10. For the Commission's opinion on this sensitive matter, see de Clercq [*1988*], and CEC [*1990*].
11. In some sense the Commission has anticipated one of the most important issues of the GATT Uruguay Round whose orientation so far has been to include services.
12. The dumping margin is defined as the difference between the export price and the overseas price.
13. The injury margin is generally defined as the difference between the EC price of the dumped good and the price in the EC markets which could eliminate the 'injury' to the EC firms.
14. A more detailed breakdown by different countries of these figures reveals that price fixing mechanisms are mostly the settlement of cases against the NICs and the LDCs [*Messerlin, 1989*].

15. For a more detailed illustration of the configuration of European and foreign industries involved in AD procedures see [*Messerlin, 1989*] and Stegeman [*1989*].
16. For this tough but precise statement see Stegeman [*1989: 32*].

REFERENCES

Alessandrini, S. and C. Secchi, 1988, 'L'unificazione del mercato interno della CEE', *Economia e Management*, 4, Sept., pp.10–19.

Bhagwati, J., 1988, *Protectionism*, Cambridge, MA: MIT Press.

Boltuck, R., 1989, 'Assessing the Effects on the Domestic Industry of Price Dumping', paper presented at the 'International Workshop on Policy Implications of Anti-Dumping Measures', European Institute for Advanced Studies in Management, Brussels, 19–20 Oct.

Commission of the European Community (CEC), 1989, 'Il commercio internazionale della CE', *Economia Europea*, 39, March.

CEC, 1990, *Settimo rapporto annuale della Commissione al Parlamento sulle attività antidumping ed antisovvenzione*, Brussels, 14 June.

Di Chiara, V., 1989, *L'antidumping nella politica commerciale della CEE*, Padova: Cedam.

de Clerq, W., 1988, '1992: The Impact on the Otside World', speech, 29 August.

Dornbush R., 1989, 'Europe 1992: Macroeconomic Implications', *Brookings Papers on Economic Activity*, 2.

The Economist, 1988, 'A True Common Market: A Survey of Europe's 1992', 48, 9–15 July.

The Economist, 1989, '1992: Under Construction: a Survey', 52, 8–14 July.

The Economist, 1989, 'A Gun that Needs to Get Knotted', 92, 9–15 Sept.

Helpman, E. and P.R. Krugman, 1989, *Trade Policy and Market Structure*, Cambridge, MA: MIT Press.

IMF, 1988, 'Issues and Developments in International Trade Policy', *IMF Occasional Paper*, 63, Washington, DC: IMF.

Instituto Nazionale per il Commercio Estero, 1989, *Rapporto sul Commercio Estero, 1988*, Rome: ICE.

Katseli, L., 1989, 'The Political Economy of European Integration: from Euro-Sclerosis to Euro-Corporatism', *CEPR Discussion Paper*, 317, London, Oct.

Krenzler, G., 1988, 'The Single European Market: a New Impetus for the Expansion of World Trade', *CBI – Chatham House Conference*, London: 11 October.

Messerlin, P., 1989, 'The EC Antidumping Regulations: A First Economic Appraisal, 1980–85', *Weltwirtschaftliches Archiv*, 125, 3.

Norall, C., 1986, 'New Trends in Anti-dumping Practice in Brussels', *The World Economy*, 9.

Ostry, S., 1989, 'The Search for Stability: Business and Government in an Interdependent World', *Council on Foreign Relations Discussion Paper*, New York.

Padoa-Schioppa, T. (ed.), 1987, *Efficiency, Stability and Equity: a Strategy for the Evolution of the Economic System of the EC*, Report of a Study Group Appointed by the EC Commission, Brussels.

Page, S., 1990, 'The Effects of 1992 on the World Trading System: a Preliminary Overview', paper presented at the 6th EADI General Conference, Oslo, 27–30 June; its revised version constitutes Chapter 3 of this volume.

Paramithiotti, G., 1989, 'Il programma di completamento del mercato interno: una verifica a metà percorso', *Il Risparmio*, XXXVII, 3.

Paramithiotti, G., 1990, 'Mercato unico del 92, relazioni commerciali esterne e nuovi strumenti protezionistici della CEE', *Studi Parmensi*, XL, 80.

Pearce, J. and J. Sutton, 1985, *Protection and Industrial Policy in Europe*, London: Routledge & Kegan Paul.
Pelkmans, J., 1984, *Market Integration in the EC*, The Hague: Martinus Nijhoff Publishers.
Regan, P., 1986, 'The Supreme Court and State Protectionism: Making Sense of the Dormant Commerce Clause', *Michigan Law Review*, 84, 1091.
Secchi, C., 1982, 'Mercantilismo, politica commerciale "attiva" e protezionismo', *Giornale degli Economisti e Annali di Economia*, July – Aug.
Secchi, C., 1988, 'Protezionismo intracomunitario, mercato interno CEE e politica commerciale verso i paesi terzi', *Diritto ed Economia*, I, 2.
Secchi, C., and G. Sacerdoti, 1987, *L'Uruguay Round del GATT*. Milan: Edizioni Bocconi Comunicazione.
Sideri, S., 1990, *La Comunità Europea nell'interdipendenza mondiale*, Milano: Unicopli.
Stegeman, K., 1989, 'E.C. Anti-dumping Policy: Are Pricing Undertakings a Legal Substitute for Illegal Price Fixing?', paper presented at the 'International Workshop on Policy Implications of Anti-Dumping Measures', European Institute for Advanced Studies in Management, Brussels, 19–20 Oct.
Tharakan, P.K.M., 1988, 'The Sector Incidence of Antidumping and Countervailing Duty Cases in the EC', in L.B.M. Mennes and J. Kol (eds.), *European Trade Policies and the Developing World*, London: Croom Helm.
Tharakan, P.K.M., 1989, 'The Political Economy of Anti-dumping Undertakings in the E.C.', paper presented at the 'International Workshop on Policy Implications of Anti-Dumping Measures', European Institute for Advanced Studies in Management, Brussels, 19–20 Oct.
Winters, A., 1988, 'Completing the European Internal Market: Some Notes on Trade Policy', *CEPR Discussion Paper*, 222, Jan.

ANNEX 1

FOR A POWERFUL, EXPORT-ORIENTED EUROPEAN INDUSTRY

Representatives of European unions and the major textile and clothing firms met with a view to harmonising their respective positions on the future of textile and clothing industries. Following the meeting, the parties:

- noted their convergent views on the importance and future of the European textile and clothing industry which is and must remain the largest European manufacturing industry.

- defined a joint stance regarding the regulation of the world textile and clothing trade. This stance will be published shortly and is based on three basic principles:

  - priority is to be given to the economic integration of the Eastern block countries rather than any new opening up of European markets to Asiatic countries;
  - conditions of fair competition are to be swiftly introduced on world markets;
  - an obligation on the part of developing countries to improve working conditions and social security for their citizens.

- reminded European politicians of the importance of the economic and social issues at stake in the Uruguay Round talks and invited them to keep a closer check – via their national governments – on the talks currently being held in Geneva, the effects of which could be quite dramatic on European jobs.

- reminded the European Commission of its duty to defend European interests first and foremost and urged the Commission to tackle the structural causes of European unemployment in a more effective manner. On the same subject, employers and trade unions are concerned by the spineless attitude shown by the Commission in the current negotiations and warned it against concluding high-profile agreements devoid of any economic substance.

- decided to mobilise employers and trade unions from the European textile-clothing industry on a long-term basis and to study all joint means of action aimed at opposing any policy of unilateral concessions to third world countries, to the detriment of European interests.

EUROPEAN LARGEST TEXTILE AND APPAREL COMPANIES
Square de Meeûs 19/20. Brussels. Belgium.

COMITÉ SYNDICAL EUROPÉEN DU TEXTILE, DE L'HABILLEMENT ET DU CUIR
Rue Joseph Stevens, 8. Brussels. Belgium.

Source: *Financial Times*, 11 July 1990.

4

The Prospects for EC–LDC Trade Relations in Traditional Consumer Goods: The Case of the Agro-industry

ANTONELLA MORI

I. INTRODUCTION

Less developed countries (LDCs) are traditionally important producers of agricultural commodities, which still remain their major exports. Several economists and policy-makers suggest that the LDCs should reduce their dependence on traditional primary product exports by diversifying the production into manufacturing. The most cited reasons vary from the negative impact of primary commodity prices instability, which causes export receipts uncertainty, to the positive characteristics of manufacturers, namely, high growth rate of demand and favourable terms of trade. A way to lower this dependence, maintaining steady growth in exports, is to move into the processing of primary commodities. A recent report by UNCTAD states:

> Increased export of domestically processed goods which are at present mainly exported in their raw or low processed form is essential to the development process and for the improvement of the external payment position of developing countries. One important factor for the attainment of this objective is the reduction, . . . of high tariff applied to imports of goods at higher levels of processing . . . [*UNCTAD, 1990: 28*].

In principle, the production of processed goods could be a right choice for a LDC producer of agricultural commodities. The agro-industry sector shows stable growth rates, although these are rather low. However, reality suggests some caution. Before choosing an industrialisation strategy, the international evolution of competition and protectionism in the sector should be considered in order to evaluate the actual prospects for the exports from the LDCs.

The unification programme in Europe is accelerating the process of structural modification of the agri-food sector and, mainly, the competitive strategy. In Europe the general trend is characterised by increasing concentration on production and retail distribution and by stronger product differentiation. Product differentiation consists in more varieties and higher qualitative and technical standards of products. As a consequence of the tightening up of European standards, the access to the Community market may become more difficult for LDCs' exports. This situation lowers the potential benefits of a liberalisation in agricultural trade within the GATT, and in particular of the elimination of the tariff escalation. The structure of tariffs in the EC, as in other industrial countries, provides zero or low tariffs for unprocessed commodities and higher duties for processed goods, with the duties escalating as the product undergoes increased manufacturing.

This chapter analyses the agro-food sector in the EC and the past food trade flows between the EC and LDCs, trying to evaluate the possible effects of the 1992 European programme. Section II describes the food and beverages sector in the Community, outlining the strengthening of the competition between producers and the important role of retailers. Section III considers the trade flows of food products between LDCs and the EC: LDCs export to the EC considerable amounts of agro-food products which, however, mainly consist of products at an intermediate level of processing for industrial uses. The final section investigates the dynamic effect of past EC protectionism, which has limited the development of LDCs processing of food. It is argued that even if the trade barriers against food exports from the LDCs were lowered, it is unlikely that LDCs will be able to compete with high quality products in the Community market. The chapter ends with some considerations on the policy implications for developing countries.

II. THE FOOD AND BEVERAGES SECTOR IN EUROPE

The EC, with a population of 320 million, is a vast and varied market for the food and drink industry. The scope of the food and drink sector includes all activities involved in the processing of agricultural products, excluding farming. Although there are strong differences in cultural values and national behaviour, some common tendencies in consumption patterns can be pointed out. First, consumers demand a wider range of products, from exotic fruits and non-traditional prepared meals to microwaveable and pre-prepared. Increasing attention is paid to freshness and to 'healthy' foods. Second, different life-styles have emerged as a consequence of the increasing number of working women and single-parent families. Third, the expenditure on foodstuffs tends to decline as a proportion of household budget. On average, in the early 1970s food budget represented one-third of the total household budget; nowadays it represents only a quarter.

Over the last few years, retail distributors have gained the key position in the food chain, becoming more powerful than the producers. A typical food chain consists of five phases: agriculture, first industrial processing, complete industrial processing, marketing and distribution. The relative importance of each phase has changed over the time; in general, the key function in one period ends up by dominating over the others. Distribution structures have moved towards increased concentration, diversification and internationalisation. However, many differences in distribution sector persist among member countries. For example, the number of small retailers varies considerably: in Italy there are 55 persons for one shop while in the United Kingdom the ratio is 165.[1]

Community industry consists of a mixture of firms and branches with very different structural and operational characteristics. There has been a tendency towards increased concentration; however, major differences between countries[2] and different branches of production[3] still remain. Parallel to the concentration, a process of diversification and internationalisation has begun within the sector. Increasing concentration on industry is apparently caused by the parallel tendency towards greater concentration on distribution, rather than by the existence of entry barriers such as high costs or complex technologies. A smaller number of larger-size retailers implies a tendency towards demand for a more limited range of substitute products.

The continuous demand for new products shows the importance of R&D activity. Firms must innovate in order to maintain their market position. Out of 100 new products launched, only three succeed commercially. Of this three per cent of new products, only 40 per cent have a life-cycle of more than five years [*European Community Commission, 1988c*]. The innovating activity being costly and risky, large firms have the advantage. Technology is evolving rapidly: the technological frontier moves towards biotechnologies.

There are some characteristics of the present interplay between distributors (retailers) and producers in Europe with interesting results for third partners, such as LDCs' producers:

(a) big retailers (supermarkets, hypermarkets) induce progressive homogenisation of consumers tastes, thus reducing variety;
(b) big retailers compete to buy both brand products and lower price products;
(c) on one hand, food processing companies tend to concentrate in order to increase negotiating power and to impose a higher number of products to retailers; on the other hand, retailers tend to increase the number of competing suppliers in order to lower negotiating power of processing companies;
(d) a concentrated food distribution sector could lower entry barriers for exporters from third countries aiming at penetrating the European market: the target of selling a certain amount of products to few big retailers can be easier than that of selling the same quantity to many small retailers;
(e) big brand companies more frequently make use of external contractors for the production, since the marketing phase has gained importance compared to the productive one.

European Internal Market

The European food industry[4] is rapidly evolving because of changes in technology and changes in structure. It appears that the coming of the Single Market will accelerate this process. The costs of non-Europe in the food industry are high, consisting of a large number of non-tariff barriers to trade, such as specific import restrictions, packaging and labelling requirements, bans on specific ingredients, regulations on product descriptions and contents, and tax discrimination. The European Commission's programme has more legislative proposals relating to food than to any other sector. The Community has already taken several steps in harmonising technical specifications, and health and hygiene regulations for food products of animal and plant origin moving between member states. The effects of higher European standards is already being felt by some LDCs. For example, Zimbabwe tobacco producers must adapt to the new low-tar standard set by the Commission. Phosphate exporters from Togo will have to invest in new equipment in response to concern about cadmium [*Matthews and McAleese, 1990*].

The introduction of the qualified majority voting, together with the acceptance of the principle of mutual recognition of product standard,[5] made it possible for the Community to address the opening of the food market. A large number of proposals have been put forward to facilitate trade between member states in meat, fruit, vegetables, cereals and food products of animal origins. The introduction of the Single Administrative

Document for customs has already helped to speed border crossing times, but the lifting of customs restrictions after 1992 will certainly stimulate further food trading across national frontiers. The coming of the single market will probably affect not only processed food trading but also primary agricultural trading. Food products of good quality are available across the EC, and if transport cost and transport times decrease, then processing companies will buy intermediate food products even more widely across the Community than they do currently. This will affect, among others, fruit, fish and seafood products.

III. PAST TRENDS OF EC AGRO-FOOD TRADE WITH DEVELOPING COUNTRIES

After reaching very high levels between 1970 and 1980, in recent years extra-EC exports of food and drink have grown more slowly. Despite the volume of international trade in foodstuffs, only a few products are marketed at long and even middle distance. There are many obstacles to marketing far from the place of manufacture: transport and storage costs, the relative fragility of the product particularly in terms of freshness, adaptation to the tastes of target populations, national regulations, customs barriers and so on. Despite the good performance records of the EC food and drink sector, the world market is still dominated by US companies of which eight are among the ten leading companies in the world.

This section describes the structure and the trend of processed agricultural product trade between the EC and the developing countries. The analysis has been carried out on a geographical basis (Asia, Africa, Latin America and the Mediterranean Countries) (see the Annex), based on Volimex NACE-CLIO (R44) (see following section), and on UN data (SITC rev.1.) (section on 'Breakdown of Food Trade').[6] It is worth pointing out that processed food is excluded from the traditional definition of manufactures (typically used by the GATT and the World Bank), which is based on categories 5–8 of the SITC. The NACE-CLIO (R44) is more appropriate since it separates food manufactures from agriculture, and includes processed food and beverages in the manufacturing sector. However, it does not allow analysis of the trade relationship at a high disaggregated level by categories of products.

Trade Relations between the EC and Developing Countries

The European Community mainly imports unprocessed products and exports processed products: unprocessed products are more than two-thirds of EC agricultural imports from the world and about one-third of exports. The gap between unprocessed and processed products is even wider in trade relations with the developing countries [*European Community Commission, 1989b*].

EC imports of agro-food products (AFPs), including intra-EC trade, has increased at a rate lower than the one relative to total trade. Table 1 shows the share of the EC trade of food manufactures in total trade:

TABLE 1
EUROPEAN COMMUNITY: TRADE OF FOOD MANUFACTURES
(1965–87)
(Imports (M) and Exports (X) as a share of total M/X with world (intra plus extra EC, percentages)

	1965	1970	1980	1985	1987
Imports	11.4	8.8	6.5	6.8	6.9
Exports	8.1	7.3	7.5	7.3	7.3

Source: Volimex.

since 1965 the AFP share of total trade has fallen by almost 50 per cent, from 11.4 per cent in 1965 to 6.9 per cent in 1987. On the other hand exports of AFPs have grown at rates similar to those of total trade, showing the aggressive competitive behaviour of the EC. Since 1965 the trade of AFPs between member countries and industrialised countries has become proportionally greater while the one between EC countries and LDCs has become proportionally smaller. In reality, however, the intra-EC trade has grown to the detriment of third countries, both industrialised and developing: from 1970 to 1986 intra-EC imports increased approximately eight-fold, whereas the extra-EC one went up three-and-a-half times (see Table 2). In 1987 AFP imports from member countries amounted to approximately 2.5 times those from third countries; imports from LDCs were slightly greater than those from industrialised countries. The Community appears not very open to extra-EC imports of AFPs: market penetration, defined as the ratio between imports and apparent domestic consumption (production plus

TABLE 2
EVOLUTION OF THE EC TRADE OF FOOD MANUFACTURES
(1963–86)
(index 1980=100)

	1963(a)	1970	1980	1986
import intra-EC	9.5	22.6	100.0	176.6
import extra-EC	32.2	38.3	100.0	131.9
export extra-EC	11.0	21.9	100.0	147.0

(a) EC of ten members.
Source: European Community Commission *1988a: 76–8*.

imports minus exports), was equal to 5.7 per cent for AFPs, while the market penetration for total manufactured goods was 12.5 per cent (1985 figure) (see Chapter 9).

Table 3 shows the trade of food products with LDCs: in 1965 the EC's imports from LDCs amounted to nearly 30 per cent of total EC agri-food imports, whereas in 1987 it amounted to a mere 15 per cent: LDCs have thus shared an increasingly smaller slice of a cake growing at below-average rate. LDCs, on the other hand, have continuously increased imports from the EC at considerably high rates: even though their share decreased from 19 per cent to 16 per cent between 1965 and 1987, their absolute value increased considerably. During the 1970s the Community turned into a net exporter of AFPs to the LDCs: in 1987

TABLE 3
EUROPEAN COMMUNITY: TRADE OF FOOD MANUFACTURES WITH DEVELOPING COUNTRIES (1965–87)
(share of LDCs in total M/X of food manufactures, for each year world=100)

	1965	1970	1980	1985	1987
Imports	29.7	30.3	18.7	19.2	14.9
Exports	19.1	15.7	21.7	19.7	16.1

Source: Volimex.

Latin America and China were the only exceptions. It is rather worrying that during the second half of the 1980s even the AFP trade balance with Africa turned in favour of the Community, whereas ever since 1965 it had been negative. The EC had the highest surplus with Mediterranean Countries and OPEC (see Table 4).

Germany, France, the United Kingdom, Italy and the Netherlands are the main EC importers of AFPs: in 1987 the share of these countries amounted to more than 80 per cent of total EC imports of AFPs and to more than 85 per cent of imports from LDCs. Each EC member tends to trade increasingly with industrialised countries (including the EC). In 1965 the first five EC countries' imports from industrialised countries amounted to two to four times the imports from LDCs; today, this gap is considerably higher and, in the case of Italy, it has reached 14 times. Nearly all EC members experienced the greatest fall in the share of imports from LDCs during the 1970s. For the United Kingdom the drop was the sharpest: in 1970 this country accounted for almost 40 per cent of total EC import from LDCs, whereas in 1980 the figure was down to 24.4 per cent. For the United Kingdom the fall was nearly entirely due to the decrease of trade with the 'Rest of LDCs' group.

TABLE 4

NET EXPORTS OF PROCESSED FOOD PRODUCTS TO DEVELOPING COUNTRIES (1987)(a)

(Million of US$)

	Medit. Countries	Latin Amer 1	Latin Amer 2	OPEC 2	Rest of OPEC	Asia 1	Africa	China	Rest of LDCs	Total LDCs	World
Belgium-Lux.	93	−173	4	120	15	−9	96	−5	51	195	2014
Denmark	67	−91	19	196	63	49	25	−96	176	408	3957
France	215	−494	21	503	135	209	38	−78	−18	532	310
Germany W.	109	−988	−1	283	10	−173	−34	−190	−82	−1068	−1377
Greece	35	−8	0	58	0	−4	−40	0	12	55	−846
Ireland	142	79	42	142	89	23	55	−0	18	589	2791
Italy	93	−341	5	275	−33	−18	45	−39	−27	−41	−6222
Netherlands	292	−348	29	523	52	−111	250	−18	613	1282	8078
Portugal	1	−23	0	5	−6	−2	−36	−2	−4	−67	−375
Spain	127	−274	4	143	−9	−39	23	−16	30	−10	−648
United Kingdom	11	−370	49	498	50	136	−342	−56	−434	−457	−3755
EC (12)	1186	−3030	173	2746	367	60	79	−500	336	1417	3927

(a) Figures refer to NACE-CLIO (R44) headings 31+33+35+37+39.

Source: Volimex.

TABLE 5

GEOGRAPHICAL COMPOSITION OF PROCESSED FOOD IMPORTS FROM DEVELOPING COUNTRIES(a) (1970–87)

1970	Medit. Countries	Latin Amer 1	Latin Amer 2	OPEC 2	Rest of OPEC	Asia 1	Africa	China	Rest of LDCs	Total LDCs	Total LDCs(b)
Belgium	4.5	73.1	0.0	0.0	4.5	4.1	7.5	0.7	5.6	100.0	122
Denmark	11.7	58.8	0.0	0.7	7.9	3.9	8.9	3.1	5.0	100.0	56
France	9.6	29.6	0.0	2.7	0.7	0.7	38.1	4.4	14.1	100.0	449
Germany W.	4.3	51.4	0.1	0.3	5.9	15.0	7.6	6.7	8.8	100.0	569
Greece	3.7	80.7	0.2	0.0	0.7	0.1	5.2	0.0	9.4	100.0	70
Ireland	9.8	33.2	0.0	4.4	3.9	3.2	15.7	0.2	29.6	100.0	34
Italy	4.7	57.6	0.0	1.7	3.6	1.5	16.5	2.4	11.9	100.0	234
Netherlands	2.6	64.2	0.0	0.1	9.0	5.5	9.8	3.2	5.6	100.0	280
Portugal	0.2	11.7	0.0	0.0	2.1	2.5	72.5	0.0	11.1	100.0	54
Spain	0.4	88.7	0.0	0.1	2.2	1.6	3.8	0.1	3.0	100.0	138
United Kingdom	2.1	21.2	0.0	0.1	5.8	4.7	14.8	0.8	50.6	100.0	1320
EC 12	4.0	40.2	0.0	0.6	4.9	5.4	16.3	2.6	25.9	100.0	3326
1987	**Medit. Countries**	**Latin Amer 1**	**Latin Amer 2**	**OPEC 2**	**Rest of OPEC**	**Asia 1**	**Africa**	**China**	**Rest of LDCs**	**Total LDCs**	**Total LDCs(b)**
Belgium	5.0	64.0	0.1	0.0	5.5	7.6	7.5	2.7	7.5	100.0	348
Denmark	5.5	38.6	0.1	0.0	6.2	8.6	5.3	28.1	7.6	100.0	342
France	9.5	42.6	0.3	0.2	1.3	2.5	27.3	4.1	12.3	100.0	2120
Germany W.	3.8	49.4	0.5	0.1	6.1	11.2	9.1	9.3	10.5	100.0	2171
Greece	5.0	12.1	0.0	1.0	0.0	7.3	67.4	0.5	6.6	100.0	70
Ireland	5.6	24.3	0.1	0.4	3.1	7.7	12.7	2.3	43.8	100.0	75
Italy	7.2	52.3	0.2	1.4	5.0	4.3	14.1	6.6	9.0	100.0	750
Netherlands	1.7	49.1	0.3	0.1	7.6	21.7	5.5	2.7	11.3	100.0	1080
Portugal	1.7	24.3	0.4	0.0	4.8	4.4	57.9	2.3	4.2	100.0	126
Spain	2.0	64.4	0.7	1.4	2.6	9.8	10.5	3.3	5.3	100.0	482
United Kingdom	8.7	29.0	0.2	0.2	2.5	4.7	25.2	3.0	26.6	100.0	2183
EC 12	6.2	43.6	0.3	0.3	4.1	8.0	17.6	5.7	14.2	100.0	9745

(a) Figures refer to NACE-CLIO (R44) headings 31+33+35+37+39.
(b) Million of US$.
Source: Volimex.

TABLE 4

TABLE 6

COMPOSITION OF PROCESSED FOOD IMPORTS FROM DEVELOLPING COUNTRIES(a) (1970–87)

1970	Medit. Countries	Latin Amer 1	Latin Amer 2	OPEC 2	Rest of OPEC	Asia 1	Africa	China	Rest of LDCs	Total LDCs	World
Belgium	4.1	6.7	2.8	0.3	3.4	2.8	1.7	1.0	0.8	3.7	6.3
Denmark	5.0	2.5	2.3	1.9	2.7	1.2	0.9	2.0	0.3	1.7	2.1
France	32.6	9.9	8.2	57.4	1.9	1.8	31.5	23.3	7.4	13.5	12.8
Germany W.	18.4	21.9	43.2	7.5	20.7	47.1	7.9	44.7	5.8	17.1	22.6
Greece	2.0	4.2	14.5	0.0	0.3	0.0	0.7	0.0	0.8	2.1	1.4
Ireland	2.5	0.9	0.0	7.0	0.8	0.6	1.0	0.1	1.2	1.0	1.0
Italy	8.3	10.1	12.6	19.0	5.2	1.9	7.1	6.5	3.2	7.0	11.9
Netherlands	5.6	13.4	4.3	0.7	15.4	8.5	5.1	10.5	1.8	8.4	8.4
Portugal	0.1	0.5	0.0	0.0	0.7	0.7	7.2	0.0	0.7	1.6	0.8
Spain	0.5	9.1	1.6	0.4	1.9	1.2	1.0	0.2	0.5	4.1	2.5
United Kingdom	21.1	20.9	10.5	5.9	46.9	34.1	35.9	11.7	77.5	39.7	30.1
EC 12	100.0	100.0	100.0	100.0	100.0	100.0	100.0	100.0	100.0	100.0	100.0
EC 12(b)	133	1337	1	21	163	181	543	85	862	3326	10993

TABLE 4

TABLE 6 (cont.)

COMPOSITION OF PROCESSED FOOD IMPORTS FROM DEVELOLPING COUNTRIES(a) (1970–87)

1987	Medit. Countries	Latin Amer 1	Latin Amer 2	OPEC 2	Rest of OPEC	Asia 1	Africa	China	Rest of LDCs	Total LDCs	World
Belgium	2.9	5.2	1.5	0.4	4.8	3.4	1.5	1.7	1.9	3.6	7.5
Denmark	3.1	3.1	1.2	0.2	5.3	3.7	1.1	17.2	1.9	3.5	2.5
France	33.4	21.2	18.9	14.1	7.0	6.8	33.7	15.6	18.9	21.8	16.6
Germany W.	13.7	25.2	37.5	4.4	33.6	30.9	11.5	36.1	16.6	22.3	20.8
Greece	0.6	0.2	0.0	2.3	0.0	0.7	2.7	0.1	0.3	0.7	2.6
Ireland	0.7	0.4	0.2	1.1	0.6	0.7	0.6	0.3	2.4	0.8	1.8
Italy	9.0	9.2	4.3	34.8	9.4	4.2	6.2	8.8	4.9	7.7	15.9
Netherlands	3.1	12.5	10.8	3.3	20.7	29.9	3.5	5.2	8.9	11.1	11.1
Portugal	0.4	0.7	1.8	0.1	1.5	0.7	4.3	0.5	0.4	1.3	1.0
Spain	1.6	7.3	12.2	23.7	3.2	6.0	3.0	2.8	1.8	4.9	3.7
United Kingdom	31.5	14.9	11.6	15.7	13.8	13.1	32.1	11.6	42.1	22.4	16.5
EC 12	100.0	100.0	100.0	100.0	100.0	100.0	100.0	100.0	100.0	100.0	100.0
EC 12(b)											

(a) Figures refer to NACE-CLIO (R44) headings 31+33+35+37+39.
(b) Million of US$.
Source: Volimex.

AFP exports are important for LDCs, although over the years they progressively diminished in importance: in the early 1970s AFPs accounted for approximately 13 per cent of total EC import from LDCs, whereas in the 1980s the figure fell to five to six per cent. The share of AFP exports varies considerably from one group of LDCs to another, ranging from an extremely high 18 per cent for Latin America to a negligible one per cent for OPEC in 1987. Latin America has always been the main AFP exporter to the EC with a share of total AFP export from LDCs to the EC always greater than 40 per cent. Second in importance comes Africa and the 'Rest of LDCs' group. Latin America is the main exporter of AFPs to all Community members except Greece, Portugal (the main exporter is Africa) and Ireland (the main exporter is the 'Rest of LDCs' group) (see Tables 5 and 6).

Breakdown of Food Trade by Level of Processing[7]

Human food is the most important product in the EC trade, accounting for 96 per cent of exports and 88 per cent of imports (figures are for 1986)

TABLE 7

MAJOR PROCESSED FOOD PRODUCTS IN EC IMPORTS FROM ALL DEVELOPING COUNTRIES (1986)

SITC,	Rev. 1	Million of ECU	% of total
1 0813	Oil Seed Cake & Meal	2369	36.2
2 0611	Raw Sugar, Beet & Cane	652	10.0
3 0535	Fruit Juces & Vegetables Juices, Infermented	502	7.7
4 03201	Prepared or Preserved Fish	318	4.9
5 4222	Palm Oil	313	4.8
6 0138	Other Prepared or Preserved Meat	242	3.7
7 0615	Molasses	239	3.6
8 0814	Meat & Fish Meal, Unfit for Human Consumption	236	3.6
9 0539	Fruit & Nuts, Prepared or Preserved	234	3.6
10 4223	Coconut Copra Oil	191	2.9
11 07232	Cocoa Butter	190	2.9
12 05552	Vegetables Otherwise Preserved or Preserved	180	2.7
13 03202	Crustacea & Molluscs, Prepared or Preserved	170	2.6
14 0713	Coffee Extracts, Essences, Concentrates	155	2.4
15 1124	Distilled Alcoholic Beverages	108	1.6
16 07231	Cocoa Paste	107	1.6
17 4214	Croundnut Peanut Oil	106	1.6
18 4224	Palmkernel Oil	101	1.5
19 0422	Rice, Glazed or Polished	79	1.2
20 09909	Other Miscellaneous Food Preparations	60	0.9
	Total	6552	100.0
	(Share of Total Imports of Food From LDC	24442	26.8
	Processed Food for Industry	4504	68.7
	Processed Food for Consumption	2048	31.3

Source: European Community Commission *1989b*.

[*European Community Commission, 1989b*]. Animal food accounts for the remaining part. Imports and exports are highly concentrated on a limited number of products: in both cases, the first 20 products account for more than 70 per cent of the total (the total number of products is more than 100).

The high proportion of unprocessed products in the total EC imports of agricultural products is explained by the destination of these imports: more than two-thirds are used in industry whereas the rest goes to household for direct consumption. The bias is even higher in the case of imports from the developing countries, albeit with major differences between the various developing countries. Not surprisingly, given the high proportion of processed products, the EC's agricultural exports are destined preponderantly for household consumption. Tables 7 and 8 list the first 20 processed food products traded with LDCs: the EC mainly exports processed food for consumption and imports processed food for industry. Thus, although LDCs succeed in exporting processed food, the level of processing of their exports is lower than that of the EC's exports.

IV. LDC EXPORTS OF PROCESSED FOOD: DYNAMIC EFFECT OF PROTECTIONISM

It emerges from the previous section that the developing countries export mainly unprocessed products or do so at a low level of processing, and that the EC is a net exporter of food products to the developing countries. This begs the question as to what the actual constraint is to having a different international division of labour with the LDCs exporting more manufactured products that are now being exported in primary form? Does the obstacle lie in the structure of tariffs and in other forms of trade barriers in the major import markets (demand-side constraints) or in the production and commercialisation skills of developing countries (supply-side constraints)? Two clear facts emerge: first, protection is generally higher the further the goods proceed up the processing chain; second, the drawing near of the 1992 deadline is speeding up changes in the food industry, both in its structure and in the competitive environment.

Table 9 shows the Most Favoured Nation post-Tokyo rates ('pre' column) and the changes in escalation of tariffs which would result from the implementation of the reductions in tariffs resulting from the concessions after the Mid-Term Review package (the 'post' column).

TABLE 8
MAJOR PROCESSED FOOD PRODUCTS IN EC IMPORTS TO ALL DEVELOPING COUNTRIES (1986)

SITC,	Rev. 1	Million of ECU	% of total
1 0222	Milk & Cream in Solid Form	1034	15.6
2 0612	Refined Sugar & Other Food of Refining	815	12.3
3 1124	Distilled Alcoholic Beverages	625	9.4
4 09909	Other Miscellaneous Food Preparations	601	9.1
5 0221	Milk & Cream Evaporated or Condensed	396	6.0
6 04601	Flour of Wheat or of Feslin	392	5.9
7 0240	Cheese and Curd	341	5.1
8 0230	Butter	295	4.5
9 08199	Sweetened Forage for Animal Feeding	278	4.2
10 4212	Soya Bean Oil	268	4.0
11 05552	Vegetables Otherwise Preserved or Prepared	238	3.6
12 11212	Wine or Fresh Grapes	219	3.3
13 4217	Rape, Colza and Mustard Oils	171	2.6
14 0482	Malt	166	2.5
15 04602	Meal & Groats of Wheat of Meslin	164	2.5
16 04842	Pastry, Biscuits, Cakes and Fine Bakers Wares	135	2.0
17 0138	Other Prepared or Preserved Meat	131	2.0
18 1123	Bear	119	1.8
19 732	Chocolate & Other Food con Cocoa	118	1.8
20 0422	Rice Glazed or Polished	118	1.8
	Total	6624	100.0
	(Share of Total Imports of Food to LDC	11363	58.3
	Processed Food for Industry	1439	21.7
	Processed Food for Consumption	5185	78.3

Source: European Community Commission *1989b*.

Developed countries have an escalating tariff structure for tropical products and the escalation will probably continue to exist. The increase in nominal duties from earlier to later stages of processing points to the existence of discrimination against exports of processed goods from developing countries. As a consequence of the escalation of duties, the effective protection or protection given to domestic value added by developed countries is much higher than the nominal tariff.

Over time, tariff and non-tariff measures have limited developing countries' exports. This trade reduction has had the dramatic effect of stopping the learning process linked to the manufacturing and marketing activities. Without competing on the international market, the LDCs have not been able to improve domestic productive capabilities. The learning effect plays a central role in explaining the pattern of trade between the EC and LDCs: increases in efficiency and in the quality of products are related to the accumulation of experience. The less a country produces, the less it is able to exploit the learning economies.

Over the past few years competition in the European food industry

TABLE 9

TARIFF ESCALATION ON TROPICAL PRODUCTS BEFORE AND AFTER THE MID-TERM REVIEW OF THE MTNs
(per cent ad-valorem or equivalent ad-valorem)

PRODUCT GROUP	EC		JAPAN		USA	
	Pre	Post	Pre	Post	Pre	Post
COFFEE						
Raw	9.0	7.0	0.0	0.0	0.0	0.0
Roasted, ground	16.5	13.5	20.0	10.0	0.0	0.0
Extracts, preparations	18.0	18.0	24.2	19.9	0.0	0.0
TEA						
In bulk	0.0	0.0	12.5	12.5	n.a.	n.a.
For retail sale	5.0	0.0	20.0	20.0	n.a.	n.a.
Extracts, essences	12.0	6.0	17.3	17.3	0.0	0.0
COCOA						
Beans	3.0	3.0	0.0	0.0	0.0	0.0
Paste	15.0	12.0	15.0	15.0	0.0	0.0
Butter	12.0	9.0	2.5	0.0	0.0	0.0
Powder	16.0	12.0	21.5	21.5	0.5	0.4
SPICES						
Unground/unprocessed	7.6	3.9	1.2	1.2	0.7	0.6
Ground/processed	11.7	5.1	6.6	4.6	4.7	4.0
ESSENTIAL OILS						
Essential oils	4.6	2.9	3.9	3.0	0.9	0.9
Preparations	6.0	3.0	5.8	5.8	n.a.	n.a.
OILSEEDS, VEGETABLE OILS						
Oilseeds	0.0	0.0	1.0	1.0	3.4	3.2
Vegetable oils	7.2	7.1	8.5	7.9	4.3	4.3
Fatty acid, fatty alchols	9.1	9.1	5.4	3.3	4.4	4.4
TOBACCO						
Unmanufactured	24.4	24.4	0.0	0.0	72.6	72.6
Manufactured	81.0	81.0	14.3	14.3	10.9	10.9
RICE						
Unmilled	12.0	12.0	0.0	0.0	5.1	5.1
Milled/processed	n.a.	n.a.	16.7	16.7	16.4	16.4
MANIOC, ROOTS, TUBERS						
Fresh, dried	6.0	6.0	11.3	11.3	13.5	12.4
Flour	n.a.	n.a.	12.5	12.5	0.0	0.0
Meals, starches	30.0	30.0	22.8	22.8	0.0	0.0
BANANAS						
Fresh, dried	20.0	20.0	25.5	25.5	1.2	0.9
Preserved	17.0	17.0	n.a.	n.a.	4.3	3.3
TROPICAL NUTS						
Unshelled, crude	2.2	1.5	7.7	4.4	5.2	5.2
Shelled, prepared	15.0	15.0	21.0	19.8	7.6	6.8
TROPICAL FRUIT						
Fresh, dried	9.7	9.7	9.1	9.1	7.9	7.9
Preserved	11.3	10.0	21.0	21.0	7.9	7.9
Prepared, fruit juices	24.6	22.2	27.5	26.6	46.7	46.6

Notes: n.a. = not available
(a) Simple averages of post-Tokyo MFN duty rates.
Source: UNCTAD (1989), computations based on GATT Tariff Study 1986 computer files.

has been remarkably aggressive. Companies compete most intensely by means of product differentiation: not only do they keep offering new products (horizontal product differentiation), which widens the range of goods offered to the consumer, but they also constantly improve the quality of existing products (vertical product differentiation). European entrepreneurs compete on the quality of products by increasing investment in research and development.

In the past the actual constraint to a different international specialisation was probably on the demand side, namely, there was a strict protectionist system that penalised the LDCs' efforts to increase domestic processing. Today, the obstacle could be on the supply side: LDCs producers can experience difficulties in competing with the higher qualitative and technical standards of products. Even if trade barriers against the LDCs' food exports were lowered or eliminated, developing countries would not be able to compete internationally because of the low levels of standards of their products and because of the lack of marketing experience (negative dynamic effect of protectionism). The outlook does not appear as unfavourable for countries which export food products destined for industry, due to the increasing oligopsonistic structure of distribution (see section II). In this case, the strengthening of the marketing structure of the LDCs becomes an increasingly important condition.

V. CONCLUSIONS

A vicious circle does exist: in order to increase exports of processed product to developed countries, LDCs should produce competitive products; however, the production of these depends partly on experience (learning by doing), which can hardly be acquired because of the current inability to export; what should LDCs do to break this vicious circle? One alternative is to boost south–south and regional trade. In fact, some attributes of food products favour trade between neighbouring countries, and between countries which have achieved similar economic development. Geographical proximity reduces transport and storage costs and similar economic development favours the existence of common tastes and habits. More intense trade between LDCs would increase productive capacity, thus making it possible to exploit fully dynamic scale economies linked to productive activity. If larger volumes are produced, companies will move down the learning curve. They will probably be able to offer better quality goods and services, eventually becoming more competitive also on the markets of developed countries. For some products it is easier to start by selling lower-quality varieties to other developing countries, before achieving competitiveness in higher-quality varieties for industrialised countries.

NOTES

1. In the EC the ratio between the population and the number of retail shops is: 55 in Italy, 62 in Greece, 81 in Belgium, 83 in France, 91 in the Netherlands, 99 in Spain, 101 in Denmark, 110 in Ireland, 125 in Portugal, 148 in Germany and 165 in the UK.
2. The UK food and drink industry is the most concentrated in the EC. In general, industry in Southern countries (Italy, Greece, Spain and Portugal) is more fragmented. Concentration levels are much higher within national markets than in the EC as a whole [*European Community Commission, 1988c*].
3. In general, the following productions tend to be more concentrated: sugar, oil, wheat, coffee, chocolate, instant products, wine, beer and spirits industries, canned soups, baby foods, frozen foods, breakfast cereals, chocolate confectionery, tinned milk, potato products, fats and margarine.
4. In this work the food industry also includes the drink industry, unless otherwise specified.
5. The principle of mutual recognition states that if a product is lawfully manufactured and marketed in one member state it should be able to move freely throughout the Community, unless a clear reason for national health prevails.
6. Under SITC, the processed agri-food products come under the 'agricultural products' heading and includes foodstuffs, beverages (most of SITC 0 and 1), flour and meal of oil-seeds, nuts . . . (SITC 2219), animal and vegetable oils and fats (SITC 4), and starches, inulim and gluten (SITC 59951 and 59952). The full list of AFPs and their assignment to product groups is in the Annex. Under the NACE-CLIO (R44) 'food, beverages and tobacco products' (groups 31+33+35+37+39) are classified as manufactures.
7. This part of the study is based on the SITC Rev.1.

REFERENCES

Cable, V., 1987, 'Tropical Products', in J.M. Finger and A. Olechowski (eds), *The Uruguay Round. A Handbook for the Multilateral Trade Negotiations*, Washington, DC: The World Bank.

CDI (Centre for the Development of Industry), 1989, 'The Role of Agro-industry in Industrial Development', proceedings of the Regional Industrial Cooperation Meeting for Central Africa, Kinshasa, Zaire 10–14 July.

CEC, 1988a, *External Trade. Statistical Yearbook*, Luxembourg: EC.

CEC, 1988b, *Industry. Statistical Yearbook*, Luxembourg: EC.

CEC, 1988c, *Panorama of EC Industry, 1989*, Luxembourg: EC.

CEC, 1989a, 'International Trade of the European Community', *European Economy*, 39, March.

CEC, 1989b, *Analysis of Agricultural Trade EC-Developing Countries, 1970–86*, Luxembourg: EC.

CEC, 1990, *External Trade. Monthly Statistics No.1*, Luxembourg: EC.

CESCOM, 1989, 'Concentrazione produttiva e distributiva nel comparto alimentare europeo', conference proceedings, Bocconi University, Milan, 12 Dec.

Cline, W.R., 1985, *Exports of Manufactures from Developing Countries*, Washington: The Brookings Institution.

Davenport, M., 1986, *Trade Policy, Protectionism and the Third World*, London: Croom Helm.
Davenport, M., *European Community Trade Barriers to Tropical Agricultural Products*, London: ODI Working Paper 27.
Davenport, M., 1989, 'The Developing Countries and 1992', *Briefing Paper*, London: ODI, November.
Dosi, G. and L. Soete, 1988, 'Technical Change and International Trade', in G. Dosi *et al.* (eds.), *Technical Change and Economic Theory*, London: Pinter Publishers.
European Community Commission CEC, 1986, *EC/Developing Countries Trade. Industrial Products Analysis 1970–84* (Theme 6, Serie D), Luxembourg: EC.
Gazzetta Ufficiale CE, 1989, 'Comunicazione della Commissione sulla libera circolazione dei prodotti alimentari all'interno della Comunita', (89/C 271/03), 24 Oct.
Golub, S.S. and J.M. Finger, 1979, 'The Processing of Primary Commodities: Effects of Developed-Country Tariff Escalation and Developing-Country Export Taxes', *Journal of Political Economy*, Vol.87, No.3.
Havrylyshin, O. and I. Alikhani, 1990, 'Changing Trade Among Developing Countries', *Economic Impact*, 69, Jan./March.
Hugon, P., 1988, 'L'industrie Agro-alimentaire Analyse en Termes de Filieres', *Revue Tiers Monde*, XXIX, 115, July–Sept.
Linda, R., 1988, 'Crescita, diversificazione e denominazione nelle strategie delle mega-aziende europee dell'industria alimentare e bevande', *Rivista di Politica Agraria*, 4.
MacBean, A. and D.T. Nguyen, 1987, *Commodity Policies: Problems and Prospects*, New York: Croom Helm.
Matthews, A. and D. McAleese, 1990, 'LDC Primary Exports to the EC: Prospects Post-1992', *Journal of Common Market Studies*, Vol. 29, No. 2.
Mennes L.B.M. and J. Kol (eds.), 1988, *European Trade Policies and the Developing World*, New York: Croom Helm.
Pellegrini, L., 1988, 'Struttura distributiva e concentrazione industriale: il caso dell'industria alimentare', *Commercio* (Milan), 31, 7–34.
Sideri, S., 1990, *La Comunità Europea nell'interdipendenza mondiale*, Milan: Unicopli.
Stewart, F., 1984, 'Recent Theories of International Trade: Some Implications for the South', in H. Kierzkowski (ed.), *Monopolistic Competition and International Trade*, Oxford: Clarendon Press.
UNCTAD, 1989, *Trade in Manufactures and Semi Manufactures of Developing Countries and Territories 1989 Review*, TD/B/C.2/228, Geneva: UN, 17 Aug.
UNCTAD, 1989, *Protectionism and Structural Adjustment*, TD/B/1240/Add.1, Geneva: UN, 14 Dec.
UNCTAD, 1990, *Selected Issues on Restrictions to Trade*, UNCTAD/ITP/24, Geneva: UN, 24 March.
Waelbroeck J. and J. Kol, 1987, *Export Opportunities for the South in the Evolving Pattern of World Trade*, Brussels: CEPS Papers No.33.
Yeats, A., 1987, 'The Escalation of Trade Barriers', in J.M. Finger and A. Olechowski (eds), *The Uruguay Round. A Handbook for the Multilateral Trade Negotiations*, Washington, DC: The World Bank.

ANNEX

Geographical Analysis

European Community:	the Community of 12.
Mediterranean Countries:	Gibraltar, Malta, Cyprus, Israel, Gaza Strip, Morocco, Tunisia, Egypt, Spanish Sahara, Syria, Lebanon, Jordan.

Latin America 1:	Latin America less Venezuela and Ecuador.
Latin America 2:	Venezuela and Ecuador.
OPEC 2:	Algeria, Libya, Iraq, Saudi Arabia, Yemen, Bahrain, Abu Dhabi, Dubai, Other UAE, Qatar, Oman.
Rest OPEC:	Nigeria, Iran, Indonesia, Gabon.
Asia 1:	Singapore, China (Formosa), Philippines, South Korea, Hong Kong, Malaysia.
Africa:	All countries except South Africa, North African Mediterranean countries and members of OPEC.

Product Classification

In this work the figures for the processed food industry refer to NACE-CLIO (R44) (section 3.1) or SITC rev.1 (section 3.2). All data are current values.
The processed food and beverages products come under the following headings:

1. NACE-CLIO (R44)

31 Meat and meat products (412)
33 Milk and dairy products (413)
35 Other food products
vegetable and animal oils and fats (411) processing and preserving of fruit and vegetables (414) processing and preserving of fish for human food (415) grain milling (416) pastes (417) amylacei products (418) bread and biscuits (419) sugar factories, refineries (420) cocoa, chocolate, sugar confectionery (421) animal and poultry foods (422) other food products (423)
37 Beverages
alcohol and spirits (424) wine (425) sidro e fruit wine (426) brewing and malt (427) mineral water and soft drinks (428)
39 Tobacco products (429)

Note: Numbers between brackets refer to NACE groups.
Source: European Community Commission.

2. Standard International Trade Classification (site) rev. 1

Processed Human Food

012 Meat, dried, salted or smoked
013 Meat in airtight containers

022 (excl. 0223) Milk and cream
023 Butter
024 Cheese and curd
032 Fish, in airtight containers and fish prepared
0422 Rice
046 Meal and flour of wheat or of meslin
047 Meal and flour of cereals (excl. Wheat and meslin)
048 Cereal preparations
052 Dried fruit
053 (exc. 05363) Fruit, preserved and prepared
05461 Frozen vegetables
055 Vegetables, preserved and prepared
06 (exc. 0616) Sugar and honey
0713 Coffee, extracts, essences, concentrates
0722 Cocoa powder, unsweetened
0723 Cocoa butter and paste
073 Chocolate
091 Margarine & shortening
099 Food preparation, nes
11 Beverages
122 Tobacco, manufactures
2219 Flour & meal of oil-seeds, nuts,
4 Animal and vegetable oils and fats
59951 Starches and inulin
59952 Gluten and gluten flour

Processed Animal Food

0813+0814+08199 Feed.-Stuff for Animals

Breakdown by Level of Use

Processed food for consumption: 012 + 013 + 0221 + 0222 + 023 + 024 + 032 + 0422 + 0481 + 0483 + 0484 + 04882 + 0532 + 0533 + 0535 + 0539 + 05461 + 0551 + 0555 + 0612 + 06201 + 0713 + 073 + 091 + 099 + 111 + 112 + 4215 + 4216− 09906− 11211

Processed food for industry: 046 + 047 + 0482 + 04881 + 04883 + 052 + 05361 + 05362 + 05364 + 0554 + 0611 + 0615 + 0619 + 06202 + 0722 + 0723 + 0813 + 0814 + 08199 + 09906 + 11211 + 2219 + 41 + 4212 + 4213 + 4214 + 4217 + 4221 + 4222 + 4223 + 4224 + 4225 + 4229 + 4311 + 4312 + 4313 + 4314 + 59951 + 59952

5

European Investment in Developing Countries: Recent Trends and the Potential Impact of Project 1992

ALESSANDRO PIO and ARIANNA VANNINI

I. INTRODUCTION

Remarkable structural changes are taking place within developed economies, which are the main sources of direct foreign investments (DFIs). The creation of a Single European Market (SEM) in 1992 and the opening of formerly centrally planned socialist economies, will bring about significant changes in firms' international strategies as well as in the macroeconomic context. Such changes are likely to affect the magnitude and direction of DFI flows in the next decade.

This is happening at a time when DFIs have become an increasingly important source of capital for developing countries due to the reduction in commercial bank lending which followed the emergence of the 1982 debt crisis. The contributions which can accompany DFIs in terms of technology, management skills and access to markets have been recognised by many developing countries in recent years, leading to a reshaping of the regulations affecting such flows. In general, one can detect the developing world's increased interest in the potential benefits of properly regulated DFI inflows.

The purpose of this study is to identify the main channels through which these changes in the economic context will influence DFI flows

This article is based on a paper presented at the 6th EADI General Conference in Oslo, 27–30 June 1990 and published in the *European Journal of Development Research*, Vol.2, 1990. While this article is the result of close co-operation and joint research by the authors, section II (whole) and the one on 'Results of the Econometric Analysis for Asia' can be attributed to Arianna Vannini and the remainder to Alessandro Pio. The authors retain all responsibility for errors and omissions.

to developing countries, and to provide preliminary estimates as to the magnitude of their impact. After a brief description of the most salient recent trends in DFI flows (section II), a theoretical framework will be presented (section III) in order to identify the effects of the creation of SEM on DFI determinants. The approach adopted for this analysis is based on Dunning's 'eclectic' theory of direct foreign investment [*Dunning, 1989*], which recognises the importance of both firm-specific factors (the existence of competitive advantages and the attractiveness of exploiting them through DFIs) and macroeconomic determinants (locational advantages in the countries of destination). However, it is argued that the analysis of the effects of SEM requires an extension of the concept of macroeconomic determinants to include relevant variables in the countries of origin of the DFI, namely GDP growth, interest and exchange rates.

Section IV presents an econometric model developed to estimate some of the impact of changes in macroeconomic variables both in home and host countries upon the magnitude of DFI flows. The model was applied to a pooled sample of four European, four Latin American and four Asian countries covering the 1970–87 period, and gave satisfactory results when appropriate lags in the explanatory variables were utilised. Section V draws on the model results and on the theoretical discussion of the previous sections to provide an assessment of the likely effect of the SEM process on DFI flows to developing countries, keeping in mind the recent developments in Eastern Europe (EE).

II. RECENT TRENDS IN DIRECT FOREIGN INVESTMENT FLOWS

World-wide DFI flows entered a renewed period of sharp growth in 1984, after the relative stagnation of the early 1980s. Annual average flows expanded from \$41 billion in 1981–83 to \$45 billion in 1983–85 and increased more than twofold to \$95 billion in 1985–87 [*IMF, 1988*]. This growth was accompanied by a shift in the relative importance of selected areas as a source or destination of foreign investments. In overall terms, the share of developed and developing countries has remained relatively stable since 1975, as shown in Table 1. Among developed countries, however, the US declined significantly as a source of DFIs, becoming the primary destination of such flows at the expense of Western Europe (although this tendency has been at least partially reversed). Japan became a relevant international investor, expanding from 6 to 12 per cent of total outward DFI stock. Among developing countries, Latin

America was able to retain its share, while Asian countries grew in the face of a decline of DFIs to African countries.

DFI flows have been attracted to the US and, more recently, to Western Europe, due to their market potential which has been the result of, respectively, the Reagan Administration's expansionary fiscal policies, and the market unification process currently under way in the European Community (EC). By contrast, many developing countries have experienced in the 1980s a period of slow growth linked to the explosion of their external debt, which has made it more difficult to attract foreign investments. The growing importance of the service sector in DFI flows can be explained, at least in part, by the relevance of the tertiary sector in the countries which are significant DFI destinations (especially the US).

DFI flows towards Developed Countries (DCs) have increased from US$7 billion in 1985 to US$ 25 billion in 1988. This increase is indicative of a world-wide trend which has been attributed to the process of 'business globalisation'. The causes of the new increase in DFIs are completely different from those which brought about the increase previously. In fact, in the 1970s DFIs were linked to import-substitution policies, and were therefore concentrated in countries with a high level of protectionism. Today, in the 1990s, DFIs flow according to the criterion of efficient resource allocation, given the increase in trade liberalisation in Latin America and Asia.

In developing countries DFIs have come to play a relevant role in net resource flows, representing 18 per cent of net flows in the 1986–88 period, up from approximately ten per cent in the first half of the decade (see Table 2). This increase in the importance of DFI is the result of both a decline in other private flows (particularly international bank lending)

TABLE 1

GEOGRAPHICAL DISTRIBUTION OF THE WORLD STOCK OF DFI

	Outward		Inward	
Region/country	1975	1985	1975	1985
Developed market economies	97.7	97.2	75.1	75.0
United States	44.0	35.1	11.2	29.0
Western Europe	43.8	44.7	40.8	28.9
Japan	5.7	11.7	0.6	1.0
Developing Countries	2.3	2.7	24.9	25.0
Latin America	n.a.	n.a.	12.0	12.6
Africa	n.a.	n.a.	6.7	3.5
Asia	n.a.	n.a.	5.3	7.8

n.a. = not available

Source: UNCTC, 1988.

and the actual increase in the amount of DFI, which grew by 44 per cent, from $1.7 billion in 1980–85 to $20.8 billion in 1986–88.

In Latin America, the net effect of these two trends caused a doubling of DFI's share, from 12.5 per cent of total flows in 1980–82 to 24 per cent in 1986–88.

DFIs to developing countries tended to be concentrated, both in terms of home and host countries. During 1981–86 the US accounted for 35 per cent of DFI flows to developing countries, followed by the UK (19 per cent), Japan (13 per cent) and Germany (eight per cent). Among individual LDCs, four accounted for over 60 per cent of DFI inflows in the 1984–87 period: China (21 per cent), Singapore (13 per cent), Mexico (16 per cent) and Brazil (11 per cent).

Foreign Investment in Latin America

The 1982 debt crisis had an adverse effect on DFI flows to the region, which shrank from an annual average of $5,454 million in 1980–82 to $3,419 million in 1983–85 [*IMF, IFS, various years*]. The decline in investors' confidence and the recessionary conditions which accompanied adjustment policies both contributed to this trend. DFI flows to the region picked up again from 1986, due to policy measures aimed at sustaining DFI inflows through both changes in regulations and the adoption of debt-equity conversion schemes. As a result of this second reversal, net DFI inflows to the Latin American region were more than twice as high in 1980–88 than in 1970–79, as shown in Table 3.

The most notable softening of Latin American regulations regarding DFI were the approval of Decision 220 by the Andean Pact countries on 11 May 1987, and the new regulations adopted by Mexico (on 17 May,

TABLE 2

NET RESOURCE FLOWS TO LDCS (1980–88)

(Annual average billion US$ and share of the total flow)

	1980–1982		1983–1985		1986–1988	
	average	%	average	%	average	%
Official Development Finance	45.2	35.4	46.4	52.6	61.2	65.1
Total Export Credits	15.9	12.5	4.9	5.6	0.8	0.8
Private flows	66.3	52.1	36.9	41.8	32.2	34.3
of which:						
Direct Investment (OECD)	13.7	10.8	9.1	10.3	16.8	17.8
International Bank Lending	46.2	36.3	21.6	24.5	5.1	5.4
Total Net Resource Flows	127.4	100.0	88.2	100.0	94.0	100.0

Source: OECD, 1989.

1989) and Venezuela. Decision 220 allows individual Andean countries more discretion in the criteria used to evaluate foreign investments; it lengthens the terms for the conversion of foreign firms into joint ventures to 30 years, and provides for more flexibility on profit remittances.

The new Mexican regulations allow 100 per cent foreign ownership of firms (with the exception of some restricted sectors), waive the National Commission on Foreign Investments' approval procedure for priority investments of a value below $100 million, facilitate foreign portfolio investments in Mexican firms and improve access to formerly restricted sectors through special arrangements. While it is generally agreed that regulations often have only marginal effects on investment flows and that their impact is not immediate, the generalised change in attitude may have contributed to the maintenance of investment flows to the region. As mentioned above, regulation changes have been accompanied by incentives granted through debt-equity conversion schemes, which are more effective than traditional tax and credit incentives.

Debt-equity conversions allow an investor to purchase part of the country's foreign debt at a discount on the secondary market and convert it into national currency at or near face value, in order to invest in the debtor country, subject to restrictions on the timing and the amount of capital and dividend repatriations. Such programmes were pioneered by Chile in 1985, and carried out intermittently by various other countries in the region including Brazil, Mexico and Argentina. According to existing estimates, conversions accounted for between one-third and one-half of DFI flows to selected Latin American countries in recent years.[1]

As in the past, investment flows to Latin America in the 1970s and 1980s were highly concentrated among a handful of countries. Brazil,

TABLE 3

LATIN AMERICA: DFI FLOWS (1970–88)

(US$ million, net flows at current prices)

Country	Total 1970–88	per cent	Total 1970–79	per cent	Total 1980–88	per cent
Brazil	31,266	40	12,475	52	18,791	36
Mexico	23,531	30	6,020	25	17,512	32
Argentina	5,509	7	568	2	4,941	9
Colombia	4.324	6	413	2	3.911	7
Chile	1.617	2	–233	–1	1.850	3
Total	66.248	85	19.243	80	47.005	87
Others	12.029	15	4.923	20	7.107	13
Latin America Total	78.277	100	24.166	100	54.111	100

Source: World Bank, 1991.

Mexico and Argentina accounted for 77 per cent of net DFI inflows to Latin America in the 1970–88 period. Colombia and Chile received another eight per cent of the flows (see Table 3). Thus, five countries accounted for 85 per cent of these resources during the decade.

Latin America has traditionally been an important destination for direct foreign investment, and European countries have played a significant role in this process (see Table 4) [*Pio, 1988; 1990*]. While the US is the largest investor in the region, with extensive interests in the primary sector (agriculture and mining), European corporations have also been particularly active in manufacturing: automotive and chemicals from Germany; food from the UK; tyres, automotive and office machines from Italy; and so on. In the case of Brazil, the share of DFIs stock originating from EC countries is higher than the share from the US. With the exception of several Andean countries (Bolivia, Chile, Colombia, Peru), where mining is important, most of the DFI stock in Latin American countries is concentrated in the manufacturing sector, though there has been recent interest in investing in banking and other financial services. This structure is the consequence of industrialisation policies based on import substitution which made production for the local market the primary target of past foreign investments in the region. This should have important consequences for the future.

Foreign Investment in Asia

During the 1980s about a quarter of all DFIs from industrialised countries was in the direction of LDCs; of this fraction Asia accounted for only one-third, which is not a very significant amount since two-thirds of the

TABLE 4
ORIGIN OF DFI IN LATIN AMERICA (1970–88)
(Cumulated net flows, current US$ mn)

Country	EC	Japan	US	Others OECD	Total
Argentina	1.946	110	2.408	205	4.669
Brazil	7.044	3.870	10.499	643	22.056
Chile	358	84	429	31	903
Colombia	144	48	−559	23	−344
Mexico	1.484	982	4.953	12	7.430
Venezuela	480	93	−183	26	416
Total	11.456	5.187	17.547	940	35.130
Latin America Total(*)	19.978	15.410	37.350	28.086	100.823

(*) Includes North and Central America.
Source: OECD data, processed by authors.

population of LDCs live in Asia. Nevertheless, compared to the 1970s, investors from industrialised countries have become more interested in this area. The high growth rate of some of the Asian countries, and the progressive liberalisation of local regulations regarding DFI since the beginning of the 1980s, are among the factors that have played a decisive role in increasing the flow of DFI to this area. The onset of the debt crisis is also a cause of this shift in attitudes, since this was a problem limited to a few countries in Asia. Only the Philippines has been subjected to strong pressure from the International Banking Community as a result of their debt exposure.

Export-led growth has characterised the development of several Asian economies, particularly the NICs (Hong Kong, South Korea, Singapore, Taiwan) where it caused an appreciation of the currencies in recent times and an increase in labour costs. As internal demand grew during the last decade due to rising per capita income levels, DFI flows towards the NICs gradually became more oriented to production for the domestic market in these countries.

The more favourable climate in terms of relaxed local regulations has caused an increase in the flow of DFI towards Asia. Different patterns can be detected at the single country level. While regional 'early starters' (Korea, Taiwan) were relatively closed to foreign capital and sustained the development of their manufacturing sector with the help of state intervention. 'Late comers' (Thailand, Malaysia, Indonesia, Philippines) relied largely on foreign investment. The fact that China opened its frontiers, after having kept them completely closed to foreign investment until 1979, is an eloquent example of the new course of events. Table 5 shows that China, which did not receive any flows in the 1970s, jumped to second place in the period 1980–88 (cumulated yearly flows) receiving 48 per cent of DFI to Asia. If we add China to the NICs (Hong Kong, Singapore, Taiwan, Korea) and to South-east Asian countries (Indonesia, Philippines, Malaysia, Thailand) we can account for 92 per cent of Asian DFI from 1970 to 1988 (Table 5). However, after the 1989 events, it seems that DFI flows to China are likely to be reduced. Our study will therefore focus on the South-east Asian countries.

As one might expect, Japan plays a leading role as an origin of DFI to this region. If we take into account the NICs plus South-east Asia, the Japanese share amounted to 45.4 per cent in the 1970–88 period, followed by the US and the EC with 37 and 14.4 per cent respectively. If we analyse separately the two decades (1970–79 and 1980–88) on the basis of unpublished OECD data we can see a decrease in Japan's share (from 63 to 40 per cent) and an increase in that of the US (from 16.5 to

43.6 per cent). Europe has not increased its share so much (from 14 to 14.4 per cent), but the European quota is decisively stronger with regard to the DFIs flows of the past few years [*Maurer and Regnier, 1988*] (see Table 6).

The recent changes in DFI flows to this area is due to the important role of the NICs in world trade. Their share in total foreign investment in four South-east Asian countries (Indonesia, Malaysia, Philippines, Thailand) in 1988 was only marginally below Japan's. At the same time, while Japanese investment in these four South-east Asian economies grew by 125 per cent in 1988, commitments from the NICs jumped by 334 per cent [*Asian Development Bank, 1990*]. Among the NICs, Hong Kong and Taiwan have been the pioneers in terms of receiving foreign investment, while Singapore and Korea are the latecomers largely because of government policy constraints. The increase in labour costs and appreciation of the local currencies in the NICs have stimulated decentralisation of labour-intensive manufacturing activities from these more developed economies in Asia to the relatively less developed ones. This new DFI flow is therefore mostly export-oriented.

Manufacturing accounts for the largest share of DFIs. The NICs are among the world's leading manufacturers in electronics, which is also becoming more important in Thailand, whereas petrochemicals play an important role in Singapore, Taiwan and Indonesia, and the motor vehicle industry in Korea, a country which did not relax foreign investment regulations until the early 1980s. Intra-Asian investments

TABLE 5

ASIA: DFI FLOWS (1970–88)

(Net inflows at current prices, US$ mn)

Country	Total 1970–88	per cent	Total 1970–79	per cent	Total 1980–88	per cent
Singapore	12.222	24	2.458	24	9.764	26
Malaysia	11.170	22	3.262	32	7.908	19
China	8.980	18	0	0	8.980	22
Indonesia	4.564	9	1.956	19	2.608	6
Thailand	3.847	8	726	7	3.121	8
Korea	2.300	4	644	6	1.656	4
Philippines	2.172	4	544	5	1.628	4
Hong Kong(1)	2.014	4	...	..	2.014	4
Total	47.269	92	9.590	93	37.679	94
Others	4.026	8	597	7	3.428	6
Asia Total	51.294	100	10.187	100	41.108	100

(1) Data include only 1980–87 because Hong Kong does not keep DFI statistics.
Source: World Bank, 1991.

from the NICs focus on the textile and garment industries, both taking advantage of lower costs and overcoming quota restrictions in overseas markets. An example of this trend is offered by Indonesia: in 1989 this country had reduced the minimum foreign investment start-up capital from $1 million to $250,000 in order to encourage small investors. This reform produced many applications from companies in Hong Kong Korea and Taiwan, eager to move into fields such as footwear, textiles, ceramics and metals.

Japan is the leading investor in services which, although less important than manufacturing, will probably gain importance among intra-Asian investment flows in the near future. On the other side, the exchange rate realignment could produce an increase in Japanese DFIs in manufacturing as Japanese firms move to Asian developing countries in an attempt to maintain their competitiveness.

Together with the increase in DFIs, Asian LDCs show a relatively coordinated development of domestic capital market. This is important for mobilising domestic resources as well as enhancing the efficiency of foreign capital. In the long run, equity investment is likely to play a more important role in foreign capital inflows. The trend towards capital market deregulation and efforts to improve capital market supervision by most Asian economies should foster more foreign investment in the future. Recent trends and signals point to an increase in European involvement in the area, spurred by the rapid growth rate of Asian NICs

TABLE 6

ORIGIN OF DFI IN ASIA (1970–88)
(Cumulated net flows, current US$ mn)

Country	EC	Japan	US	Others OECD	Total
Hong Kong	2.295	3.875	4.022	753	10.942
Indonesia	211	3.090	2.715	209	6.225
Korea	231	2.425	603	0	3.258
Malaysia	200	1.040	789	324	2.353
Philippines	138	651	626	106	1.521
Singapore	1.739	2.733	2.639	220	7.331
Thailand	227	1.179	736	99	2.241
Taiwan	168	1.381	1.149	−491	2.207
Total	5.209	16.371	13.279	1.220	36.078
Total Asia(1)	8.303	20.892	21.055	17.206	67.456

(1) Includes other Asian countries, such as China, differences with World Tables data are due to the lack of data in the period 1970–79 for US DFI in all countries except Indonesia and Philippines.
Source: OECD data, processed by authors.

(6.5 per cent on average in 1989) and by the cost advantage and reliability in terms of quality that have been secured by decentralising production in these countries. The annual average investment flow from Europe to the Asian NICs (excluding Hong Kong) grew from $230 million in 1982–85 to $648 million in 1986–89. In 1989, Western Europe became for the first time the leading foreign investor in Singapore with US$291 million. Japanese and American investments in the same year were $289 and $278 million respectively.

While European corporations are becoming increasingly interested in the domestic market potential of these countries (which are slowly becoming more open to external influence), decentralisation of production in both high – (electronics, computers) and low-tech sectors (garments) are still the main motives for European presence through DFIs. This explains why in Korea, Indonesia and the Philippines the share of DFIs originating in Europe grew from 3.4, −1.4 and 2.6 per cent of total net flows in 1970–79 to 8.3, 9.5 and 24.5 per cent respectively in 1980–88 [*OECD data*, processed by authors]. The fast growth rate of the most recent period can also be explained by the need to fill in the gap, with the US and Japan having been active for a long period. This growing interest also translated itself into closer institutional co-operation, as witnessed by the ASEAN–EC bilateral agreement signed in March 1980 and renewed in October 1985.

Foreign Investment in Africa

During the last decade, Africa received a smaller share of DFI flows from the industrialised countries. In the 1970s Africa's share of net DFI flows was only slightly smaller than Asia's, that is, US$8.79 million versus 10.19 million (excluding Hong Kong) [*World Bank, 1991*]. The 1980s witnessed a rapid decline of the annual flows, with a trough in 1980, a year when disinvestments by foreign countries were particularly high. Cumulated net flows between 1980 and 1988 show a nominal value which is even lower than the one for the period 1970–79. This decrease in DFI is due to the economic climate that became progressively more unfavourable. The onset of the debt crisis in 1982 closed off access to the international credit market, making balance of payments constrains more binding.

Reduced levels of economic activity made profits more difficult to achieve, while foreign reserve scarcity made their repatriation more problematic. Besides, the largest share of DFIs in Africa was either import-substituting investments or directed to the primary sector. DFI associated with import substitution does not generate exports covering the costs of servicing the investment, while its dependency on imports for inputs, spare parts and equipment made it vulnerable to foreign exchange shortages as export commodity prices fell and oil prices rose. Only in a few cases (such as Malawi, Botswana, Zimbabwe and Senegal) did DFI lead to a significant increase in the export of manufactured goods. Therefore, while in some cases DFIs acted as a stimulus for economic activity (and this was undoubtedly true for countries such as Kenya, Nigeria and Botswana), it had a negative impact on the balance of payments in many African countries since the 1970.

As Table 7 shows, seven countries account for about 82 per cent of net DFIs flows during the 1970–88 period. Nigeria ranks first with 39 per cent, followed by Tunisia with 13 per cent, while all the other countries individually account for less than seven per cent of inflows. Botswana, ranking sixth, seems to be an especially interesting case. Its good standing is due to DFI in the diamond industry, but the country is also characterised by an unusually high level of education when compared with the averages of other African countries. A relatively high percentage of DFI in Africa comes from Europe (see Table 8). If we only consider the three most important home areas – Europe, US and Japan totalling $15,361 of net inflows – Europe accounts for more than 60 per cent of the cumulated DFI flows between 1970 and 1988. The US and Japan account for approximately 28 and 10 per cent respectively. The percentage would be even higher with reference to the total of net DFI, due to the heavy disinvestment originating from 'other' countries.

TABLE 7

AFRICA: DFI FLOWS (1970–88)
(Net inflows at current prices, US$ mn)

Country	Total 1970–88	per cent	Total 1970–79	per cent	Total 1980–88	per cent
Nigeria	6.020	39	3.140	36	2.888	43
Tunisia	2.019	13	539	8	1.480	22
Algeria	1.094	7	906	10	188	3
Gabon	1.032	6	405	5	627	9
Botswana	935	6	357	4	579	9
Zaire	792	5	731	8	61	1
Morocco	701	5	215	2	485	7
Cameroon	564	4	165	2	399	6
Total	13.156	85	6.458	73	6.699	100
Others	2.363	15	2.335	27	28	0
Africa Total	15.520	100	8.792	100	6.727	100

Source: World Bank, 1991.

The relevant role of European investments can be easily understood if we consider Africa's geographical position, its consequent historical and cultural links and colonial heritage. The colonial origins of the links between Europe and African countries explain a net differentiation in the role played by each European country. The UK ranks first with a share of 44 per cent in the cumulated DFI flows from Europe followed by France with 32 per cent.

Future prospects are definitely linked with the ability of African countries to create a more favourable climate for DFI, which can be achieved both via a greater liberalisation of present regulations and via an effective economic recovery. Political stabilisation would also be a relevant factor, especially to attract foreign investors in the high risk and capital intensive mining exploration and exploitation.

The potential of debt for equity conversions in Africa, as a means to reduce the burden of interest payments and as a source of investment capital from industrialised countries, is quite limited since only about 30 per cent of total external debt derives from commercial sources.

From this brief review one can conclude that DFI flows in recent years have become a more relevant component of financial flows to developing countries and though the picture is evolving (in some cases with remarkable speed), the motivation of DFI in the three continents is still fairly different: extraction of natural resources from the primary sector (agriculture or mining) in Africa, production for protected host market in Latin America, decentralisation due to cost advantages or

TABLE 8

ORIGIN OF DFI IN AFRICA (1970–88)
(Cumulated net flows, current US$ mn

Country	EC	Japan	US	Others OECD	Total
Nigeria	1.891	24	1.143	−237	2.820
Tunisia	222	223	/	−185	259
Algeria	118	0	/	0	118
Gabon	661	11	/	58	731
Botswana	5	/	/	0	5
Zaire	56	−14	/	518	560
Morocco	160	2	/	1	163
Cameroon	346	0	/	15	361
Total	3.460	245	1.143	169	5.016
Africa Total (1)	9.353	1.518	4.490	−8.234	7.126

(1) The difference between the first six host countries and the overall total is due to the high share of unallocated and unspecified direct investment to Africa.
Source: OECD, 1989.

as a strategy to overcome third country import restrictions in the case of Asia.

In spite of significant international competition and sluggish domestic economic growth, regions such as Latin America have been able to retain their share of foreign investments by developing appropriate policies, while Asia has become a more attractive destination for DFI than in the past, trying to carve a role as the world's 'workshop', thanks to its relatively low cost and highly qualified work force. It is within this internationally competitive environment that the unification of the EC market will exert its impact.

III. THE DETERMINANTS OF FOREIGN INVESTMENT: POSSIBLE EFFECTS OF THE SINGLE EUROPEAN MARKET

Economic literature concerning the determinants of international direct investment has focused on a variety of approaches, ranging from firm characteristics to market imperfections and macroeconomic conditions (for a relatively recent and comprehensive survey on the topic see Agarwal [*1980*]). Summarising briefly, one can distinguish between those authors who pay close attention to the firm's characteristics and decision-making processes ('defensive' *vs.* 'offensive' DFIs, etc.) and those who focus their analysis on country-specific conditions which encourage or discourage foreign investments (labour costs and skills, market potential, regulatory environment, etc.).

The most successful attempt to integrate the microeconomic and the macroeconomic approach can be attributed to Dunning's 'eclectic' theory of foreign investments (for a recent and more systematic presentation, see Dunning [*1989*]). According to Dunning, a firm deciding to invest in a foreign country must have a competitive advantage over its foreign competitors, and must have decided that internalising the benefits of this advantage through DFIs is more profitable than exploiting them otherwise (through licensing or sale of a patent for example). At the same time, the country of destination of the investment must offer some locational advantage over the firm's home country, such as lower labour costs, availability of raw materials, etc.

The following analysis tries to extend the scope of Dunning's approach by scrutinising more closely the impact of changes in the DFIs' region of origin on the magnitude of these flows, whereas most previous analyses focused on conditions in the country of destination. One can easily argue that the SEM process will significantly affect firm strategies and macroeconomic conditions in Europe, and that DFI flows will respond to such changes. While many of the previous studies are devoted to US investments abroad, an innovative aspect of this study lies in its attempt to provide empirical information on the sensitivity of European investments in Latin America and Asia to macroeconomic changes. Whereas the quantitative estimates are only devoted to studying the impact on DFIs of changes in macroeconomic variables in both the areas of origin and of destination, it will be useful to initiate the discussion with a qualitative review of the likely impact of the SEM process on individual firms' internationalisation strategies.

Internationalisation Strategies of European Firms

The accelerated integration process induced by the creation of the SEM is likely to result in the opening up of formerly captive markets, causing a reduction of intra-EC price differentials and increasing the level of competition [*Cecchini et al., 1988*]. The impact on European firms and their strategies is likely to be threefold:

(a) increased competition will cause the failure of a number of protected firms dependent on national or local captive markets, often linked to government procurements;
(b) large and medium-sized firms will be encouraged to restructure and merge in order to face this increased competition, with the greater efficiency which derives from economies of scale and of scope;
(c) small and medium-sized firms which are able to efficiently specialise in specific niches (high-technology components or high-skill services, for example) will be encouraged to begin or to expand international operations.

The first signs of these trends can already be detected: mergers and acquisitions involving the first 100 European firms increased from 227 in 1985–86 to 383 in 1987–88 [*Jacquermin, Buigues and Ilzokovitz, 1989*]. Firms have also tried to strengthen their international competitive position by forming strategic alliances aimed at acquiring new technologies or gaining shares of foreign markets, as evident by the sharp increase in European acquisitions in the US since 1985.

The renewed dynamism of European firms is also reflected by the growth of intra-EC cross-border investments, acquisitions, joint ventures and other cooperative agreements aimed at creating better scale and scope economies within a context of increasing regional integration. If we consider a sample of five countries (UK, Germany, France, Netherlands and Denmark), intra-EC investment flows grew from an annual average of $16.1 billion in 1981–83 to $25.5 billion in 1984–87 and increased from 22 per cent to 30 per cent of total DFI outflows originating in the five countries [*UNCTC. 1988 and national data*]. While in the past, most intra-EC investments were oriented towards serving domestic markets, European corporations are now aiming at specialising production facilities within a global perspective. This tendency increases the attractiveness of production locations in several Community member countries, such as Portugal, Spain, Greece and Ireland, which offer cost advantages as well as state incentives to foreign investors. As a result, one should expect a trend towards growing intra-firm trade within the EC.

This tendency to divert DFIs away from developing countries and toward peripheral EC members could be aggravated in the coming decade by recent economic and political developments in EE. Although the short-term impact should not be overestimated, as discussed in section V, it is undeniable that EE countries have some of the same attractive features as developing countries in terms of labour costs, market potential and inability to compete in advanced sectors, coupled with the advantages of relatively high labour skills and close geographic and cultural proximity to the European Community. In fact, a look at the data presented in Table 9 shows that, in the 1980s, the LDC's share of DFI outflows from the leading European countries has already declined sharply. When looking at absolute figures, however, this decline in percentage terms takes the form of substantially stable flows in a situation of rapidly growing DFIs to industrialised countries.

A review of the internationalisation strategies enacted by European firms in response to the SEM process therefore lends support to the conclusion that, in the initial stage, attention will be focused on the opportunities and risks present in the SEM. DFI flows to external developing areas will probably continue due to past momentum, but geographical diversion effects resulting in the reduction of such flows are quite possible. In this sense, regions such as Latin America which

TABLE 9

LDC's SHARE OF DFIs FROM THE EC (1980–87)
(Percentage of DFI outflows)

	1980–81 average	1982–84 average	1985–87 average
United Kingdom	18.5	20.1	13.4
Germany	37.7	28.1	2.7
France	19.8	14.9	12.7
Nertherlands	6.1	9.3	9.6
Italy	26.5	22.1	14.5
5–country total	20.3	17.5	10.6

Source: IMF, OECD.

have, in the past, resorted to less capital intensive 'new forms' of productive co-operation such as joint ventures, technology licensing, technical assistance contracts, etc. (see Oman [*1984*]), should be in a better position to maximise the benefits from limited amounts of financial resource flows.

While initially one can foresee a reduction in DFI flows to developing countries for the above mentioned reasons, it would be reasonable to expect that, as European corporations become more efficient and better able to compete internationally, their international operations, including those in developing countries, will expand. This process, which should also involve highly specialised small and medium-sized firms, will be accompanied by an increase in foreign investments, thus producing what could be compared to a 'J' effect in the temporal sequence of European investments in LDCs after 1992. A similar behaviour can be expected from other international investors, such as the US and Japan, which have already started (and will continue for some years) to focus their efforts on the establishment of productive and commercial bases within the EC.

Changes in the Macroeconomic Context

The influence of macroeconomic variables on the level of foreign investment flows is not a direct one. Macroeconomic variables affect the level of DFIs as a result of the investing firms' reactions to the modified macroeconomic environment, such as the reduction in flows triggered by higher interest rates which would make financing more onerous. Strictly speaking, therefore, all changes in investment flows can be brought back to the firm level.

Within the present study's context, we will refer to 'macroeconomic' determinants of DFIs in order to differentiate them from other factors such as firm size, expenditures on advertising or research and development at the firm level, the degree of managerial skills within the firm, profit levels and industrial concentration in the sector. All the latter, which have been extensively investigated in the literature (Blomstrom and Lipsey [*1986*], Grubaugh [*1987*], Lall [*1988*] and Santiago [*1987*] to mention just a few relevant recent contributions) can be considered 'microeconomic' determinants, in the sense that they analyse specific characteristics of individual firms or sectors, which make them more or less likely candidates to engage in foreign investments. The analysis of macroeconomic determinants, in turn, focuses on the conditions within the macroeconomic context which make DFIs more or less likely to happen.

Most of the existing literature has examined the effects of conditions in the host country. It has been demonstrated that foreign investments are attracted to countries which have a large [*Culem, 1988*; *Reuber et al., 1973*; *Scaperlenda and Balough, 1983*] and/or growing [*Agarwal, 1980*; *Root and Ahmed, 1979*; *Schneider and Frey, 1985*] domestic market, or access to a larger regional market through integration agreements (again [*Root and Ahmed, 1979*]). A positive correlation has also been demonstrated between economic and political stability in the host country and foreign investment flows, even though the evidence is weaker. In the empirical analyses [*Agarwal, 1980*; *Schneider and Frey, 1985*], economic instability has been equated with high levels of inflation and balance of payments deficits. Political stability has been measured in terms of politically inspired riots and strikes [*Schneider and Frey, 1985*], peaceful changes in government [*Root and Ahmed, 1979*] or political risk indices [*Juhl, 1977*].

A second series of macroeconomic factors commonly considered in the literature concern the attractiveness of the host country for the decentralisation of productive activities. Such decentralisation can be pursued in order to serve the host country's market, or with the objective of re-exporting production to the home country or to a third area. Most European manufacturing investments in Latin America fall under the first category, while those directed to the Asian countries belong to the second, just like US, 'maquiladora' plants in Mexico. Finally, many Japanese investments in emerging Asian countries can be classified in the third category, given their purpose of taking advantage of the preferential access to the US, granted to manufactured exports from developing countries.

According to economic theory, the decentralisation of productive activities should be induced by cost savings resulting from lower wages and salaries (once differences in productivity are accounted for), lower prices of raw materials and intermediate outputs (once differences in quality are accounted for) and incentives provided by local governments (concessional credit, tax exemptions, subsidised utilities, etc.). Unfortunately, empirical evidence does not lend strong support to the importance of these determinants, although methodological problems in accounting for productivity and quality differentials and the lack of complete and reliable data may have negatively affected the results. While several authors have found a positive correlation between low labour costs and DFI flows [*Culem, 1988*; *Cushman, 1987*; *Riedel, 1975*], others [*Agarwal, 1980*; *Kravis and Lipsey, 1982*; *Santiago, 1987*] cannot confirm the hypothesis. Both Reuber *et al.* [*1973*] and Balasubramanyam [*1984*] find scant evidence concerning the effectiveness of incentives in attracting foreign investments, and indicate that other factors such as market size and dynamism or political stability have a greater impact on DFI flows.

Most of the macroeconomic factors examined up to this point bear little relationship to the likely impact of the unification of the European market in 1993, since they are primarily related to conditions in the host country. It is therefore necessary to identify linkages between macroeconomic conditions in the country of origin of DFI flows and the level of these investments. Unfortunately, very little economic literature exists on this topic. A review of the short and medium-term impact of the SEM (as identified in the Cecchini Report [*European Economy, 1988*]), however, does provide some guidance on possible outcomes and linkages.

The Cecchini report estimates that cost reductions combined with increases in efficiency will give an impulse to growth and employment in Europe, with relevant side benefits which include price reductions and improvements of the public budget and in the balance of payments of EC countries as a whole *vis-à-vis* the rest of the world. The report's mid-range estimate projects: a growth of 4.5 per cent in GDP, accompanied by the creation of 1.8 million new jobs; a drop of 6.1 per cent in consumer prices; a decline in public sector deficits totalling 2.2 per cent of the European GDP; and a balance of payment surplus equivalent to one per cent of GDP.

These changes in macroeconomic conditions at the European level could affect DFI flows to LDCs in the following ways:

(a) Income growth in Europe and the rationalisation of the productive structure will require considerable domestic investments and reorganisation of production on a global scale. As a consequence of the restructuring strategies pursued by European firms (described in the previous section), only limited managerial and financial resources will be available for foreign investments in developing countries beyond the maintenance of existing levels, with exceptions existing for especially attractive or strategic sectors or countries. Therefore, the hypothesis is that national and international investment flows will be competing somewhat for the limited financial and managerial resources available to the firm, and that in the near future the attractiveness of the European market will cast a shadow over potential flows to developing countries, unless such flows are part of a strategy aimed at decentralising production to serve more efficiently the home market.

(b) Economic growth in Europe will be partially exported to LDCs through trade creation effects. As a consequence, DFIs could also grow, either to serve European markets or in order to cater to the LDC's domestic markets. This effect would counter the expected decline discussed above, and the impact of European growth on DFI flows in Europe would therefore depend on the relative strength of the two outcomes. This topic will be addressed in the following empirical analysis, but a preliminary assessment would lead us to believe that the first 'distraction' effect will be stronger where investments are geared to producing for the host market (that is, in Latin America) than in the case of export-oriented DFIs (Asia). This conclusion is supported by recent estimates [*IMF, 1989*] which indicate that a growth rate of one per cent in the developed countries leads to 0.5 per cent growth in LDCs as a whole (and only 0.2 per cent in the case of Latin America). The five per cent additional GDP growth attributed by the Cecchini estimates to the effects of SEM, would result in a one per cent additional growth rate for Latin American countries. Given the excess capacity existing in some of these countries as a result of the debt-induced recessionary environment of the 1980s, it is doubtful that significant increments in DFIs would take place as a consequence of this modest growth, with the possible exception of sectors and countries which show capacity constraints. In the case of Asian countries, on the contrary, increased decentralisation of production from Europe coupled with domestic market expansion in Asia (as the fruits of growth become more evenly distributed domestically) could have a more positive impact on DFI growth.

(c) An improvement in the European aggregate balance of payments would make European currencies appreciate with respect to the dollar, since within a system of freely floating exchange rates (as is the case between the EC and other countries, most notably US and Japan), a balance of payments surplus causes the appreciation of the currency of the surplus country(ies). With the advent of the SEM, the EC balance of trade should improve by approximately one per cent of GDP [*Commissione delle Comunità Europea, 1988*], while capital inflows are also likely to be positive for the EC as a whole. The existence of the exchange rate stabilisation agreement within the European Monetary System should guarantee a fairly even diffusion of this appreciation among EC member states, while the persistence of the US trade deficit seems to indicate that no strong appreciation of the dollar should be expected within the near future.

Appreciation of European currencies would favourably influence

DFI flows to third countries, since it would make such investments relatively less costly in terms of the home country currency. As a consequence, exchange rate appreciation could play a positive role in stimulating DFI flows to 'dollar area' developing countries. Recent evidence concerning this matter, however, is mixed. Cushman [*1980*] found a positive correlation between real exchange rate appreciation and DFI flows, while Solocha *et al.* [*1989*] found that Canadian investments in northern New York in the 1961–85 period grew when the Canadian dollar depreciated, possibly because of the higher value in local currencies of future dividends streams.

(d) The rationalisation of financial services in Europe will reduce the cost of capital, thereby making it possible to borrow at more convenient rates in order to finance investments, among them DFIs. The linkage between the cost of capital and DFI flows has already been suggested in the literature [*Kravis and Lipsey, 1982*] and recently tested empirically [*Cushman, 1987*]. The SEM should permit a reduction in the cost of financial services of around ten per cent, although the most significant impact should be on the consumer rather than the business services. As a consequence, one can expect a modest reduction in the cost of borrowing. The impact on DFI flows, however, is likely to be modest. Given the high risk margin involved in overseas operations, firms usually base their decisions on a rate of return on investments, which will not be significantly affected by marginal changes in the cost of financing. Besides, multinational corporations are able to secure financing at the most convenient conditions on international markets, and, therefore, are not bound by the conditions prevailing on their home credit markets.

While in theory we can expect all the macroeconomic variables identified thus far to play a role in DFI flows, the sign and magnitude of their impact needs to be tested through empirical analysis. This is the object of the following section.

IV. AN EMPIRICAL TEST OF THE SENSITIVITY OF FOREIGN DIRECT INVESTMENT TO CHANGES IN MACROECONOMIC CONDITIONS

In the previous sections, three sets of factors which have an impact on DFI flows were identified: firm and sector-specific microeconomic factors, host country macroeconomic conditions and home country macroeconomic determinants. In this section, the effects of some of the second and third kind of (macroeconomic) factors will be tested empirically. Considering Latin America and Asia as receiving areas and using data for the 1970–87 period which cover four European countries (France, Germany, Italy and the UK). The four home countries are the most relevant ones within the European Community in terms of GDP. In the case of Latin America, the four countries selected (Argentina, Brazil, Colombia and Mexico) are the main destination of DFIs accounting for 85 per cent of net inflows in the region in the 1980–88 period [*IMF, IFS various years*]. In the case of Asia, four South-east Asian countries (Indonesia, Malaysia, Philippines and Thailand) were considered, because of their openness to DFIs in recent years. In the case of other Asian countries, changes in attitude and regulation towards DFIs have a far greater explanatory potential than the analysis of macroeconomic determinants which we are concerned with in this case. The sample should therefore allow us to draw on inferences concerning the more general topic of European DFI flows to Latin America and Asia.

The Model

Since the object of the study is to assess the likely impact of SEM on DFI flows, explanatory variables on the home country side are fundamental. They include GDP growth rates, exchange rate appreciation over the previous year and interest rates (both on the national currency and on the US dollar, in consideration of the possibility that a multinational corporation may seek financing on international markets), in line with the theoretical formulation used in the section on 'changes in the Macroeconomic context'.

As we have noted in that section, macroeconomic variables in the host countries are also important and should be included in the analysis. The GDP growth rate, inflation rate, balance of payments and net financial transfers excluding DFIs were considered. The first variable (GDP growth) measures the attractiveness of the host market. The following two (inflation and balance of payment conditions) give indications concerning the country's economic stability. In particular, chronic balance of payment deficits may foster restrictive foreign exchange measures which could, in turn, endanger capital and dividend remittances. Net financial transfers were taken as signs of (1) the overall confidence of the international community in the host country's economy, and (2) the availability of additional resources which, if invested in infrastructure or human development, would improve overall economic conditions and the likely profitability of foreign investments.

In this approach, it was decided not to consider variables such as labour cost and productivity differentials or incentive programmes (such as debt-equity swaps) in order not to excessively dilute the results, also because of the poor performance of previous analyses regarding these topics, as discussed in section III.

In its basic formulation, the model can be summarised as follows. (Signs in parenthesis [ ] near the variables indicate the expected sign of the coefficient)

$$\begin{aligned} \text{DFIECRA} = {} & a + b1{*}\text{GREC}(-t) + b2{*}\text{IREC}(-t) + b3{*}\text{IRUS}(-t) \\ & + b4{*}\text{ERECUS}(-t) + b5{*}\text{GRRA}(-t) + b6{*}\text{INRA}(-t) \\ & + b7{*}\text{BPRA}(-t) + b8{*}\text{NTRA}(-t) + \epsilon \end{aligned}$$

where

DFIECRA	FDIs flow from the EC country to the host receiving area (RA) in millions of US dollars at 1980 prices
GREC[+/−]	GDP growth rate in the home (European Community) country (expected sign is minus for Latin America; plus for Asia)
IREC[−]	interest rate (lending rate) on the home currency in the home (EC) country
IRUS[−]	interest rate (lending rate) on the US dollar
ERECUS[−]	exchange rate variation over the previous year between the home (EC) country currency and the US dollar (units of home currency per US dollar: an increase indicates depreciation of the home currency)
GRRA[+]	real GDP growth rate in the receiving areas (RA)
INRA[−]	inflation rate (GDP deflator) in the receiving areas
BPRA[−]	balance of payments balance (total balance, equivalent to change in net reserves; a positive value indicates a balance of payments deficit)(*) of receiving areas at 1980 prices
NTRA[+]	Net transfers (official financing + private flows – interest payments) to receiving areas at 1980 prices.

All data utilised have yearly frequencies. DFIECRA was obtained from the OECD data-bank on DFI flows reported by member countries. Interest rate data are from IMF, International Financial Statistics or national sources, while the remaining macroeconomic data come from World Bank sources: World Debt

Tables for NTRA and World Tables for the remainder.

The model is built on the assumption that a time lag elapses between the moment in which investment decisions are taken (on the basis of current macroeconomic information) and the moment when investment flows materialise. This delay is due to the timing requirements of phasing in an investment project, which lengthen in the case of a distant location, and includes the DFI regulatory processes required by host countries. In many countries these processes often involve submitting an application which must be reviewed by competent national bodies, a negotiation phase and, finally, registration with the Central Bank. For this reason, current investment flows are regressed against lagged (−t) values of the macroeconomic explanatory variables, which were the observed values at the time when the original investment decision was reached. One of the purposes of the model is to identify the duration of such lags, which one expects to be short in Asia given the more streamlined procedures and greater efficiency of public administration.

The model has been estimated using ordinary least squares. Since the objective of the analysis is to provide aggregate estimates for European DFI flows to Latin America and Asia, data for the four host countries in each area were aggregated. Level variables (BPRA, NTRA) were simply added together, while growth and inflation rates for the region (GRRA, INRA) were computed using a weighted average with each country's GDP as a weight.

In order to retain sufficient degrees of freedom for the estimation of the coefficients, data for the four European countries were not aggregated. Instead, a pooling approach was followed, whereby data for each country of origin are 'stacked' under a common variable name. Thus, for example, variable DFIECRA contains data on German investments in Latin America/Asia, followed by data on British investments to the same area and so forth. In turn, the home country explanatory variables refer to each specific European nation: GREC associates German GDP growth rates with German DFI flows, British rates with British flows, and so on. This approach requires the introduction of dummy variables to correct for differences in the order of magnitude of the constant caused by differences in DFI levels by country of origin.

An advantage of the pooled approach is that it forces regression coefficient estimates to represent an 'average' value for all home countries, thus approaching our goal of identifying 'European', rather than national, sensitivities. Where national patterns are markedly diverse and the estimation of a common coefficient becomes problematic, it is possible to resort to country-specific multiplicative dummy variables which allow for coefficient corrections in order to account for national specificities.[2]

Results of the Econometric Analysis for Latin America

The model was estimated using constant lags for all explanatory variables, assuming a delay of one, two and three years between the investment decision (that is, the value of the independent variable) and the observed financial flow (that is, the value of DFIECRA). After several runs, it was decided to drop the variable INRA (the Latin American inflation rate) from the regression, due to the distortion in the results caused by its inclusion. Estimates including INRA had less significant regression coefficients, and the sign of INRA was generally positive, implying a direct relationship between Latin American inflation and DFI inflows. While we can offer no clear explanation for this relationship, we can at least conclude that no evidence was produced to support the hypothesis that inflation has an adverse impact on DFI flows.

Equations using one, two and three-year lags showed similar explanatory power. R-squared values ranged from a minimum of 0.549 to a maximum of 0.657, depending on the exact model specification, and F values for the whole equation ranged from 6.57 to 8.68 with 36 or more degrees of freedom, comfortably beyond the 95 per cent confidence level. An R-squared level around 0.6 can be considered satisfactory, since many other variables at the firm level also contribute to explain DFI decisions.

The best results (shown in Table 10 and discussed in the following paragraphs) were obtained with three-year lags. The only variable with

TABLE 10

RESULT OF LEAST SQUARE REGRESSION FOR LATIN AMERICA

(Three-year lags on explanatory variables)

Variable	Coefficient	Std. Error	T-Stat.	2-Tail Sig.
C	242.5331	65.6757	3.69283	0.001
DF	−108.6915	36.6207	−2.96803	0.005
DI	−168.4591	37.7397	−4.46371	0.000
GREC	−10.0800	8.6822	−1.16099	0.253
DGRG	22.8746	12.0323	1.90110	0.065
IRUS	−6.7556	4.7765	−1.41434	0.166
ERECUS	2.2389	1.7966	1.24620	0.221
GRRA	14.6928	6.5578	2.24050	0.031
NTRA	0.0073	0.0029	2.48284	0.018
BPRA	0.0044	0.0047	0.92886	0.359

R-squared	0.65743	Mean of dependent var	167.6279
Adjusted R-squared	0.57179	S.D of dependent var	138.9669
S.E. of regression	90.93659	sum of squared resid	297700.7
F-statistic	7.67656	Number of observations	46

a sign that differed from our expectations was ERECUS (European exchange rate depreciation), whose coefficient was positive though not very significant, and BPRA, also positive and not significant. The specification with two-year lags produced all the expected signs. The level of significance of the individual coefficients, however, was not as satisfactory. Finally, one-year lags produced some unexpected signs in the coefficients (GRRA, GREC, BPRA, IRUS depending on the exact model specification) and still lower individual significance regarding the estimators. We can therefore conclude that a long time interval seems to elapse between the investment decision and its execution, probably as a result of the technical and regulatory delays discussed in the previous section.(Insert Table 10)

The model specification presented in Table 10 shows a positive constant (242.5) which should be corrected downward in the case of France and Italy by the respective dummies (DF and DI). The dummy for the UK was omitted because it turned out to be small and not significant, since the latter is a large investor in Latin America, with DFI flows of the same order of magnitude as Germany.

As expected, European GDP growth has a negative impact on DFI flows to Latin America (US$–10.08 mn for every percentage point of GDP growth), even though there are some doubts about the significance of the coefficient, which differs from zero with only a 75 per cent level of confidence. This value of the coefficient holds well for three of the four countries studied, while in the case of Germany it is appropriate to use the country-specific multiplicative dummy (DGRG), which yields a positive coefficient of 22.87. This result implies that, in the specific case of Germany, there is a positive correlation between home GDP growth and outward DFI flows, and that each percentage point of home GDP growth translates itself into a US$12.79 mn increase in DFIs to Latin America. With the exception of Germany, we have therefore found a weak confirmation of our hypothesis that internal growth has a 'distraction' effect on DFI flows, because it absorbs financial and managerial resources for domestic expansion goals.

The model specification presented in Table 10 excludes home country interest rates (IREC) from the explanatory variables. European interest rates were generally dropped from the equation because they had positive signs and lower significance than US dollar interest rates, which suggests that either European firms are not particularly sensitive to interest costs when making DFI decisions (possibly because they engage in joint ventures or make contributions primarily under the form of physical capital, such as machinery), or that they finance their investments on international markets, using the US dollar as the currency of reference. The dollar interest rate, on the contrary, has a negative coefficient (−6.75) which is significantly different from zero at the 83 per cent confidence level.

Depreciation of the exchange rate (ERECUS) is the only variable whose sign differs from that expected (+2.23), although the coefficient does not significantly differ from zero. The results therefore weakly confirm those obtained in several previous studies [*Solocha et al.. 1989*], indicating that depreciation of the home currency makes investors more, rather than less, willing to invest abroad, perhaps as a result of expected exchange rate gains on future dividend streams resulting from further depreciation. Our results may be weakened by the fact that depreciation was measured against the US dollar, assuming that Latin American countries belong to the dollar area and follow a stable real exchange rate policy *vis-à-vis* the US currency, in order to compensate for high internal inflation rates. Since exchange rate adjustments between Latin American currencies and the dollar take place discontinuously, the parity between European and Latin American currencies may not have been accurately represented by our proxy.

Latin American variables confirm the importance for Latin America of host country growth in attracting foreign investments. The GRRA coefficient is positive (+14.69) and significant at the 97 per cent level. Other net resource flows (NTRA) also have a positive effect on DFIs both by providing a demonstration of the international financial community's confidence and by contributing complementary resources which increase investment profitability. While the regression coefficient is highly significant, its dimension is rather small, indicating that only seven million DFIs are induced by a US$1 billion flow of other resources. The small size of the coefficient is probably a consequence of the great quantity of commercial lending received by the region in the 1970s, and we would expect that a repetition of the estimation for other countries and/or more recent periods (after 1982) would yield higher values.

Finally, the balance of payments situation has an unexpected impact (a positive coefficient of .004 for BPRA), but again the coefficient is rather small and does not differ significantly from zero, indicating that concerns regarding the impairment of profit remittances do not seem to rank highly among foreign investors' criteria when assessing the host country's situation.

Results of the Econometric Analysis for Asia

As in the case of Latin America, the model was estimated using constant lags for the explanatory variables assuming that a delay should occur between the investment decision and the observed financial flows. The best results were obtained with a delay of one year, confirming our hypothesis that investment decisions materialise faster in Asia, possibly as a result of smoother regulatory processes and better functioning of the local public administration.

In the case of Asia, the variable NTRA was not included, given the limited importance of such resource flows for the four countries considered, with the exception of the Philippines. BPRA was included in the regression but was later dropped because the coefficient, though of the expected sign, was not significant. The direction of causality between balance of payments surplus and foreign investment is not so easy to determine in this case, since DFIs from developed countries to Asia are export-oriented and therefore generate current account surpluses which increase foreign currency reserves. Variable ERECUS (the exchange rate) was also dropped from the analysis due to a lack of significance.

Although one could expect the four countries to peg their exchange rate to the yen rather than to the dollar, because of their geographic location, preliminary analysis showed no greater correlation with the Japanese currency, probably because stability *vis-à-vis* the US was important, given their relevance as an outlet market.

Inclusion of the exchange rate between EC currencies and the dollar in early versions of the model for Asia produced a small negative coefficient (ranging from -0.4 to -1.5) with low significance, pointing to a moderate increase in DFI flows when European currencies appreciate (and investing abroad becomes cheaper). The low significance of this explanatory variable led to its exclusion from the final version of the model.

The equation which best explains European DFI flows to Asia is presented in Table 5.11. R-squared for the equation is 0.34, considerably below the value of 0.66 obtained for Latin America, and the F value for the equation is 2.41 with 33 degrees of freedom, which ensures an overall significance above 95 per cent, while most individual coefficients are also significant.

The fact that investment flows can not be explained as well by the fluctuation in macroeconomic variables is probably due to structural determinants of such flows, for example differences in labour costs between home and host countries. The relative 'novelty' of European DFI flows to Asia is confirmed by the negative sign of the constant, which must be further corrected downwards to account for differences among home countries. The UK appears to be the most prone to invest in the four countries considered, followed by Germany, Italy, and France.

The European growth rate is a relevant determinant of DFI flows to Asia (US 12 million for each percentage point), thus confirming the hypothesis that decentralisation of production to supply the home market at low cost is a significant factor behind these flows. This conclusion is confirmed by the positive and significant coefficient of European interest rates (IREC). European DFIs to the four Asian countries were also positively correlated to the US lending rate (IRUS) in earlier versions of the model, but the coefficient of IRUS was smaller and not significant, which led to its abandonment. On the whole, the results of the regression for Asia indicate that the cost of financing DFIs is not a deterrent to investment flows. In fact, one can explain the positive correlation with IREC as a sign of increased decentralisation of production in Asian countries when home production costs (among them interest rates) increase.

The positive and high value of the coefficient for INRA together with the negative (and high) value of the coefficient for GRRA are somewhat puzzling. We would have expected investment flows to decline as inflation erodes the cost advantage of decentralising production to the four countries considered. While local growth should stimulate investment to the extent that it gradually aims at supplying growing domestic demand of the Asian host countries. Domestic growth in Asia seems, on the contrary, to be associated with declining DFIs flows, perhaps because it produces skilled labour shortages or bottlenecks in strategic infrastructures, which negatively affect production in the export sector. Inflation may be the result (rather than the cause) of strong DFI inflows which generate trade balance surpluses and to the extent that Asian exchange rates have not been allowed to appreciate, balance of payment surpluses have not been sterilised by the central bank, and has therefore resulted in a higher money supply and in higher inflation.

TABLE 11

RESULTS OF LEAST SQUARE REGRESSION FOR ASIA

(One-year lag on explanatory variables)

Variable	Coefficient	Std. Error	T-Stat.	2-Tail Sig.
C	−59.013905	65.641400	−0.8990348	0.375
DG	−53.716627	35.904610	−1.4960928	0.144
DF	−143.94204	47.930714	−3.0031275	0.005
DI	−88.907763	45.889702	−1.9374299	0.061
GREC	11.997833	6.342231	1.8917369	0.067
IREC	8.624974	4.331252	1.9913349	0.055
INRA	407.93082	143.835650	2.8360898	0.088
GRRA	−399.57684	188.258620	−2.1224889	0.041

R–squared	0.338861	Mean of dependent var	25.54395
Adjusted R–squared	0.198619	S.D. of dependent var	74.30218
S.E. of regression	66.515230	Sum of squared resid	146001.1
F–statistic	−225.821300	Number of observations	41

While this explanation is only tentative and requires further investigation, it is worth pointing that the magnitude of the two coefficients is roughly similar (+408 for INRA and −400 for GRRA), and therefore given the positive correlation among the two variables (faster growth is normally accompanied by higher inflation), we can expect the two effects to closely balance each other, in spite of the conflicting economic explanations behind the observed trend.

V. THE LIKELY IMPACT OF SEM ON INVESTMENT FLOWS TO DEVELOPING COUNTRIES

The analysis developed in the previous paragraphs has identified, from a theoretical viewpoint, some of the implications of the creation of SEM for DFI flows to developing countries. Several of the relationships between macroeconomic variables and European DFIs in Latin America and Asia were empirically tested as well. The sample period under consideration (1970–87) covers an array of fairly heterogeneous economic conditions, including two oil shocks (1973 and 1979), periods of high and low inflation in industrialised countries, periods of rapid economic expansion in Latin America (the 1970s) followed by other years of slow or negative growth (the 1980s), as well as the steady appreciation (1980–85) and depreciation (post-1985) of the US dollar. For this reason, the results of our estimations should be relatively robust, in the sense that the data cover a period that experienced many fluctuations in the economic conditions.

As in all cases, however, inferences can only be drawn with confidence for values of the explanatory variables within the sample boundaries, assuming that no underlying structural changes are occurring. The creation of SEM is likely to be one of the significant structural changes of the decade, and it is therefore difficult to assess the extent to which past trends can still be assumed to be useful in predicting the future behaviour. With this warning in mind, we can nevertheless attempt to discuss the impacts of SEM on DFI flows to LDCs.

The Impact of the Single European Market

The first conclusion which can be drawn from the empirical evidence presented in the previous section is that a large share of European DFIs to Latin America can be considered 'autonomous', as evidenced by the large value of the regression constant. This finding is further supported by the significance of the country-specific dummies (DF and DI). Each European country has reached an average level of DFI flows which fluctuates mildly in response to changes in macroeconomic conditions, and whose momentum is based on past DFI history. In this sense, changes brought about by SEM process should not have a devastating effect on DFI flows.

In the case of Asia, on the other hand, such long standing tradition of European DFI is lacking. The phenomenon is considerably more recent and responds to a larger extent, to structural conditions which go beyond the macroeconomic determinants examined in the present study (only one-third of investment flows is explained by the model). Rather than a point of weakness, this may be a strong point for Asian countries, which may prove more dynamic in capturing a larger share of future European DFI flows, in comparison with the more steady (but stationary) role of Latin American countries.

The Cecchini Report [*European Economy, 1988*] estimates that the creation of the SEM will have a medium-term impact of approximately five per cent on EC's GDP growth, spread over several years. Other authors [*Baldwin, 1989*] regard these estimates as too cautious, since they do not consider the dynamic effects of European integration. Rather than siding with one or the other projection, we can assess the net impact of a given growth in the EC GDP level, say, of one per cent. GDP growth in the EC has a different impact on the two regions considered. In the case of Latin America it has two contrasting effects: it diverts financial and managerial resources away from the region, orienting them towards EC home country markets, while at the same time promoting growth in Latin America through 'transmission of growth' effects, thereby encouraging DFIs.

In the case of the South-east Asian countries, EC growth leads to expanded DFIs to the region in order to serve the growing EC market through low cost decentralised productive facilities, while the 'transmission of growth' effect is ambiguous because of the relationship between Asian GDP growth and inflation. A separate discussion of the impact of the two areas helps to clarify matters further.

If we accept IMF indications [*IMF, 1989*] which suggest that one per cent GDP growth in industrialised economies will produce 0.2 per cent expansion in Latin America, we can provide a rough estimate of the net impact of such growth on DFI flows to the region. If we assume that the German deviation from the European pattern is confirmed, we need to re-estimate our equation eliminating the dummy variable DGRG in order to count with a single sensitivity parameter for Europe as a whole. The resulting coefficients are -3.52 for growth in Europe (GREC) and

12.68 for Latin American expansion (GRRA). The net impact of one per cent GDP growth of EC could therefore be estimated at -0.984:[3] European growth would have a mild diversion effect on DFI flows to Latin America, in the order of US$1 mn for each percentage point. If, on the contrary, Germany were to align itself with the European average (as a result, for example, of the increase in resources being devoted to East Germany's modernisation), and the coefficients of the original equation were to be utilised, the diversion effect would be seven times greater (US$7.14 mn), but would still remain relatively mild (three per cent of the baseline annual DFI level).

In the case of South-east Asia, the direct effect of European GDP growth is to stimulate GDP flows to the four countries in the region for an amount equivalent to US$12 mn for each percentage point. The indirect effect is harder to estimate, due to the opposite influence of Asian growth and inflation. According to our model the former depresses DFIs while the latter stimulates them, with the net effect depending on the extent of inflationary pressure which can be expected to accompany growth. The net indirect effect could turn positive if Asian growth were accompanied by European investments aimed at serving the expanding Asian market, which is quite possible if the EC as part of its new trade policy begins to push for an expansion of domestic markets in Asia, along the line of US requests towards Japan.

Our estimates indicate that neither interest nor exchange rate variations at the European level would have a significant impact on outward DFI flows, towards Latin America and a positive effect on flows to Asia, thereby contradicting some of the hypotheses advanced in section IV. US dollar interest rates are, on the contrary, more relevant for Latin America, and a one per cent variation in their level would exert an impact which is of the same magnitude as a one per cent variation in EC's GDP growth.

It must be finally pointed out how the resumption of growth in Latin America and of financial flows to the region would be the most relevant contribution to a prospective increase of DFI flows. This finding is in line with our knowledge regarding the host country market orientation of European DFI flows to Latin America, and suggests that a common European initiative for the solution of the debt problem, or an increase in export flows from Latin America to Europe, would be the most significant incentive for increasing DFI flows. Finally, in assessing the overall situation, one must not forget that European investments (analysed in this study) are only a fraction of total foreign investments to developing countries and are surpassed by the US and challenged by the dynamism of Japan. Flows from these other regions are also likely to continue unaffected by developments in the EC, following an initial period where some diversion effects are likely to occur.

Other Relevant International Factors

In this study we have concentrated specifically on the impact of SEM on DFI flows to Latin America and Asia. It is undeniable, however, that recent developments in the international economic situation are just as likely to affect such flows, and it seems useful therefore to devote a few paragraphs to recent events in EE countries.

The latest changes in EE countries have caught international attention, leading to comments regarding their negative impact on developing countries. The impact, however, must be assessed realistically, differentiating between short and medium-term effects and between East Germany's situation and that of the other EE countries.

The opening of EE countries will affect DFI flows to developing countries primarily through diversion and indirect macroeconomic effects. EE countries have an income level per capita that is two to three times as high as Latin America's (US$6,216 in 1988 excluding the Soviet Union and $5,737 including it) and therefore represent an attractive potential market. Labour costs are comparable to those of some Asian countries (South Korea and Taiwan) and the labour force is relatively skilled. Distances from Western European countries are much smaller. For all these reasons, EE countries will be an attractive competitor for DFI flows both to middle-income developing countries and to some peripheral regions and countries in Europe, such as Turkey.

At the same time, obstacles must not be underestimated. In many cases plants and infrastructure are obsolete, and will require considerable capital for modernisation; currencies are not convertible, new laws regulating foreign investments are in their infancy and the flow of sensitive technology is still restricted for security reasons. In general, these countries will require considerable institutional, social and 'cultural' adjustment in order to be able to operate according to free market criteria. For all these reasons, one may expect that integration with Western Europe, particularly including direct investment flows, will proceed somewhat cautiously for an initial period of at least four to five years.

Furthermore, the opening of EE countries will affect macroeconomic conditions in the rest of Europe as well, thus indirectly influencing foreign investment flows. Greater competition for capital on international markets may result in increased interest rates which could offset the reduction in the cost of borrowing produced by the liberalisation of financial services within the EC. The monetary integration of the two Germanies will cause an expansion in liquidity, which could in turn lead to inflation and increasing interest rates. Concerning East Germany, the additional expenditure required by the unification process will increase the public deficit, leading to fiscal austerity measures or to monetary expansion. In the first case, a slower GDP growth rate for both Germany and Europe will result, while in the second case inflationary pressures will increase.

On the other hand, development in EE is likely to affect Latin American and Asian countries' trade positively. EE countries will diversify trade patterns away from their previous concentration on the socialist bloc, and economic growth will increase their demand for raw materials and foodstuffs. Asian exporters could also benefit from increased demand for their manufactured products and technology. In summary, it can be expected that the opening of EE countries will increase competition for DFIs and other financial flows, but that this effect will be more significant in the medium than in the short term, once the initial hurdles have been overcome.

Concluding Remarks

The purpose of this study was to analyse the impact of the SEM process on European investments in developing countries, particularly in Latin America and South-east Asia. It was first necessary to develop a theoretical framework in order to do so, since economic literature on this topic is fragmentary. The main direct macroeconomic effects were identified in relation to economic changes within the EC, such as the expected acceleration in GDP growth rates, decline in interest rates and exchange rate appreciations.

The relationship between macroeconomic variables and the level of DFI flows was tested with the help of an econometric model. As expected, it was found that European growth and the level of interest rates on the US dollar affected European DFI flows to Latin America negatively, but affected DFIs flows to Asia positively.

With reference to Latin America, European interest and exchange rates had no significant effects on the flows, while GDP growth in the host countries and net financial resource flows to the region exerted a positive effect. In the Latin American case, all the macroeconomic variable tested produced mild fluctuations around a fairly stable level of DFI flows to the region. In the Asian case, the potential for more rapid expansion of such flows is linked to the growing process of decentralisation of production, as European firms strive for greater efficiency and cost reduction. Export oriented DFIs could be complemented by investments aimed at production for the Asian market, depending on the extent that domestic demand in these countries expands as a result of the 'trickle down' effect of economic growth and of increasing EC pressure.

NOTES

1. Chile's plan, aimed at attracting both national flight capital (Chapter 18) and foreign funds (Chapter 19) was responsible for the conversion of US$6,198 mn in 1985–88, according to Chilean Central Bank data. In 1987, for example, Chapter 19 investments were slightly superior in quantity (US$555 mn) to direct investments under normal D.L. 600 regulations (US$497 mn).
2. Dummy variables to correct for the value of the constant have the traditional form, being a vector of 1s for the observations which refer to the home country and of 0s for all other observations. Multiplicative dummies have 0s in all observations concerning other countries and the value of the specific explanatory variable (multiplied by 1) in observations concerning the specific home country. The same value of the explanatory variable therefore appears twice in one observation: once to explain the European 'average' value of the coefficient, and again to explain the deviation of the specific home country from the norm. Thus, if the IREC coefficient is −5 and the coefficient of the dummy for France DIRF is +2 we can interpret the result as saying that a one per cent increase in interest rates causes European DFIs to decline by US$5 mn, but that in the case of French investments the impact is more limited and equivalent to a decline of US$3 mn (−5 +2).
3. The result is given by −3.52 (direct effect of European growth) + 12.68*0.2 (effect of Latin American growth induced by economic expansion in Europe) = −0.984.

REFERENCES

Agarwal, J., 1980, 'Determinants of Foreign Direct Investment: A Survey', *Weltwirtschaftliches Archiv*, 116, 4.

Asian Development Bank, 1990, *Asian Development Outlook*, Manila: ADB.

Balasubramanyan, V., 1984, 'Incentives and Disincentives for Foreign Direct Investment in Less Developed Countries', *Weltwirtschaftliches Archiv*, Vol.120, No.4.

Baldwin, R., 1989, 'The Growth Effects of 1992', *Economic Policy*, Oct.

Blomstrom, M. and R. Lipsey, 1986, 'Firm Size and Foreign Direct Investment', Washington, DC: NBER Working Paper n. 2092.

Cecchini, P. *et al.*, 1988, *The European Challenge 1992: The Benefits of a Single Market*, Aldershot: Wildwood House.

Cockcroft, F.L., 1989, 'The Past Record and Future Potential of Foreign Investment', Prepared for the Workshop on 'Alternative Development Strategies in Africa', Oxford, 11–13 Dec.

Culem, C., 1988, 'The Locational Determinants of Direct Investments among Industrialised Countries', *European Economic Review*, Vol.32, No. 4, April.

Cushman, D., 1980, 'Exchange Rate Uncertainty and Foreign Direct Investment in the United States', *Weltwirtschaftliches Archiv*, 124, 2.

Cushman, D., 1987, 'The Effect of Real Wages and Labor Productivity on Foreign Direct Investment', *Southern Economic Journal*, Vol.54, No. 1.

Dunning, J., 1989, *Explaining International Production*, London: Allen & Unwin.
European Economy, 1988, 'The Economics of 1992, 35, March.
Grubaugh, S., 1987, 'Determinants of Foreign Direct Investment', *The Review of Economics and Statistics*, Vol.69, No. 1, Feb.
IMF, 1988, *Balance of Payments Statistics*, Washington, DC: IMF.
IMF, 1989, *World Development Outlook*, Washington, DC: IMF.
IMF, *International Financial Statistics*, Washington, DC: IMF, various years.
Jacquermin, A., Buigues, P. and F. Ilzkovitz, 1989, 'Concentrazione orizontale, fusioni e politica della concorrenza nella comunità europea', *Economic European*, No.40, May.
Juhl, P., 1977, 'Prospects for Foreign Direct Investment in Developing Countries', in H. Giersch (ed.), *Reshaping the World Economic Order*, Tubingen: Mohr Siebeck.
Kravis, I., and R. Lipsey, 1982, 'The Location of Overseas Production and Production for Export by U.S. Multinational Firms', *Journal of International Economics*, Vol.12, 3–4.
Lall, S., 1988, 'Monopolistic Advantages and Foreign Involvment by US Manufacturing Industry', *Oxford Economic Papers*, Vol.32, No. 1, March.
Maurer, J.L. and P. Regnier, 1988, *Investment Flows between Asia and Europe, what Strategies for the Future?*, Geneva: Modern Asia Research Centre, April.
Naya, S., 1990, 'Direct Foreign Investment and Trade in East and Southeast Asia', in R.W. Jones and A. Kruger (eds.), *The Political Economy of International Trade*, Cambridge, MA: Basil Blackwell.
OECD, 1989, *Development Cooperation in the 1990s*, Paris: DAC-OECD.
Oman C., 1984, *New Forms of International Investment in Developing Countries*, Paris: OECD.
Pio, A., 1988, *Europa-America Latina, nuove forme di cooperazione*, Milan: Unicopli.
Pio, A., 1990, 'The Impact of the 1993 Single European Market on Investment Flows Between the European Community and developing countries: The case of Latin America', *European Journal of Development Research*, Vol.2, No. 2, Dec.
Reuber, G., H. Crokellel, M. Emersen, G. Gallias-Hamono, 1973, *Private Foreign Investment in Development*, Oxford: OECD Development Centre.
Riedel, J., 1975, 'The Nature and Determinants of Export-Oriented Direct Foreign Investment in a Developing Country: a Case Study of Taiwan', *Weltwirtschaftliches Archiv*, 111, 3.
Root, F. and A. Ahmed, 1979, 'Empirical Determinants of Manufacturing Direct Foreign Investment in Developing Countries', *Economic Development and Cultural Change*, Vol.27, No. 4, July.
Santiago, C., 1987, 'The impact of Foreign Direct Investment on Export Structure and Employment Generation', *World Development*, Vol.19, No. 3.
Scaparlenda, A. and R. Balough, 1983, 'Determinants of U.S. Direct Investment in the E.E.C.', *European Economic Review*, Vol.21, No. 3.
Schneider, F. and B. Frey, 1985, 'Economic and Political Determinants of Foreign Direct Investment', *World Development*, Vol.13, No. 2.
Solocha, A., M. Soskin and M. Kasoff, 1989, 'Canadian Investment in Northern New York: Impact of Exchange Rates on Foreign Direct Investment', *Growth and Change*, Vol.20, No. 1.
UNCTC, 1988, *Transnational Corporations in World Development*, New York: UN.
World Bank, 1989, *Sub-Saharan Africa, From Crisis to Sustainable Growth*, Washington, DC: World Bank, Nov.
World Bank, 1991, *World Tables 1991*, Baltimore, MD: Johns Hopkins University Press.

6

The Single European Market and Latin American Trade

ESPERANZA DURÁN

I. INTRODUCTION

The creation of the Single European Market (SEM) from 1993 raises a number of questions regarding the future of economic relations between the European Community (EC) and Latin America. In particular, the area where changes are going to be more visible and are likely to be felt soon is trade. In this regard, the deeper integration and increased commercial exchanges within the Community will result in some amount of trade diversion away from extra-regional trade flows. But similarly, improved growth prospects may be a countervailing factor in the medium and longer term. Questions arise as to whether Latin American countries will be worse off than they are at present in their access to the European market for their exports; which products are likely to face difficulties and which on account of policy decisions or technical harmonisation have improved access opportunities. And ultimately whether and how Latin America can take advantage of the creation of this large single market, which will retain its common external tariff.

In considering these questions, attention has to be given not only to the intra-community dynamics and their direct effect on relations with Latin America, which is the focus of this chapter, but, also to the extent that these issues may be complicated by an increased eastward vision of the EC and the seemingly irresistible push for closer links with the rest of Europe. In particular, Eastern European countries may be well placed to take over some business – or prospective business – from Latin America, some of whose comparative advantages are similar to Eastern European countries, as a result of a somewhat similar relative abundance of energy and resources as well as a reasonably skilled labour force available at competitive wages.

The European process of unification, with the imminent creation of the SEM and the much more ambitious plans and prospects that exist for fuller economic and political unification, is followed with great interest – and some apprehension – by governments throughout Latin America. Indeed, the EC is, overall, second only to the US (and in some aspects ahead of the latter) in its aggregate importance as a trade and investment partner for the countries of the region. EC's trade with Latin America is of some importance, though limited, amounting to no more than four to six per cent of its total trade. By contrast, for the Latin American countries this trade with the EC represents between 18 and 21 per cent of their total trade, and for some major countries of the region it is even greater. Furthermore, in a majority of cases and for the region as a whole, there is trade surplus for Latin America in its trade with EC.

How this important relationship may develop in the medium term will depend not only on the evolution of EC trade rules and policies in the coming years, and will be largely dictated by the SEM and broader European policies, but will also depend on the outcome of crucial negotiations currently under way, at the bilateral level and the ongoing Multilateral Trade Negotiations (MTNs) of the Uruguay Round. However, it would be unrealistic, or naive, to think that certain major thorns in Euro-Latin American commercial relations will be dramatically altered, let alone removed, whatever the outcome of the major processes just mentioned. Amongst long-standing commercial grievances of Latin America against the EC, one may mention the preferential agreements the EC has with the African, Caribbean and Pacific (ACP) countries participating in the Lomé Conventions, which Latin America considers discriminatory; the Common Agricultural Policy (CAP) with its negative effects on the region's exports and price instability for the sector; and, indeed, the overall European protectionism.

Latin American countries have remarked that the problem of protectionism is not so much of tariff barriers because these have, in nominal terms, decreased considerably over the years in most products. Instead, the growing perception is that European protectionism has evolved into, and is manifested in, the use and development of diverse forms of non-tariff barriers (NTBs), both traditional and novel, including trade quotas and other quantitative restrictions (QRs) or voluntary export restraints (VERs), as well as an increasingly assertive use of defensive trade instruments.

The aim of this chapter is to examine the consequences of the unification of the European market on the trade with Latin America. The first section briefly sets the background, trying to summarise the problems that have existed in EC–Latin American commercial relations, in order to identify the main issues at stake and how they will be affected, if at all, by the new rules of the SEM. The second section deals with some of these rules themselves, that is with the objectives and some key implications of the SEM for EC policies and regulations. These rules, of course, will be directly affected by the accords that may be reached within the framework of the MTNs of the Uruguay Round, currently under way. The possibilities of furthering exports from Latin America to the EC, and more generally, the impact of the SEM on interregional trade opportunities will be examined in the third part of the chapter. The final section presents a summary assessment of the prospective effects of the SEM for future commercial relations between the EC and Latin America.

II. THE EURO-LATIN AMERICAN TRADE LINK

There is no doubt that at present the EC is the most important trading bloc in the world. It represents three times the US global trade and approximately four times Japan's; the EC's export flows amount to 38 per cent of the world's total while its imports account for 37 per cent of total international trade. But Latin American participation in total EC trade has been negligible. Although EC imports from Latin America increased by five per cent between 1979 and 1988, the Latin American share in the EC's total imports from third countries decreased to 5.5 per cent, compared with 6 and 7.5 in 1979 and 1985 respectively [*von Gleich. 1990: 1–3*].

The diminishing-share trends have been a long-term constant since the signing of the Treaty of Rome, even though in the first half of the 1980s the fall was contained as the Community's imports from Latin America stabilised.[1] Indeed, during this period, EC's annual imports from Latin America remained more or less stable around $22 billion: $22.7 billion in 1980; $21.3 billion in 1982, again $22.7 billion in 1985. In contrast, in the second half of the decade Latin American exports to the EC, whilst limited to the same orders of magnitude as indicated above, have shown greater variability. So, in 1986 the region's exports reached their lowest level: $20.1 billion, accounting for a 2.6 per cent participation in European imports, whilst by 1988, the relative success for the region's export-oriented policies can be discerned and Latin America's total exports to the EC amounted to $26 billion.[2] Nonetheless, even though in relative terms Latin America fared reasonably well over the decade, as its share in EC imports held its ground against further advances by those from other regions, in absolute terms, Latin America's exports to the EC have not been very dynamic, and their overall level is disappointing.

European exports to Latin America have also shown declining trends, particularly during the period 1980–85. This was directly related to Latin America's external debt crisis, which dramatically affected the region's capacity to import: from $18.3 billion in 1980, to $11 billion in 1983, a level which remained unchanged in 1984 and 1985. In 1986, however, EC exports to Latin America increased slightly, reaching $13.4 billion, but even then, taking into account the increase, EC exports to Latin America accounted for 1.7 per cent of total EC exports. This is a clear illustration of the insignificance of Latin America for the EC as a market at present, and the asymmetry in Euro-Latin American commercial relations.

An interesting characteristic of the trade links between the two regions, which cannot be observed by looking only at overall figures, is that the EC countries have been selective in developing their trade interests in Latin America. They have focused their attention on two types of countries: their former colonies (as has already been remarked with regard to the ACP countries) and the countries representing the more economically advanced countries in the region, namely Argentina, Brazil, Mexico and Venezuela. Dramatic illustrations of the strong preference of the EC countries to establish trade links with their former colonies are not hard to find. In 1980–83 France exported more to Guadeloupe and Martinique combined than it did to Brazil. Similarly, in 1981, the UK exported more and imported more from Jamaica than from Chile, Colombia, or Peru. On the other hand, merely three countries, together, account for two-thirds of EC's imports from Latin America: Brazil, Mexico and Argentina. Nevertheless, it should be noted that the share of Argentine exports to the EC has been showing a persistent decline over the last ten years or so: from 20 per cent of Latin American exports in 1979 to 10 per cent by 1987.

In qualitative terms, commercial relations between Latin America and the EC have been most conflicting. A recurrent cause of complaint on the part of Latin America is that the bulk of the products they export, notably tropical products (specifically coffee and cocoa) plus sugar, iron ore, blister copper and cotton, cannot compete effectively with those from the ACP countries, which receive preferential treatment under the Lomé Conventions. These stipulate that most of the ACP products can enter the EC market without tariffs or restrictions, on a non-reciprocal basis. They also introduce a system of stabilisation of export revenues (STABEX), to ensure that these countries will not suffer excessive fluctuations in the prices of their exports.

Another Latin American grievance stems from what is regarded as growing European protectionism. Indeed, the EC has made increasing use of a series of defensive trade instruments, such as anti-dumping measures, safeguards and surveillance procedures, for restraining imports which are regarded as harmful to its domestic producers or that are considered as traded unfairly, not to mention the whole gamut of NTBs. Products that have been particularly affected by NTBs are agricultural, textiles and clothing, ferrous metals and non-electrical machines.[3]

Latin American exports which are subject to EC's NTBs are: meat, which faces tariff quotas or variable levies and licences; tuna fish products, which are subject to reference prices and to growing technical barriers; cut flowers, again subject to technical barriers and seasonal tariffs; oranges, grapes, apples and pears, subject to seasonal tariffs, reference prices and licences; maize and sugar, subject to variable levies and licences; and many others. Similarly, in manufacturing, major sectors of interest to Latin American countries are in many cases subject to various restrictions, notably textiles and clothing under the Multi-Fibre Arrangement (MFA); footwear, iron and steel, the latter under VERs and otherwise both under Community surveillance.

On the other hand, as the leading industrial countries drastically reduced their tariffs and their formal NTBs as a result of the Kennedy and Tokyo Rounds, pressures began to build, for them to continue to protect their industries through less conspicuous, often technical means. One such has been the anti-dumping charges. The EC has imposed anti-dumping duties on products such as chemicals, synthetic fibres, construction materials, and steel. Several Latin American countries have been affected by these charges, notably Mexico and Brazil on their steel exports to the EC.

However, the most visible area of conflict between the EC and some countries in Latin America has been that of agricultural trade. The countries most critical of the EC have been Argentina and Uruguay (and more recently, Brazil and Chile), and have traditionally been competitive producers of agricultural exports. However, not only have their products limited access to the EC market, but their overall capacity to export has also been hindered severely by the effects of the CAP on international agricultural prices. Latin Americans have pointed repeatedly to the adverse effects that the EC's CAP, with its generous internal support (and border protection) for its farmers and consequent export subsidies, has had on their agricultural exports [*SELA, 1984: 25–33*]).

But the implications of the CAP are wide-ranging. One of the stumbling blocks in the Uruguay Round negotiations has been the state of negotiation in agriculture. As negotiations have unfolded and, one way or another, advanced, it has become clear that agriculture holds the key to the success or failure of the Uruguay Round. At present, the virtual impasse and uneven pace reached on this issue make it rather difficult to foresee a successful end to this latest round of MTNs.

The Europeans do not consider the Latin American criticisms to be fair. They repeatedly point to their trade deficit with Latin America, which they claim would invalidate the complaint that the EC is protectionist or that Latin American products cannot enter the European market. The EC also points out its generous use of the Generalised System of Preferences (GSP), which could facilitate the entry of Latin American exports to the Community market. Latin Americans argue that the GSP, established in 1971 (modified in 1981, which is currently under revision and will come into force in 1991) has had limited coverage and is granted on a temporary basis.[4] Furthermore, industrial products, most of which are included in the system, are classified as sensitive, semi-sensitive and non-sensitive. Only the last do not face import limitations. As a result of the 1981 revision, the relative weight of non-sensitive products decreased while that of the sensitive ones was significantly increased. In 1985, for instance, 132 products were classified in the sensitive industrial products list, of which 58 had ceilings established. Imports beyond the ceiling imposed faced non-preferential tariffs. Preferential treatment under the GSP has also been eroded by the yearly transfer of 'non-sensitive' products to the sensitive product list [*Canela, 1988: 44*].

The EC's perception is that Latin Americans have not taken full advantage of GSP, either because they are ignorant of how to make full use of it, or because in any case their products are not price-competitive. Partially valid as this argument would seem to be, Latin America's conviction is that the GSP is neither a permanent solution to their commercial problems, nor are its effects far-reaching in increasing the access of Latin American products to the EC [*Canela. 1988: 53*]. These issues are constant concerns that come up in bilateral negotiations time and again.

III. ON THE WAY TO 1992

The cornerstone for the establishment of a European Communities' market without frontiers as from December 1992 was the adoption of the European Single Act (ESA) on 1 July 1987. This document included, amongst other important reforms, 279 specific directives – the blueprint to achieving the desired aim. The ESA was based on the European Commission's White Book, which was published in 1985. The ESA, apart from laying down the basis for European unification, was the first fundamental reform to the Treaty of Rome, geared towards the adaptation of the Community's institutions for the 'new Europe'.

The ESA granted to the European Parliament, greater capacity of intervention in the legislative process of the EC; it reformed the voting system, eliminating the principle of unanimity and introducing that of a qualified majority when each member state's vote would be proportional to its population. These fundamental changes introduced a new dynamism to the European unification process, lending renewed credence to the most ambitious expectations as to the pace of progress in the current state of creation of a single Europe. The sense of urgency for completing the process towards unification was in good measure due to the realisation that the so-called Euro-sclerosis might be directly traceable to the inefficiency of having a highly fragmented EC 'market', which implied substantial economic costs. Indeed, a 1988 report on the *Cost of Non-Europe* [*Cecchini, 1988*] estimated the overall cost of existing barriers at approximately ECU 200 billion. Although the Common Market established in theory a customs union without tariff barriers, divergent national product standards, technical regulations, conflicting business laws, widely differing VAT rates, etc., meant that goods sold in one country could not be exported to others.

In order to remove all existing obstacles to intra-European trade, the completion of the European single market will take place under the principle of 'mutual recognition'. This implies that goods produced or consumed in an EC country will circulate freely within the EC and will have to be accepted for consumption in any other Community country. The main agreed ingredients to guarantee the free flow of intra-Community trade are:

(1) the removal of physical (or direct) barriers to the free circulation of goods, services, capital and people;
(2) the elimination of technical (or indirect) barriers, including non-tariff measures as well as local requirements in a large range of areas, where certification processes are typically carried out in both the exporting and importing countries; the key targets here are regulations on public health, security, environment, and consumer protection; equally, public procurement would be liberalised;
(3) the dismantling of fiscal obstacles, including the harmonisation of indirect taxes.

The fourth report of the European Commission of 1989 with regard to the achievements since the adoption of the ESA, indicated that the Commission had drafted almost all of the 297 directives foreseen, 60 per cent of which had been approved by the Council of Ministers. Nevertheless, despite the general background of Euro-dynamism, progress in the unification process has not been uniform. More has been achieved on questions of principles and long-term direction, than with regard to the adoption of specific measures on, for instance, veterinary, health and environmental issues, or in achieving harmonisation of regulatory and fiscal policies.

A general practice contained in EC legislation is that once a product enters the EC, it has free circulation in all EC countries. However, a number of articles in the Treaty of Rome permitted departures from this provision. Namely, first, Article 36, which justifies restrictions to internal trade on grounds of public morality, public policy or public security. In the same vein, article 109 permits protective measures in balance-of-payments crises. And article 115 authorises member states to carry out intra-Community surveillance on particular sensitive goods from outside the community to prevent these goods from being imported from another member state, after request of a waiver by the Commission [*Pearce and Sutton, 1985: 46–50*].

Equally, there are sectors on which a system of national quotas prevails; this adds to the difficulties of the unification of the European market. National quotas presently apply to more than 700 tariff lines; 550 relate to manufactures and 150 to agriculture. Those currently in place in the manufacturing sector, and on whose eventual post-1992 elimination EC member states have expressed concern, apply to sensitive industrial products: steel, with import quotas by country; automobile industry, particularly of France and the UK, where quotas and bilateral arrangements seek to limit Japanese imports; textiles and clothing, in which countries apply quotas under the MFA; footwear and electronic components. On tropical products the EC Commission foresees the removal of all national quotas, except for bananas.

One factor that has in the recent past arguably hindered the abolition of the national quota systems is the existence of the ongoing Uruguay Round of MTNs. The logic is twofold. First, it makes sense to wait and see what the new rules of the game in the international trading process will be, so as to ensure consistency and efficiency of the measures taken. Secondly, and perhaps more importantly, the Community is all too well aware of the demands that will inevitably come its way at the end of the day in the negotiations. Any single quota given up outside or ahead of the MTN framework, is one chip less for the eventual hard bargaining there.

Similarly, the sudden, unexpected and dramatic events in Eastern Europe in 1989 represented another major distraction from the Twelve's hitherto smooth handling of their own adjustment process. Wide-ranging factors, such as the potential complementarities of the two sets of economies; a historical, cultural and political importance that the new partners in the East represent for their Western European neighbours; the Eastern European countries' grave financial, industrial, technological and environmental predicament and needs, have all led the EC to be distracted from its own integration process and, alas, from opportunities and interests elsewhere in the world, including in Latin America.

IV. 1992 AND TRADE WITH LATIN AMERICA

What then are the foreseeable effects of the creation of the SEM on the commercial relations between the EC and Latin America? Any answer to this frequently raised question must inevitably be speculative. There are too many deep changes under way, and their effects are not separable – not even independent of each other. Within the EC alone, the unfolding picture is complicated by the coexistence, alongside the European Monetary Union (EMU) process, of EC relations with EFTA countries, both collectively and, in several cases, singly. Finally, there is attention of the ongoing, dramatic developments in Eastern Europe and the USSR. And beyond the European sphere, within the realm of international trade, established patterns and interests are under fundamental revision, with Japan's final accession into the category of commercial superpower; the continuing trend towards the formation of regional trade groupings; the rising tide of protectionism throughout the industrial world and, also, the MTN of the Uruguay Round.

The stakes at present being negotiated within the Uruguay Round are high, not only for the industrialised world, but equally for the LDCs, including those within Latin America, which are taking an active role in defence of their own trading interests. The overwhelming importance of the Uruguay Round stems from the fact that, compared to previous rounds, this is the first time that vital topics which were outside the scope of the GATT system are being negotiated, notably agriculture and textiles and clothing (both formally in the GATT but subject to pervasive distortions under old regimes of exception), as well as a whole gamut of so-called 'new issues' which relate to investment questions (TRIMs: trade related investment measures), patents and brands (TRIPs: trade related intellectual property rights) and the whole universe of service sectors – notably finance in all its forms, telecommunications, transport and so on. In addition, this is the first of the eight rounds so far of MTNs where LDCs are actually taking part in the negotiations – and in an important way – with far-reaching implications for both the substance and the conduct of the exercise.

With such a charged and even confused international agenda, it would be brave to assert unequivocally what the outcome of each of these elements in the game will actually be, especially for European or any other region's trade and prosperity. However, it seems safe to surmise that, despite the profound changes taking place for the future of Europe, the direct effects of these developments on trade with Latin America are unlikely to be dramatic. Problems that have plagued Euro-Latin American commercial relations in recent decades are likely to remain as continuing leitmotifs of the relationship beyond 1992, notably the preferential, unfavourable competitive conditions Latin America faces in the EC *vis-à-vis* the ACP countries as well as those of the CAP, at one end of the production spectrum – primary products – coupled with increasing protectionism where manufactures are concerned.

Even if the main lines of the interregional bilateral agendas remain the same, the likely significant effects from the single-market process can be identified. On the negative side, the harmonisation of sanitary measures and provisions for environmental and consumer protection could affect existing Latin American exports to the EC, if the countries in the region fail to adapt to the new EC requirements. The other side of the coin is that access to the European market will be assisted in some measure, by the 'mutual recognition' principle because, once an export has passed the certification process, it is free to circulate in any EC member state, thus facilitating exporting to these countries. Equally, the increase in demand and the greater economic momentum of Europe '92 offers possibilities for greater export prospects from non-EC countries.

Regarding the system of national quotas, there is reluctance on the part of EC member states to eliminate those on products they regard as sensitive; common policies and commitments at the level of detail are in many cases still to be reached. However, the momentum of the unification process will doubtless be decisive in most cases here: the elimination of customs barriers within the Community would make it difficult to administer national quotas and enforce their implementation, hence creating a formidable pressure for further harmonisation and probable liberalisation of quotas. One of the Latin American exports which could be positively affected by the streamlining or elimination of national quotas is crude oil from Mexico and Venezuela.

Nevertheless, even where national quotas eventually do disappear, they will in many cases be translated into equivalent provisions at the EC level, even though this will hardly be the case where the national quotas exist only in a few of the EC's twelve countries. Similarly, in some products intra-Community surveillance is feasible and the quotas are likely to continue. Some goods of great exporting interest to a number of Latin American countries are likely to be included in the EC quota system, for instance, bananas, where the UK, France, Italy, Greece, Spain and Portugal have quantitative restrictions or prohibitions, to limit banana imports from the so-called 'dollar zone' (Latin America and the Caribbean and the Philippines). It is clear that, in a free trading system, bananas from certain ACP countries or from offshore island provinces (in the case of Spain and Portugal) would not be able to compete in price or quality with those from the dollar zone. In this respect, 1992 is unlikely to alter the status quo [*Cárdenas, 1990: 15*].

Another potentially beneficial effect from the harmonisation of Community policies, post-1992, refers to products exported under the GSP. At present, quota percentages and ceilings differ from one EC member state to another. For instance, the percentage of products imported by the EC as a whole under this system is 41 per cent on average. However, this percentage is as high as 51 per cent for Germany and as low as 20 per cent for Greece. One of the objectives of 1992 is to eliminate these differences, and this will mean changes and rearrangements that Latin American countries with a vigorous export drive (Chile and Mexico) will be able to seek and take advantage of. But the future of the GSP will be decided before 1992. Indeed, the present system lapsed in 1990, and its revision or sequel, as a useful instrument for Latin American countries to increase their exports to the EC market, will depend on the outcome of the negotiations for the post-1990 system.

Similarly, there are areas where the harmonisation of the EC's regulations, standards, testing and certification procedures could mean certain advantages for the Latin American countries, in their efforts to increase their exports to the EC. The harmonisation of standards for imports of preserved food, for example, would offer countries with diversified or flexible production capabilities an advantage over others (in this case ACP countries) for EC market penetration. Indeed exports of processed food products is an area where the Latin American countries are becoming increasingly competitive. If they manage to adapt swiftly and efficiently to the Community's requirements in this line of products, the EC could well become an important market for Latin American processed food exports.

V. CONCLUSIONS

An important debate has emerged on the effects of the imminent creation of the single market in the EC after 1992. There are two schools of thought on the general trend this will entail for world trade. On the one hand, there are those who believe European protectionism and inward looking policies will turn the EC into 'Fortress Europe', with the consequent negative trade diversion effects for non-regional suppliers. On the other, one can also find those who, more optimistically, express their conviction that the greater economic dynamism of a unified EC will result in greater internal demand, with concomitant trade creation effects for the benefit of the keener and more able extra-regional exporters. Both views are wrong for being simplistic, and are certainly partial. But they both contain elements of truth.

In parallel, almost hand in hand with the European unification process, there are a number of factors changing the face of Europe, and changing the face of international trade. The outcomes from these processes are still far from clear. It is thus still too early to assert with any confidence what the effects of Europe '92 will be on the EC's commercial relations with non-EC countries.

As regards EC–Latin American trade, it is foreseeable that the commercial problems that have existed between the two regions in recent decades will not be dramatically altered after 1992. The main reason for this is that the elements which have been in place for creating trading difficulties in Euro-Latin American trade, are likely to remain after 1992: namely, the privileged relation between the EC and ACP countries which discriminates against Latin American exports; the CAP, with its negative effects on Latin American – and other countries' – agricultural trade; and certain areas where there is reluctance on the part of the European Commission to alter the *status quo* (which includes a number of traditional manufactures and banana trade).

Admittedly, it is to be expected that, on many trade-related aspects, the EC will find increased opportunities within itself after 1992. But it is just as true that many reforms and changes are in the making and that, thereby, new opportunities will emerge and become available for extra-regional agents. This will be brought about, first, through innumerable side-effects of the European unification process, but equally, by the overall changing circumstances taking place, both in Europe as well as on other fronts. For instance, the harmonisation of the EC's regulations will simplify the exporting process, and will also result in new rules of the game for trade with the emerging trading giant that the unified community will be. This will provide those countries and agents better able to adapt to the new EC requirements with a new competitive edge over those less able to make timely changes in their production or marketing processes. At the same time it must be mentioned, even if only in passing, that a successful outcome of the Uruguay Round negotiations would result in overall tariff reductions and improved trading possibilities which would provide the Latin American countries (and other LDCs) with better and more reliable access to the EC (and other industrialised countries') markets.

The beneficial or negative effects of the accelerated process of European integration will, in the end, depend on the ability of Latin American countries to adapt to the new EC rules. It is of the utmost importance that the Latin American governments, and their exporters, follow closely the process of creation of the EC single market, in a keen search for ways to adapt and take advantage of the opportunities this far-reaching event will in the end provide.

NOTES

1. There are several sources for the trade figures used for less recent years: Eurostat [1985]; Sistema Económico Latinoamericano, [1984–85]. Current figures are from the UNCTAD Data Base.
2. This total includes Latin American exports of petroleum products (HS2709 and 2710). Excluding tariff lines related to petroleum and derivatives, Latin America's exports to the EC amounted to $23.6 billion.
3. A recent study [*Laird and Yeats. 1990: 299–325*] on non-tariff barriers concludes that industrial countries' imports affected by NTDs increased from 25 per cent in 1966 to approximately 48 per cent in 1986. Also that trade covered by NTBs has increased more rapidly in EC countries than in the US or Japan.
4. As a means to help the Andean countries in their fight against drug production, the EC came up in 1990 with a scheme according special GSP treatment to four countries: Colombia, Peru, Ecuador and Bolivia. It has been argued by trade experts that this is a 'perversion' of GSP, as it distorts the system of preferences granted to these *vis-à-vis* other countries.

REFERENCES

Canela, S.M., 1988, '¿Por qué no comerciamos más con Europa? Proteccionismo y discriminaciones de la Comunidad', *Síntesis*, Madrid, 4.

Cardenas, J.M., 1990, 'Europa 1992 y los países en desarrollo con especial énfasis en américa Latina', *Integración Latinoamericana*, 15, 158.

Cecchini, P., 1988, *The European Challenge 1992*, Aldershot: Wildwood House.

Eurostat, 1985, *Analysis of EEC–Latin American Trade. Recent Trends*, Luxembourg: EC.

Laird, S. and A. Yeats, 1990, 'Trends in Non-tariff Barriers of Developed Countries, 1966–1986', *Weltwirtschaftliches Archiv*, 126, 2.

Pearce, J. and J. Sutton, 1985, *Protection and Industrial Policy in Europe*. London: Routledge & Kegan Paul.

Sistema Económico Latinoamericano (SELA), 1984–85, Secretaría Permanente, *Relaciones Económicas América Latina–CEE. 1984–1985*, Caracas: SP/XI.O/DT no. 13.
Sistema Económico Latinoamericano (SELA), 1984, *América Latina y la Comunidad Europea*, Caracas: Monte Avila Editores.
von Gleich, A., 1990, 'Continuidad y cambio en las relaciones económicas Europeo-latinoamericanas', paper presented at the AIETI/IRELA seminar, Barcelona, 4–7 Oct.

7

The Effect of Project 1992 on the ASEAN

JAYSHREE SENGUPTA

I. INTRODUCTION

A group of South-East Asian countries called the ASEAN (Association of South East Asian Nations), has emerged as important exporters of manufactures in the last decade following the footsteps of the four East Asian Tigers: South Korea, Singapore, Taiwan and Hong Kong or the Newly Industrialising Countries (NICs). For the European Community, the ASEAN has been an important region for direct foreign investment (DFI), industrial co-operation and technical assistance in the past and the EC has been absorbing increasing amounts of ASEAN exports. Thus it is of interest for both the ASEAN and the EC to see how this regional grouping of countries is going to be affected by the Single European Market (SEM) of 1992.

II. THE ASEAN

The ASEAN comprises six countries: Brunei, Indonesia, Malaysia, the Philippines, Singapore (which is also one of the NICs), and Thailand. These countries have an overall area of three million square kilometres and is roughly equal to 2.3 per cent of the entire world and nearly four per cent of the developing world. All the countries except Thailand have come under the influence of European countries since the early sixteenth century.[1] The Association came into being on 8 August 1967 with Indonesia, Malaysia, the Philippines, Singapore and Thailand as the five founding members. Brunei joined the ASEAN in 1985 immediately after independence.

The region is rich in oil, natural gas, tin, nickel ores, bauxite, copper, manganese, gold, silver and iron ore. The region is also rich in agricultural cash crops and forestry products – natural rubber, timber. It exports coconut, palm oil, tea and coffee, cotton, jute, tobacco, pineapple, sugar, tapioca, oil seeds and rice. During the 1970s and early 1980s, EC (EUR 10) trade with the ASEAN increased rapidly. The annual rate of growth of EC imports from the ASEAN between 1970 to 1984 was around 17 per cent as against a 13 per cent increase in imports from all developing countries as well as from the rest of the world. Only imports from the East Asian NICs – Hong Kong, South Korea, and Taiwan – as a group to EC grew at a higher rate of 19 per cent per annum.

In 1980 the EC–ASEAN Cooperation agreement was concluded (renewed and extended in 1986 and 1990) which provided a framework for political and economic consultation as well as technical assistance, but the agreement neither provides for trade preferences nor for bilateral trade negotiations of any kind. However, the Cooperation Agreement was instrumental in increasing the total trade between the two regional groupings substantially. In 1980 the total trade was worth 12.226 ecu million (mn) between EC (EUR 9) and it increased to 18.931 ecu mn EUR 12) in 1987, an increase of 55 per cent. EC exports rose during this period from 5.369 ecu mn to 8.904 ecu mn, an increase by 65.8 per cent and imports from the ASEAN by the EC increased from 6.857 ecu mn to 10.027 ecu mn which is an increase of 46.2 per cent (see Table 1). The increase in trade between the ASEAN and the EC continued for five years 1980–85, after which the decline of the US dollar triggered off a decline in exports and imports in 1986 in ecu terms. This development strengthened the position of Japan and the US in their trade relations with the ASEAN. Japan has been an important trading partner of the ASEAN countries. For Brunei, whose exports are largely of fuel, the main partner is Japan and both the EC and US are less important. For Indonesia, in 1970, Japan was the largest market and has remained so. But US is the second largest market replacing EC. For Malaysia too, Japan is the main market, US is second in importance and EC, third. For the Philippines, the US is the number one market followed by Japan.

TABLE 1

TRADE BETWEEN ASEAN AND EC (ECU mn) (1980–87)

	1980	1981	1982	1983	1984	1985	1986	1987(1)
EC Exports	5.369	7.152	8.470	9.269	9.886	9.810	8.495	8.904
EC Imports	6.857	6.646	7.104	7.920	9.662	9.972	9.212	10.027
Balance	−1.488	506	1.368	1.349	224	−162	−717	−1.123

(1) Excluding data from Greece for the period Oct.–Dec. 1987

Source: Eurostat, *External Trade – Statistical Yearbook*, Luxembourg, EC, various years.

For Singapore, EC is second only to the US market. But for Thailand, EC has emerged as the largest market replacing Japan which was the main market in 1970; now US is the second biggest market and Japan the third [*The EC and Asean, 1988*].

In 1986 Japan and the US took 26.8 per cent and 24.7 per cent of ASEAN's exports respectively while EC was the third biggest export market, absorbing 15.7 per cent of ASEAN's total exports. Similarly on the import side, the EC is ASEAN's third largest supplier after Japan and the US. In 1986, the EC accounted for 16.5 per cent of ASEAN's total imports with Japan supplying 26.0 per cent and the US 19.1 per cent. Trade with Japan in non-manufactures is somewhat exceptional, partly because of Japan's large direct investment in the ASEAN. Japan was one of the first to invest heavily in the ASEAN to exploit their comparative advantage for relatively labour-intensive products. Japanese were followed by Taiwan, South Korea and even Hong Kong despite their increased subcontracting in China. Japan has also traditionally invested in the ASEAN to gain access to raw materials and fuels.

In 1988, 55 per cent of Japan's bilateral exports with the ASEAN was in ores, minerals and fuels (see Table 2). Manufactures are highest in USA's bilateral exports, second only to EC.

There has been a qualitative change in ASEAN's exports to the EC as

TABLE 2

PRODUCT COMPOSITION OF ASEAN EXPORTS (1975–88) (Percentage of total bilateral exports)

Year	EC	US	Japan
Food			
1975	42.5	19.8	19.2
1988	24.5	9.0	13.2
Raw Materials			
1975	25.6	7.7	10.4
1988	13.0	5.1	14.8
Ores, Minerals, fuels			
1975	8.4	52.2	67.5
1988	1.7	8.2	54.7
Manufactures			
1975	23.0	19.2	2.8
1988	59.1	75.9	15.8
of which Textiles/clothing			
1975	4.1	3.8	0.5
1988	13.9	13.2	1.5

Source: Eurostat, *External Trade – Statistical Yearbook*, Luxembourg, EC,various years.

there has been a steady growth in the production of manufactured goods in the ASEAN countries. In 1986, exports of manufactured products represented 50 per cent of the total exports to the EC, exceeding in value for the first time the value of primary product exports (see Table 3).

III. EXPORT GROWTH TRENDS

All the five ASEAN countries experienced impressive GNP per capita during 1970–84, with Indonesia having a growth rate of GNP per capita of 9.4 per cent, Thailand 9.2 per cent, the Philippines 6.6 per cent, Singapore 13.3 per cent and Malaysia 9.9 per cent. Malaysia experienced a surge in machinery and electronic components exports and the manufacturing sector is the most dynamic sector of the economy in recent years. Both Malaysia and Thailand have experienced an increase in output of 15 per cent in 1989. Singapore has benefited from the expansion in other countries of the region, such as a strong demand by assembly plants for components of electronic and telecommunication equipment and refined petroleum products. Increased ship repair business, active banking and financial services and an important increase in tourism, helped the service sector to expand at 14 per cent in value terms in 1989. Indonesia grew at 7.3 per cent in 1989 as compared with 5.7 per cent in 1988, due to non-oil/gas export expansion and financial stability and declining lending rates, low inflation and high savings rates. Philippines has experienced a slow-down in recent years with imports increasing more than exports and some deceleration in the manufacturing sector. In all the countries there was an increase in imports of capital and intermediate goods as well as consumer goods as a result of higher wages and employment. Agricultural output grew by 5.5 per cent in Malaysia and 4.1 per cent in Thailand [*UNCTAD, 1990*].

TABLE 3

ASEAN EXPORTS TO EC BY PRODUCTS (1980–87)

	1980	1984	1985	1986	1987(1)
% Share of Primary Products	60.9	54.7	54.3	47.2	43.3
% Share of Agri. Products	27.2	31.3	31.0	29.6	23.0
% Share of Raw Materials	30.8	21.7	20.9	17.2	15.8
% Share of Mfd. Products	28.7	44.3	44.4	49.3	53.3

(1) Provisional estimate (January/ September 1987)
Source: Eurostat, *External Trade – Statistical Yearbook*, Luxembourg, EC.

IV. OPENNESS OF THE ASEAN ECONOMIES

The ASEAN members do not owe their growth to the integration of the ASEAN into a free trade area, a customs union or a common market. Intra-group trade liberalisation and economic co-operation among members are modest. The strong export performance of the ASEAN has been due to the policies they followed in the past which have an 'outward orientation'. The export orientation and the export success of these economies have been strongly correlated with superior overall export growth and increase in employment as well as reduction in poverty. In all the countries except Singapore which has always remained open, there was a shift towards higher levels of protection in the 1970s. During this period high rates of investment were financed through rises in oil and commodity earnings, as well as by external borrowings and DFI by European, American and Japanese firms.

Much of the new investment aimed at creating additional capacity in the industrial sector and some of it was directed to export industries. But the prime motivation was to quicken the pace of import substitution both in traditional manufactures and in new areas such as intermediate goods and transport equipment. The import-substituting investment phase was supported by protectionist barriers that raised the overall level of protection in these countries. Tariffs were imposed often in response to specific situations so that there was a tendency towards variation in the structure of protection.

The countries in the region began with a protective regime but gradually favoured an open trading system. The average level of tariff has been between 15 per cent to 34 per cent and the dispersion of tariffs has been lower than in other countries of South Asia. While Malaysia has the most uniform tariff structure by levels of industrial processing, Indonesia, the Philippines and Thailand have considerable escalation in their tariff structures. Since exemptions allowed on inputs can offset the anti-export bias created by the protective structure, such exemptions on machinery and other inputs were offered as investment incentives in Malaysia and also in Thailand. Quantitative Restrictions (QR) on imports have been important in the Philippines and Indonesia as compared to Malaysia and Thailand, but the overall role of QRs in the region has been less important as compared to some other developing countries [*Sengupta, 1988*].

V. LIBERALISATION AND EXPORT PROMOTION

In liberalising their trade regime, the ASEAN countries have replaced quotas with tariffs and reduced the level of nominal tariffs followed by a move towards uniform tariff structure. The Philippines and Indonesia have removed QRs on inputs first and such liberalisation has led to an improvement in capacity utilisation while keeping the balance of payments pressure in check. In the Philippines, the average level of tariff was reduced and the dispersion of rates narrowed from 0 to 100 per cent to 10 to 50 per cent. A large number of consumer goods were also removed from the banned import list but balance of payments difficulties caused a reversal to take place in 1983.

In Malaysia, there were lesser trade distortions and the weighted average level of effective protection in the manufacturing industries was estimated at 23 per cent in 1983 which is not much as compared to other developing countries. Thailand's trade reform focused on tariff reduction but the main constraint to tariff reduction was the need to generate fiscal revenue to cover growing budget deficits. In manufacturing, which was the main target of reform, there was a reduction in the level and dispersion of protection.

In Indonesia, high and disparate tariff rates coupled with non-tariff restructuring covered one-fifth of all import categories and this was reflected in the high and variable rates of effective protection. The government first eased the import curbs in 1985 and announced an across-the- board reduction in the range and level of nominal tariffs. The number of tariff categories was also reduced but the full benefit of the liberalisation programme was not realised because of the proliferation of licence restrictions. The licensing restrictions have recently been removed. Another way of import control reduction was through a major overhaul of the customs procedures and placing the job of certifying imports and assessing tariffs in the hands of private surveyors. The reduced number of customs officials and the average time spent helped in decreasing the freight costs. The openness of the ASEAN is reflected in the export/GDP and imports/GDP ratios of the member countries (see Table 4).

All the ASEAN countries gave incentives to exports in order to promote

TABLE 4

EXPORTS AND IMPORTS AS A PERCENTAGE SHARE OF GDP (1979–87)

Country	Exports/GDP		Imports/GDP	
	1979–81	1985–87	1979–81	1985–87
Indonesia	30.5	21.4	21.9	20.1
Malaysia	56.8	71.3	53.0	52.4
Philippines	19.6	25.4	25.6	22.4
Thailand	24.2	30.1	30.1	26.7

Source: UNCTAD, 1990, *Trade and Development Report, 1989*, New York: UN.

higher export growth and in order to compensate for the negative effects of taxes, tariffs and the high cost of export finance. All of them also gave some financing support to exporters most commonly pre-shipment short-term credit [*Rhee. 1986*]. In addition, like the East Asian NICs, ASEAN countries also established export processing zones. Thus ASEAN has followed closely the pattern of exports of the East Asia NICs.

VI. ASEAN EXPORTS AND ACCESS TO EC MARKET

As pointed above, EC–ASEAN trade has strengthened because the ASEAN's share in overall exports to the EC in 1975 was 1.8 per cent but became 3.4 per cent in 1989 and ASEAN imports into EC as a share of all developing countries rose from 3.9 per cent in 1975 to 6.8 per cent in 1985 and 10.8 per cent in 1988. Since the ASEAN has followed the same patterns of export growth as the East Asian NICs, the same curbs as applied to the East Asian NICs will be applicable to the ASEAN after 1992.

As a result of the changes in trade policies and incentives given to the manufacturing sector by all the countries of the ASEAN, the group has been producing more manufactures than primary goods and raw materials. Textile and garments account for a large share of its manufactured exports. Imports into the EC of textile and clothing products from the ASEAN countries grew rapidly with an increase in volume terms of 43 per cent in 1986 and a further 42 per cent increase in the first six months of 1987, as compared to the first six months of 1986. In value terms between 1980 and 1986, ASEAN's exports of textiles and clothing to the EC increased by 67 per cent from 4.737 ecu mn to 7.896 ecu mn [*The EC and ASEAN. 1988*]. Singapore and Indonesia and the Philippines have achieved huge gains in textile and clothing exports to the EC (see Table 5).

VII. ACCESS TO EC AND GSP

In broad terms, access for ASEAN exports to the EC is as summarised in Table 5.

Of the total exports of the ASEAN countries to the EC in 1986, 34.4 per cent entered duty free under the Most Favoured Nation (MFN) treatment, 13.8 per cent entered duty free under GSP (non-agricultural products), 8.7 per cent got preferential access under GSP (agricultural products) and 45.1 per cent were subject to MFN duty. Thus 46.2 per cent of ASEAN exports entered the EC duty free underscoring the fact that the ASEAN is a major beneficiary of the EC's GSP treatment. Total (100 per cent) ASEAN exports eligible under GSP increased from 3.494 ecu/mn, in 1980 to 3.97 ecu/mn in 1983, and to 5.112 ecu/mn, in 1986. But only 34 per cent of ASEAN exports actually benefited from GSP in 1980 (1.192 ecu/mn), 44 per cent in 1983 (1.752 ecu/mn), 40 per cent in 1986 (2.066 ecu/mn). Agricultural exports benefiting from GSP amounted to 15.8 per cent (0.553 ecu/mn) in 1980, 19.7 per cent (0.785 ecu/mn) in 1983 and 15.6 per cent (0.800 ecu mn) in 1986. Industrial exports benefiting from GSP amounted to 18.2 per cent (0.639 ecu mn) in 1980, 24.3 per cent (0.968 ecu/mn) in 1983 and 20 per cent (1.022 ecu mn) in 1986.

The EC's GSP applies to all industrial products and include textiles,

TABLE 5

INCREASE IN ASEAN TEXTILE AND CLOTHING EXPORTS TO EC (1985–86)

	1986/85	1987/86
Thailand	+52%	+20%
Singapore	+44%	+96%
Indonesia	+40%	+74%
Philippines	+27%	+64%
Malaysia	+27%	+25%

Source: Eurostat, *External Trade – Statistical Yearbook*, Luxembourg, EC, various years.

	ecu mn	%
Total exports to the EC in 1986	9.21	100
Duty free under MFN	2.99	32.4
Duty free under GSP (non-agricultural products)	1.27	13.8
Preferential access inder GSP (agricultural products)	0.80	8.7
Subject to MFN duty	4.17	45.1

ASEAN exports under GSP are:

			in ecu mn	
	1980	1983	1986	1987
Total ASEAN exports eligible under GSP	3.494(100%)	3.978(100)%	5.112(100%)	6.504
ASEAN exports benefiting from GSP	1.192(34%)	1.752(44%)	2.066(40%)	n.a.
Agricultural exports benefiting from GSP	0.553(16%)	0.785(20%)	0.800(16%)	n.a.
Industrial exports benefiting from GSP	0.639(18%)	0.968(24%)	1.022(20%)	n.a.

Source: Eurostat, *External Trade – Statistical Yearbook*, Luxembourg, EC, various years.

clothing, footwear, leather goods and timber which are excluded from the GSP schemes operated by the US and Japan. However, the GSP has remained largely unexploited by the ASEAN countries, due to a complex system of exceptions, quotas, and GSP alterations imposed by the EC.

There are 133 items which come under the sensitive products and ASEAN exports to the EC under the GSP are subject to limitations in the form of tariff quotas or ceilings. Of the 133 sensitive product groups, there were 11 quotas on ASEAN exports to the EC in 1988. These were glutamic acid (from Thailand and Indonesia); urea and sacks of polymers of ethylene (Malaysia, Singapore); plywood and wood marquetry (Indonesia, Malaysia, Philippines and Singapore); glazed paving flags and tiles (Thailand); pumps and compressors, ball bearings (diametre not exceeding 30 mm); TV receivers, radio, telegraphic receivers, electric capacitors, thermonic, cathode valves/tubes and diode transistors (Singapore). Other products in the sensitive products list were subject to ceilings but in 1987, MFN duties were reimposed for the ASEAN on only 35 of these products.

VIII. THE SEM AND THE ASEAN

The question whether united Europe will offer the ASEAN countries improved trading prospects and market access will depend on the barriers which they will encounter while entering the SEM. The ASEAN does not receive preferential treatment like the ACP and the Mediterranean countries and benefits only from GSP. In the past, as pointed above, agreements between the EC and the ASEAN incorporated a general loosening of quotas with growth ceilings in the four to six per cent range depending on the product and the country. But non-tariff barriers (NTBs) have affected the exports of electronics, wood products, ceramics, machine tools and chemicals. In addition, the ASEAN countries may encounter fresh barriers to entry as a result of integration.

The barriers to entry for the ASEAN to the SEM may include the following:

(1) As many of the ASEAN exports will directly compete with member countries of the EC, additional protective measures are likely to be granted to give members a more sheltered market. The inefficient industries in consumer electronics, telecommunications and cars in the EC are likely to be replaced by more efficient concentrated industrial sectors of Europe itself. This will increase the competitiveness of European industries through more efficient

production techniques which the ASEAN countries may find hard to beat.

(2) The imposition of uniform standards by the EC in 1992 will make entry more difficult by the ASEAN countries, and more investment will be needed by them to comply with stricter standards which may not be possible for the less advanced ASEAN countries as they may not have the means for monitoring the latest developments.

(3) Fewer bilateral relations will be in effect between trading partners after 1992. In the past, bilateral relations between ex-colonial powers and their territories in the ASEAN enabled ex-colonies to gain access in the markets of industrial countries more easily and sometimes on concessional terms. These privileges are likely to go with Europe 1992 and will be replaced by more uniform policies requiring much harder lobbying and analyses of market trends.

(4) Anti-dumping laws and more NTBs will be imposed to restrict entry of cheap imports. On a larger scale, this will discourage the entry of the ASEAN exports on grounds of local content. In order to circumvent this type of discriminatory practice, the ASEAN countries ought to be able to set up plants in Europe, even though this may not always be acceptable or possible. Another alternative is to have joint ventures with European companies. This will affect the East Asian NICs more.

(5) The screwdriver rule and the safeguard rule have been adopted by the EC to endure varying levels of European content in products assembled inside the EC, on the basis of supplies from elsewhere, and a European firm assembling parts made in Singapore or Malaysia will be affected. Criticism has been directed at the inconsistencies between the local content requirement set up by the EC, for example, a draft proposal on video recorders has a provision for 45 per cent local content requirement, while proposals for photocopiers and semi-conductors use different criteria of technological significance applied slightly differently in each case. This type of inconsistency means unpredictability which can act as a NTB for non-EC companies.

(6) The EC is often accused of denying national treatment to non-EC firms in so far as they are treated differently from domestic firms. It is not that non-EC companies are losing anything that they have previously enjoyed; rather they may miss out on the new benefits and opportunities against products having less than 50 per cent European content. If an EC government or purchasing entity decides to accept a foreign proposal which has less than 54 per cent EC content, they must grant a three per cent price preference

to equivalent offers with 50 per cent EC content [*Featherstone, 1990: 158*].

IX. COMPETITION FROM EC MEMBERS

In the past, the EC's external trading policy with the ASEAN was based on free trade or aspirations to achieve it, specially in manufactured goods. However, in the case of goods in which the ASEAN products compete directly with products from the member countries, the attitude has been and will be cautious. In textile and clothing and in electronic goods ASEAN imports will compete directly with products from the EC.

The EC textile and clothing industry has undergone considerable restructuring in the last two decades, the main reason being the influx of cheap imports from East Asia, slow-down of consumption in industrial countries and sustained technological change in the production process of the textile industry. As a result of the imports and slow-down in consumption, the Community's production of textiles and clothing stopped rising in the mid-1970s. Between 1975 and 1985, employment fell by 38 per cent in textiles and 40 per cent in the clothing industry with a loss of a million jobs. In 1985, one-fourth of EC's apparent consumption in textiles was met through imports. From 1978 to 1985, the proportion of imports rose from 19.2 to 24.2 per cent. In clothing, half of the consumption was met through imports and this has remained a much less integrated sector [*European Economy, 1988: 74*].

Within the EC, Italian producers have improved their relative positions at almost all levels of the textile and clothing sector and have become very competitive. In textiles, production capacity was reduced primarily in France and in the UK, and in clothing, the largest capacity reduction took place in Germany. Thus there is likely to be marginal change in the exports within the EC countries in textiles after 1992 as the industry is already well integrated. The pattern of imports from ASEAN is not likely to change substantially. But in the clothing industry there is scope for increasing imports because production of clothing cannot be automated too much or mechanised, and hence the European industry has not been integrated to the same extent as the textile industry. The production of one segment of the market has been transferred in the past to ASEAN members who have become important suppliers. European producers are increasingly specialising in the manufacture of high-quality fashion goods. This segment of the market has to be very flexible in order to cope with rapid changes in consumer tastes, and hence is likely to remain with the EC countries. Thus the more competitive environment induced by an integrated internal market will most likely favour increased recourse to DFI and contracted processing work in the ASEAN countries.

As for the quotas, in 1986 about 70 per cent of the EC imports of textiles and clothing from third countries were covered by bilateral textile agreements within the MFA of the GATT and other arrangements. Under this system, imports into EC countries are limited by bilateral quantitative restrictions. There exists a price differential between the members as a result of the differences in import restrictions as commodity arbitrage is difficult. Enforcement of quotas *vis-à-vis* third countries and different interpretations of the country of origin rule by individual members have made border controls necessary. Quotas thus impose extra cost to the intra-community trade and will be incomp atible with the abolition of the intra-community frontiers by 1992 and will have to go. Hence the completion of the SEM will necessitate the removal of the differences in the import regimes of the member states resulting from quantitative import restrictions. The problem may come from Spain and Portugal which have experienced a huge increase in clothing imports from non-EC countries (82 per cent in 1987 and 75 per cent in 1988) as a result of joining the EC which forced them to reduce tariff and quantitative protection. In textiles, growth of imports have been 40 and 30 per cent for 1987 and 1988. If these countries are unable to compete in the future with the ASEAN countries in textiles and clothing, they may press against further liberalisation.

In the case of agricultural products, ASEAN exports to the EC are of non-competing kind – tropical products. Thailand, Malaysia and Indonesia may benefit when the excise duty of tea and coffee go after 1992, but on the whole, the impact will be marginal because the quantity exported of processed products is small.

In manufactured products, Malaysia's small export of cars has enjoyed free access to EC markets. In footwear, too, ASEAN exports are small, although Indonesia is aspiring to expand its footwear exports. In jewellery, a major export item for Thailand, 1992 may bring forth some additional requirements that will go to raise the average standards, although this does not necessarily mean a ban or substantial reduction in imports. Exporters will be required to appoint authorised representatives and this might inhibit small suppliers from the ASEAN. There may be a new directive specifying minimum gold carats requirement, test methods and advertising for jewellery. These are unlikely to affect exports adversely [*Pelkmans, 1990*].

In electronics there are three subsectors of importance for ASEAN exports to the EC-semiconductor, consumer electronics and telecom components (mostly) for terminal equipment. Semiconductors and consumer electronics are GATT-controlled, but in semiconductors, EC policy may run into conflict with the GATT. This is because in 1989 EC sought price undertakings from Japanese producers in order to protect the interests of the EC domestic industry from a flood of cheap imports. The EC's price undertakings were discriminatory and its content was not negotiated or concluded in a transparent manner nor was it publicly debated. This non-transparency aroused suspicions of some protectionist designs in the agreement [*Murphy, 1991*]. Thus the EC's strategy towards high technology illustrates an uneasy compromise between open trade and protectionism.

In consumer electronics, there are issues such as anti-dumping, (TV) standards and tariff reshufflings. Quotas and VERs have been applied by Italy, France, Spain but have been directed mostly against Japan and the East Asian NICs and not against ASEAN. Already some common VERs have been imposed *vis-à-vis* Japan and South Korea. Removal of quotas and liberalisation may have a positive effect on ASEAN exports. In telecommunications, removal of public procurement by member countries of EC and the introduction of free competition will give new opportunities to the ASEAN.

On the whole, after 1992, all NTBs can be replaced by new EC-wide restrictions instead of the existing national barriers. While desirable, this may not be politically feasible. Member states may also exert pressure to extend their own restrictive regimes to the community as a whole. Member countries with a relatively high level of QRs are in fact demanding that Community-wide restrictions should replace their national protective measures in 'sensitive' areas. Some member countries are asking for compensation for the loss of national NTBs which they are now applying. Such compensations could be in the form of tariff equivalents of abolished QRs or import quotas set at the EC level. It could be based on the fulfilment of reciprocal demands urging trade partners in ASEAN or the NICs to make concessions on their part and liberalise trade. Thus, only if liberal tendencies dominate among the EC members will the ASEAN countries gain after 1992.

Some estimates [*Cecchini, 1988*] indicate that the completion of the SEM will reduce imports from developing countries by ten per cent and even as much as 15 per cent on the assumption that the long-run dynamic gains of the SEM are fully realised. On the other hand, according to the same estimates, as a result of higher incomes, imports from developing countries into the EC could increase by about 15 per cent provided income in the EC increases by about five per cent which corresponds to the estimate by the European Commission of the impact of 1992.

Hence, on the aggregate level, the net impact on developing countries could be small. In any case, for commodities and manufactured products with relatively low income elasticity of demand (clothing, textile), both trade creating and trade diverting effects are likely to be marginal.

X. DFI IN THE ASEAN

How will the creation of the SEM affect direct foreign investment (DFI) in the ASEAN countries? As pointed above, much of the fast rate of growth in the ASEAN region has been due to the inflow of DFI which helped in the transfer of technology, know-how and in establishing marketing channels for the manufactured products. For the ASEAN's sustained growth in the future, continued DFI flow is important. However, there is likely to be a change in the DFI flow as a result of the integrated market because, not only will the region compete with investments in the newly opened Eastern Europe, but there is also likely to be an increased flow of foreign investment by American and Japanese firms in Europe itself.

Japan and US have been the main sources of DFI in the ASEAN in the past. The ASEAN countries undertook many reforms to attract DFI as a result of which DFI flows increased significantly in the past two decades. The EC's share of DFI in the ASEAN has been less than 20 per cent of the total DFI in the past two decades (see Table 6).

From $158 million annually in the 1965–70 period DFI increased to $3,014 million in the 1981–85 period. In the 1986–88 period, DFI fell by almost eight per cent to $2,775 million. The share of ASEAN countries in DFI inflows to Asia reached its highest level in 1971–75 at 73 per cent. Since that period, there has been a decline in DFI to 30 per cent in 1986–88 as shown in Table 7.

A united Europe will have a magnetic effect of pulling investment into the region that would otherwise have been located elsewhere. This will be more so because less industrialised countries (Spain and Portugal) are included in a regional grouping of industrialised nations; it is then more likely that the integrated area will be perceived as comparable to developing countries as possible locations for DFI and this could cause investment diversion to occur. DFI coming from the US may relocate in Spain and Portugal as an alternative to the ASEAN because 1992 can improve their investment climate and infrastructure significantly. This, however, may be quite unrelated to investment prospects in the ASEAN because investors from EFTA, Japan, US and Canada expect Spain and Portugal to have sustained growth in the future and, hence, find it worthwhile to invest in marketing, distribution or local manufacturing, specially if proximity to customers is of critical value. Investment in the services sector in EC is also strong and responds to the deregulation initiated by 1992 and opportunities arising from it.

XI. COMPETITION FROM EASTERN AND WESTERN EUROPE

In recent times, Eastern Europe has accounted for only seven per cent of EC's total imports and 5.5 per cent of its exports [*CEPR, 1990: 14*], but current events point towards greater trade and investment relationships between the two European regions. Most East European countries offer foreign investors a low-cost, highly-skilled labour force and a basic industrial infrastructure, as well as close proximity to the EC. The major constraints are the non-convertibility of their currencies, unstable macroeconomic conditions, low profit prospects and incompatible regulatory environment. Eastern Europe, however, offers prospects for establishing industries producing goods and services that could be exported back to Western Europe.

DFI flows into Eastern Europe would rise if the border of the SEM is kept open to imports of components and final goods from non-EC countries of Europe. For example, General Electric's investment of $150 million in a factory in 1990 as part of its strategic planning for 1992, if proved successful in the next few years, will promote DFI in the region thus competing directly with the ASEAN for foreign capital.

Local content requirements may force Japan and American transnational corporations (TNC) that were hitherto investing in the ASEAN, to divert their DFI to European locations. Local content requirement sets down the percentage of value added that has to be performed within a country or region in order for a product to qualify for duty-free entry to that country or region. Rules of origin establish the criteria used for determining the exporting country from which a product originates so that quotas or tariffs could be imposed if applicable. Both these policies

TABLE 6

DFI BY COUNTRY OF ORIGIN IN ASEAN (1967–87)

	Indonesia (Rupiah mn)	Malaysia M$ mn	Philippines Thousand Pesos	Singapore S $ mn	Thailand Baht mn (EFTA+EC)
Total DFI	17,640.0	--	25,775,344	1448.0	54,400.0
EC	2,242.4	63.1	4,416,728	241.0	6,900.6
Japan	5,458.9	230.1	4,141,515	601.1	23,548.0
US	1,021.9	61.3	9,724,261	543.5	5,025.0
EC share	12.71	--	17.12	16.67	12.67

Source: Europe Information (External Relations).

will affect the sourcing activities of TNCs which operate within a national or regional market. For example, EC-wide local content rules of origin could be set in such a way that a car which has been assembled in the UK from Japanese and Malaysian parts, and shipped to France, would have to submit to EC quotas or tariffs on imported cars rather than enter duty free and quota free into France as a UK-made car. Thus, depending on the level of external tariffs on car imports, such treatment would induce TNCs to shift their operations from ASEAN to EC locations [*UNTC, 1990: 16*].

In the local content rule, certain additional requirements can have an adverse effect on DFI which has been directed to cheaper locations like the ASEAN countries. For example, integrated circuits manufactured partly in the EC by a non-EC supplier can be treated as imports because the most technology-intensive portion of production (diffusion) has not been performed within the EC. As a result of the diffusion decision, much DFI from US and Japan has already moved to EC in a big way – Intel, the world's largest manufacturer of computer chips recently invested about $400 million in a facility in Ireland. Sony is going to invest several hundred million dollars in Europe, but the head of Sony said 'If we followed just the economics of manufacturing, we'd ship the lot from South-East Asia.' All this would translate to a decline in real opportunity costs for ASEAN in the form of declining flows of DFI.[2]

The ASEAN would therefore lose substantially on Japanese and American investment if these went into the production of goods which were later exported to Europe. In fact the Japanese have a trade-based rather than an investment-based relationship with the EC. Affiliates of Japanese TNCs are therefore implementing defensive export-substituting investment strategies to protect themselves against the possibility of future barriers to Japanese exports after 1992. Japanese investors are locating not only more production in the EC but also more research and engineering facilities as well. As a result of all these changes, there has been an increase in Japanese investment in the UK (the most favoured location by Japanese investors in the EC) by 30 per cent, whereas investment in North America fell by 19.8 per cent in 1990

TABLE 7

DFI INFLOWS INTO ASEAN (1965–88) ($US mn and percentage)

1965–70	1971–75	1976–80	1981–85	1986–88
158.1	790.5	1547.2	3014.3	2774.9
		Percentage		
69.0	72.9	61.6	56.0	29.8

Source: IMF, 1989, *Balance of Payments Tapes*, Washington: IMF, Oct.

from 1989 and investment in Asia also fell by 14.4 per cent [*International Herald Tribune, 1991*]. But most Japanese and American TNCs in the ASEAN have invested in factories producing goods aimed for exporting to neighbouring Asian countries and to home countries, frequently as intra-firm trade, and this is unlikely to change substantially after 1992.

The possibility of achieving European Economic Space by January 1993 is another attraction for the American and Japanese TNCs to come to Europe. The European Economic Space will be based on the current negotiations taking place between the EC and EFTA for the extension of the existing bilateral free trade arrangements to all essential features of the SEM. Such an arrangement will result in a substantial extension of the present preferential EFTA–EC relations to cover areas such as agriculture, trade, government procurement, services, investment and others. EFTA countries have also been investing in the ASEAN countries in the past. Europe 1992 may induce them to bring back their investments closer to their home countries.

After 1992, Europe will be transformed into a single, open and extremely large market space which will also be one of the most strategically important markets to sell to by foreign firms. For the European TNCs, there will be a large enough home market for the first time, which will enable them to reap economies of scale and increase the volume of sales, thus enabling them to compete more successfully with the US and Japanese TNCs in the world markets.

The TNCs from the EC are engaged in cross-border asset restructuring because they are more diversified than their US and Japanese competitors, and are therefore likely to be at a cost disadvantage in a unified market. Some are pursuing strategies of integrating disparate European affiliates and reorganising them to prepare them for the SEM. To increase their competitiveness they could be looking for low – cost export bases in industries such as automobiles, office equipment, micro electronics and consumer retailing. They could increase their investment flows into the ASEAN. Resource-based as well as manufacturing DFI could rise if the overall demand in the EC rises significantly.

XII. IMPLICATIONS FOR THE ASEAN

On the whole the implication of the integrated market on EC's trade with the ASEAN is hard to assess because reforms within the EC have not taken their final shape. Potentially, however, all developing countries may benefit from the creation of new trade, particularly if the process of European integration is accompanied by a strengthening of the multilateral system. However, if this does not happen then developing countries could suffer setbacks as a result of trade diversion. The extent of trade creation will depend on the extent to which economic growth in the EC accelerates and the responsiveness of imports to such acceleration.

There remains perhaps an expectation by the ASEAN that after 1992 the European markets will perform a 'vent for surplus' function under the diversification policy of the ASEAN countries. For the ASEAN countries, the EC is much more important an outlet than the ASEAN is for the EC and it is expected to serve as an alternative to the restricted Japanese market and as a substitute for slower expansion of exports to the US market. On the other hand, the EC also has a stake in gaining an increasing share in the Pacific Basin countries' (ASEAN, Japan and the NICs) trade in the future as this area is expected to have the fastest rate of growth.

But if the EC implements policies promoting European sourcing, then the export-oriented DFI in the ASEAN could weaken. The TNCs could move plants making components located in the ASEAN for sale in the EC to less industrialised parts of EC itself, even though the ASEAN may be a more suitable location for such investments (for example, semiconductors, automotive parts and consumer appliances). The location could also be in other developing countries in the Mediterranean region because it enjoys trade preferences with the EC and countries benefiting from the Lomé convention which could also be suitable hosts [*Lorenz, 1986*].

In the past, the ASEAN countries have closely followed the export-led growth path of the NICs by undertaking trade reforms, improving their macroeconomic strength and exploiting their skilled labour force. These led to productivity gains despite competition from industrialised countries. It may not be possible for them to continue with export-led growth to boost their economies in the future if they face protectionist barriers or a fall in the level of DFI. They may turn inwards again and this will not be desirable for the world trading system itself. Much, of course, will depend on the success of the multilateral trade talks under GATT.

NOTES

1. First among the present-day ASEAN members, the Philippines came under Spanish domination and remained under Spanish rule until June 1898 when the US gained control. Political sovereignty was granted in 1946. The Dutch came to Indonesia in 1609 in Java and remained until 1959 when it was granted independence. Singapore was founded by the British in 1819 after which Malaya was annexed and remained a

part of the British Empire until 1957. Japanese occupation of the region took place during the Second World War only and was short-lived.

2. Quote by the Chairperson of Sony Europe, J. Schmuckli, 'Emergence of a Global Company', *Financial Times*, 2 Oct. 1990.

REFERENCES

Cecchini, P., 1988, *European Challenge 1992. The Benefits of A Single Market*, Aldershot: Wildwood House.

CEPR, 1990, *Monitoring European Integration – A CEPR Annual Report – The Impact of Eastern Europe*, London: CEPR, Oct.

The EC and ASEAN, 1988, Brussels: Europe Information (External Relations), April.

European Economy, 1988, 'The Economics of 1992', 35, March.

Featherstone, K., 1990, *The Successful Manager's Guide to 1992. Working in the New Europe 1992*, London: Fontana.

Financial Times, 2 Oct. 1990.

International Herald Tribune, 6 June 1991.

IMF, 1989, *Balance of Payments*. Tapes, Washington, DC: IMF, Oct.

Lorenz, D., 1986, 'New Situation Facing the NICs in East Asia', *Intereconomics*, Nov./Dec.

Murphy, A., 1991, 'The European Community and the International Trading System', in *The European Community and the Uruguay Round*, Vol. II, Brussels: CEPS Paper No. 48.

Pelkmans, J., 1990, 'ASEAN and EC 1992', *National Institute Economic Review*, London: Nov.

Rhee, Yung Whee, 1986, *A Framework for Export Policy and Administrative Lessons from East Asian Experience*, Washington, DC: World Bank, Industry and Finance Series, Vol. 10.

Sengupta, J., 1988, 'Trade and Industrialization Experience in East Asia–Malaysia, Thailand, the Philippines, Indonesia and Korea', in J. Roy and J. Sengupta (eds.), *Trade and Adjustment in European Countries*, Washington, DC: EDI (World Bank).

UNCTAD, 1990, *Trade and Development Report 1990*, Geneva: UN.

UNTC, 1990, *Regional Economic Integration and Transnational Corporations in the 1990s: Europe 1992. North America and Developing Countries*, New York: UNTC Current Studies No. 15 (Series A), July.

8

Africa and Project 1992

MICHAEL DAVENPORT

I. INTRODUCTION

The Community makes up some 60 per cent of Africa's export markets and exports remain the major source of resources for development finance. Africa's financing gap, the difference between the amount required 'to restore the prospects for development and growth' [*Wass Report, 1988*] and the aggregate of expected financial flows, including multinational and bilateral aid, direct foreign investment and export earnings, is expanding. The significance of Project 1992 to Africa lies, firstly, in its effect on that financing gap, either widening it further or narrowing it. However, Project 1992 will not simply make it easier or more difficult to expand exports to the EC. Through its differential effects on different product groups, it will change the mix of African exports and, in doing so, it has implications for development strategy.

This chapter looks at those implications. It concentrates on those aspects of the Project 1992 where something fairly precise – although not necessarily quantifiable – can be said: diversion and creation in merchandise trade, the elimination of existing member state quotas or privileged access for goods from particular countries, the harmonisation of indirect taxes in the EC and the establishment of EC norms and standards. It considers briefly the impact of Project 1992 on trade in services and on direct foreign investment. It ignores the elimination of monetary compensation amounts which, while it is a Project 1992 effect, is only of significance to the outside world so far as it makes a decision about the Community-wide price levels for Common Agricultural Policy (CAP) goods unavoidable, but that decision will be influenced by the Uruguay Round and CAP reform rather than by Project 1992.

It also ignores the implications of European monetary integration. Although clearly inspired by progress towards the Single Market, the new initiatives in this domain are formally distinct. Monetary integration has a specific impact on the 13 African countries that use the CFA (Communauté Financière Africaine) franc, which is fixed in terms of the French franc. As the French franc has strengthened through being effectively tied to the Deutschemark, these countries have experienced problems of overvaluation. If, and when, the French franc disappears altogether through European Monetary Union, these countries will have to establish new exchange rate regimes [*ODI, 1990*].

II. GENERAL TRADE EFFECTS

Table 1 gives a snapshot of the evolution of Africa's trade with the Community between 1970 and 1987 – the last year for which comprehensive data are available. Clearly massive swings in the price of oil have had a major impact on the value figures, in particular, the fall in the value of trade between 1980 and 1987 and the share of fuels in African exports.

In looking at the shares by broad commodity groups after oil is excluded (panel III), the most striking feature is the rise in the share of manufactures. This seems to contrast with the general gloominess about the recent performance of Africa on the EC and world markets. In fact, while Africa increased its share in EC imports of manufactures up to 1980, its overall share in EC imports fell. The decade of the 1970s was good for African manufactured exports to the EC but, except for oil, disastrous for all other categories. The rise in the share of manufactures primarily reflects the poor performance of exports of primary goods. Moreover, the share of Africa in EC imports of manufactures has now fallen back once again. Indeed, relative to EC imports as a whole, Africa's share has fallen by 50 per cent since 1970.

To complete the picture Table 8.2 gives data on Africa's imports from the Community. The most striking feature is the increased dependence on imports of food. Imports of food and raw materials have squeezed out imports of manufactures which are needed to build up the infrastructure and productive base for development.

The Project 1992 will alter trade flows between the EC and the rest of the world through trade creation, through trade diversion and through terms of trade effects. Trade creation stems from the once-and-for-all increase in Community GDP which the SEM will generate, estimated at four-and-a-half to seven per cent in the Cecchini Report [*Cecchini, 1988*] and, for the purposes of this chapter, taken as five per cent.[1]

Much of the impact of Project 1992 on EC investment may have already taken place. Firms have been preparing for the SEM by rationalising and restructuring their productive apparatus. Investment has been strong and above-trend in the last three years. Intra-EC trade has picked up as a share of member state exports after declining between 1973 and 1985. The continuation of the investment boom through 1989 gives further credence to the anticipation of Project 1992 effect, although obviously towards the end of that year the 1992 effect was becoming concatenated with the impact of the political developments in Eastern Europe.

TABLE 1
AFRICA'S EXPORTS TO THE EC (1970–87)
(ecu mn and per cent)

	1970	1980	1987
Total, ecu mn	7201	29180	25983
I. as % of total			
food	25.7	13.6	17.8
agric. raw material	7.0	3.7	4.7
ores and metals	20.0	7.8	6.8
fuels	43.1	69.5	58.5
manuf.	4.1	5.4	12.1
total	100	100	100
II. as % of total excluding fuels			
food	45.2	44.6	42.9
agric. raw materials	12.3	12.1	11.3
ores and metals	35.2	25.6	16.4
manuf.	7.2	17.7	29.2
total	100	100	100
III. as % of Africa's world exports			
food	54.1	54.5	59.1
agric. raw materials	39.3	51.1	52.9
ores and metals	63.8	55.8	54.3
fuels	78.3	38.9	59.0
manuf.	35.9	56.7	52.7
total	61.2	42.8	57.5
IV. as % of EC imports (fob)			
food	9.8	6.6	4.7
agric. raw materials	7.1	5.7	4.4
ores and metals	14.2	7.9	6.4
fuels	29.4	17.2	19.9
manuf.	0.5	0.6	0.6
total	6.6	5.8	3.3
V. as % of the EC imports excluding fuels (fob)			
food	10.8	8.6	5.2
agric. raw materials	7.9	7.4	4.9
ores and metals	15.8	10.3	7.0
manuf.	0.5	0.8	0.6
total	7.3	7.5	3.6

Source: as for Table 2.

The SEM is founded on the belief that the EC must make a quantum leap in productivity if it is to compete effectively with the United States, Japan and the NICS, but this also means an improvement in competitiveness *vis-à-vis* the other Third World exporters. Other things being equal, this would mean a further redirection of trade away from traditional suppliers and towards partner EC members, analogous to the redirection that occurred after the initial elimination of internal tariffs. This is the trade diversion effect of Project 1992. Trade diversion is only likely to have a major impact in the manufacturing sector. As regards primary goods exported by Africa to the EC, the Community is generally (i) not itself a producer, or (ii) is a small producer and can only sell to third countries at the world market price, or (iii) manages internal production through the CAP, where the internal price mechanism is divorced from the world market. In none of these cases will trade diversion operate.

Trade creation[2] for Africa will be most important in exports of fuels. As Table 3 indicates, nearly 70 per cent of trade creation derives from fuels, that is, oil exports from Nigeria, Libya, Algeria, Egypt, Gabon and Angola and natural gas exports from Algeria.[3] Without the contribution of fuels trade creation would only sum to ecu 423 mn or 3.9 per cent of African non-oil exports. Of course, a boost to exports to the EC of this size is not to be trivialised but it will occur over several years, and is 'once and-for-all'. The low income elasticity for primary products means that, although African exports of these to the EC are more than double

TABLE 2

AFRICA'S IMPORTS FROM THE EC (1970–87)
(ecu mn and per cent)

	1970	1980	1987
Total, ecu mn	5428	30938	28165
as % of total			
food	11.4	13.4	14.4
agric. raw materials	1.0	0.7	1.3
ores and metals	1.5	1.2	1.4
fuels	2.5	5.4	3.0
manuf. c	83.6	79.2	79.8
total	100	100	100
as % of Africa's total imports			
food	36.8	42.7	44.6
agric. raw materials	19.5	17.9	24.3
ores and metals	46.9	40.8	41.6
fuels	24.9	40.8	41.6
manuf.	51.8	57.4	58.6
total	46.9	51.1	50.5

Source: UNCTAD, 1990, *Handbook of International Trade and Development Statistics 1989*, New York: UN.

those of manufactured goods, the trade creation effect is approximately equal for the two categories.

Trade diversion in manufactures is estimated at somewhat more than ecu 200 mn. For sub-Saharan African manufactures diversion is likely to be concentrated in chemicals whose high 'diversion elasticity' stems from the potential for economies of scale and other available gains from restructuring of the industry in the EC. For North African manufactures refined oil, chemicals and machinery and transport equipment will suffer from trade diversion.

The SEM is expected to reduce production and distribution costs, increase competition among EC producers and lead to the rationalisation of plant, economies of scale and other advances in efficiency. The Commission [*CEC, 1988a*] estimates the reductions in average costs three per cent in agriculture and four to six per cent in manufactures. These cost reductions have positive implications for LDC import prices. Moreover, reductions in EC export prices on world markets might in some cases bring down the prices charged by non-EC suppliers, by forcing them to engage in restructuring to capture economies of scale, or to reduce X-inefficiencies in production or producer rents.

However, the link between lower EC costs and LDC import prices depends on a large number of factors, some of which are themselves enmeshed in the Project 1992 process. For example, the degree of industrial concentration is important in determining the extent to which cost reductions are passed on to final consumers. Also important is the degree to which EC producers can price discriminate between the internal and the world markets. To the extent that Project 1992 leads to

TABLE 3

TRADE CREATION AND TRADE DIVERSION IN AFRICAN EXPORTS TO THE EC

I.	Income elast. of demand	Trade creation ecu mn	% expts.
food	0.46	101	2.3
agric. raw materials	0.80	49	4.0
ores and metals	0.70	62	3.5
fuels	1.22	924	6.1
manuf.	1.32	207	6.6
total		1347	5.2
II.	Diversion elasticity	Trade diversion ecu mn	% expts.
manufactures	1.52	−239	−0.9
III *Total*: trade volume change		1108	4.3

a: the method and elasticities used to estimate the trade effects is discussed in the Technical Appendix.

the restructuring, it may increase the concentration of EC industry and thus oligopolistic power. Moreover it might be argued that, since Project 1992 is all about maintaining the EC's competitive position in the world economy, it will not offer a significantly cheaper source of imports for the LDCs. At best it will meet the competition from Japan, the NICs and newly emerging nations of South-East Asia and so on.

In any event these terms of trade gains are unlikely to occur in those primary goods where the Community is a relatively small exporter and has little impact on world prices. In the case of CAP goods – the only primary goods in which the EC is a major exporter – the Community tends to 'dump' large quantities on the world market and thus depress the world price. But changes in productivity in the production of CAP goods are determined in the main by a combination of technological change and structural subsidies on the supply side and the administered price system with its panoply of incentives to produce and penalties for overproduction on the other. The impact of the SEM on productivity in the CAP sector will be insignificant unless there is a major shift to a market system which seems improbable.

As a result of these considerations, reduced prices have only been included in the case of manufactured exports to the LDCs, and then only the reductions associated with the direct effects of the SEM on costs. That is, the efficiency gains from abolishing internal borders, member state public procurement restrictions and national standards have been included, while those from the restructuring of production, in particular, economies of scale, reductions in X-inefficiency and monopoly rents have not.[4] The former set of export price reductions on manufactures as calculated by the Commission were then weighted by LDC imports from the EC to arrive at an average reduction in-LDC import prices of 1.6 per cent.

There will also be a terms-of-trade effect from higher prices as higher EC demand pushes up world prices for goods for which there is an efficient international market. This gain will depend on the share of the EC in LDC exports, the income elasticity of demand and the price elasticities of import demand and export supply. Details of the calculations are given in the Appendix. Fuels are not included in the terms-of-trade effects since supply from each oil-producing country is primarily determined through the OPEC quota system, which means that output is no longer price-sensitive, even though there may be considerable 'cheating' on the quotas themselves.

Putting together the different trade effects, the net gain to Africa is in the order of plus ecu 1.6 bn, based on 1987 trade data. This is about six per cent of African exports in that year. Of the gain, more than half derives from increased volumes of fuel exports to the Community and so will be concentrated in a few oil and gas producers in North Africa and Nigeria, Gabon and Angola. On balance trade creation in manufactures is estimated to be more than offset by diversion. The Project 1992 programme is unlikely to give a net boost to industrialisation. On the other hand, most of the terms-of-trade effect is in the reduction in the price of EC manufacturing exports, although this is also the most uncertain of the estimates.

Individual countries will be affected in different ways by trade creation, trade diversion and the terms-of-trade effects associated with 1992. Five countries have been selected to illustrate the diversity of Project 1992 effects. They are Morocco, Tunisia, the Côte d'Ivoire, Kenya and Zimbabwe. Between them, they export a wide range of goods, including a number which will be directly affected by new legislation on agricultural products, by the harmonisation of taxes in the EC, and by the elimination of member state quotas on clothing and other products. As a group they have gone further towards industrialisation and establishing exports of manufactured goods than Africa as a whole. This makes them atypical of the continent today but their experience of the SEM, and their response to the challenges that it raises, may be more informative for development policy for Africa than would be the experiences of a less developed sample of countries. Table 5 shows estimates of the general trade effects on these countries.

Tunisia's crude oil exports, for which the income elasticity of demand

TABLE 4

TERMS OF TRADE EFFECTS FOR AFRICA

I. Rise in export values from increase in primary product prices

	EC share in LDC exports %	Incr. in world demand %	Incr. in world price %	Terms of trade gain to Africa ecu mn	% expts.
food	29.9	0.7	0.4	30	0.4
agric. raw materials	26.0	1.0	1.0	24	1.0
ores and metals	30.2	1.1	1.0	31	1.0
total				85	0.3

II. Reduction in import values from lower EC export prices

	African impts. from EC ecu mn	Reduction in import price %	Terms of trade gain to Africa ecu mn	%
expts.				
manufactures	22194	2.03	451	1.7
III. *Total*: terms of trade effects			536	2.1

a: the method and elasticities used to estimate the terms of trade effects is discussed in the Appendix.

is greater than for most other primary goods account for Tunisia's strong trade creation in primary goods. Morocco only exports refined oil and oil products to the EC, which are treated under manufacturers. In the case of Morocco the primary sector contributing most to trade creation is minerals, including fertilisers and, in particular, phosphates. Morocco is the world's largest exporter of phosphate rock, with the EC taking some half of the exports. For these countries trade creation in manufacturing mainly comes from chemicals and clothing and textiles. The two sectors where trade diversion in favour of EC producers is likely to be most serious are chemicals (including processed fertilisers) and machinery and transport equipment. Morocco had been hoping to export increasing amounts of phosphatic fertilisers to the EC. It currently enjoys a cost advantage, although this could be eroded through Project 1992-led restructuring in the EC fertiliser sector.

Of the total estimated trade creation in the Côte d'Ivoire of 41 mn ecus of exports of primary goods, 13 mn and 9 mn ecus respectively derive from increased exports of cocoa beans and wood. Trade creation in manufactures is estimated at 12 mn ecus, or 9.3 per cent of manufactured exports. Of this total, eight million ecus comes from 'manufacturers classified by material', including processed wood, wooden articles and paper pulp. Trade diversion in manufactures is estimated to exceed trade creation. Diversion in wood processing is largely the cause. The

TABLE 5

ESTIMATES OF TRADE CREATION AND DIVERSION AND TERMS OF TRADE EFFECTS ON FIVE AFRICAN COUNTRIES
(ecu mn and per cent)
(based on 1987 data)

	Morocco	Tunisia	C. d'Ivoire	Kenya	Zimbabwe
I. Trade creation					
Primary gds.	23.7	26.4	41.1	9.2	9.5
% expts. to EC	3.1	5.0	2.7	2.3	3.1
Manuf. gds.	99.0	96.4	11.8	5.1	14.3
% expts to EC	9.6	9.6	9.3	9.6	9.3
total	122.6	122.8	52.8	14.3	23.8
% expts to EC	6.8	8.0	3.2	3.2	5.1
II. Trade division					
total	105.9	107.9	15.8	7.4	19.6
% expts. to EC of manufactures	10.2	10.8	12.5	13.8	12.7
III. Terms of trade effects					
total	32.8	22.0	18.0	8.2	7.6
IV. Overall total	49.5	36.9	55.0	15.1	11.8
% expts to EC	2.7	2.4	3.3	3.4	2.5

Sources: see text and tables above.

Côte d'Ivoire exports significant quantities of semi-processed products – wooden panels, plywood, veneers and similar products – where there is likely to be more acute competition in the EC market, particularly from French firms. The Commission studies foresee a reduction of imports from third countries of wood products of five-and-a-half to seven-and-a-half per cent owing to direct cost savings from market integration [*Cawley and Davenport, 1988*].

The only significant sources for Kenya of trade creation in primary goods are coffee and tea; altogether they are estimated to yield six million of the nine million ecus of trade creation. This might be something of an underestimate since Kenya has taken to specialising in out-of-season vegetables (like green beans) and 'exotic' fruit and vegetables, including passion fruit, avocados and cherry tomatoes. The income elasticity of demand for these goods is probably somewhat higher than that for fruit and vegetables as a whole. Trade creation in manufacturing is estimated at five million ecus or 9.6 per cent of manufacturing exports to the EC – of which sisal, pyrethrum and rotenone are significant components. These are all subject to competition from synthetics, and trade diversion is in fact estimated at seven million ecus.

For Zimbabwe trade creation is calculated at only nine million ecus, of which five million is attributable to tobacco. Owing to exports of ferro-alloys and other steel products, Zimbabwe could experience significant trade creation in manufactures (estimated at 14 mn ecus or 9.3 per cent of exports to the EC). However, the continued rationalisation in the EC steel industry could result in a negative balance – trade diversion exceeds trade creation in the sector 'manufactures classified by materials'.

III. SECTORAL ISSUES: (1) ELIMINATING QUANTITATIVE RESTRAINTS

There are several different sets of quantitative restraints (QRs) on imports which are inconsistent with the SEM. From the point of view of Africa it is helpful to distinguish those established under the umbrella of the MFA, the member state QRs on horticultural and fishery products, and separately the special arrangements for imports of bananas from EC's overseas territories and the ACP states. In all cases the QRs depend to varying degrees on the use of article 115 which allows member states to suspend free circulation of goods within the EC where outside exporters are circumventing, or threatening to circumvent, member state quotas by transhipping goods through another member state. Article 115 will no longer be available once internal border controls are removed. Enforcement would become difficult in the absence of frontier controls and, in any event, any derogation from the SEM would certainly be subject to legal challenge from interested parties.

Clothing and Textiles

Traditionally the production of clothing and textiles has been the entrée into manufacturing for developing countries. However this route has long been made more difficult by the Multifibre Arrangement (MFA), through which the EC, the United States and most other developed countries regulate LDC imports to protect their domestic industries. The present EC MFA (MFA IV) is particularly complex in that the quotas are generally subdivided into EC member state shares or 'subquotas'. These quotas cover the imports of up to 93 products from each of 17 LDCs (including China and Taiwan which were not MFA signatories) and 5 centrally planned economies, though in earlier EC MFAs several additional LDCs were included.[5]

The African countries are not subject to the MFA though exports of textiles and clothing by the Mediterranean countries are subject to restrictions through their various co-operation and preferential agreements with the EC. Neither are the sub-Saharan countries (other than South Africa) directly affected since they are within the group of ACP states. Indeed in not only being free of quotas but also of tariffs on their exports of these goods to the EC they appear to enjoy considerable advantages over the other developing countries.

But textiles and clothing are not major exports for the sub-Saharan countries, with the single exception of Mauritius for which they comprise over a third. McQueen and Stevens [*McQueen and Stevens, 1989*] have identified some products where sub-Saharan countries, other than Mauritius, have begun to export on a non-negligible scale. The most important country is Zimbabwe. However, these exporters do not clearly do better in products controlled by the MFA. Another study [*Agarwal et al., 1985*] concludes that the principal obstacles to ACP exports lie on the supply side and are not due to protection, thus the marginal erosion of ACP preferences from eliminating member state shares in the EC MFA will have little impact. At most Mauritius, Zimbabwe and other aspiring exporters will have to compete more aggressively on those EC markets where lower-cost producers have hitherto been restricted.

The Mediterranean countries on the other hand have expanded their exports to the EC more rapidly than the MFA-controlled LDCs since 1973. Over the period 1985 to 1987, countries under the MFA increased their exports to the EC by 23.5 per cent in volume for all textiles and clothing and by 25.4 per cent for categories subject to quota. Over the same period the Mediterranean countries increased their exports by 47.0 per cent and 47.3 per cent respectively. Textile and clothing exports are of particular significance to the Maghreb (Algeria, Morocco and Tunisia) countries. Morocco exported textiles worth 110 mn ecus and clothing worth 541 mn ecus to the EC in 1987. For Tunisia the respective figures were 62 mn and 560 mn ecus. Textiles and clothing represented 34 per cent and 40 per cent of Moroccan and Tunisian exports to the EC in that year [*Erzan et al., 1989*] suggest that the Mediterranean countries' exports may have gained from the EC MFA restrictions as a whole, although they do not appear to have improved their penetration significantly more in non-MFA categories. In any event, to the extent that the MFA restrictions are marginally eased through dropping the member country shares, the Mediterranean suppliers may stand to lose somewhat.

Bilateral Restrictions on Horticultural and Fishery Products

Right from the outset of the EC, certain member states and, in particular, France, insisted on 'grandfathering' their QRs on horticultural produce and fish.[6] These QRs were allowed to continue 'temporarily', even though they implied restrictions on free circulation of goods within the EC. A new set of transitional restrictions were established after the accession of Spain and Portugal. Now both sets of restrictions are due to be eliminated, the earlier ones probably by 1993, and those protecting Spain and Portugal by 1996, although this date might well be advanced. The Commission had promised to table some proposals by the summer of 1989 on how the QRs might be phased out but has so far failed to do so.

In any event beyond 1992 it is unlikely that these QRs can be sustained. Except those cited in the Acts of Accession of Spain and Portugal, they would be difficult to defend against a legal challenge (even now they are legally questionable), they would lack the sanction of article 115 and the exporting countries will probably be less prepared to enter informal voluntary restraint arrangements with individual member states where the latter lack the sanction of imposing even tougher restraints.

Recourse to article 115 for agricultural goods has been limited. Other than bananas, which are treated separately, the only cases since 1979 concern potatoes (from Spain to France in 1983 and 1984 and from Cyprus to Ireland in 1985), tomatoes (from Spain to France in 1982, 1983 and 1984 and from Spain to Benelux from 1981 to 1984) and honey (from Mexico to France in 1981 and 1985, from Hungary and China to France in 1985 and from Hungary to Italy in 1982 and 1983). The fact that article 115 has not been used more often may be because most exporters are aware of the restrictions and do not consider worthwhile the extra costs of transhipping through another member state, particularly in the case of perishable goods. Most of the goods are only excluded for certain seasons of the year and the suppliers may consider that accepting the QRs is better politics than creating a stir and perhaps having their access further restricted.

The only way to assess the significance of these QRs to the producing countries is to go through them one by one, looking at the value of imports by the non-restrictive state are being restricted and by how much. Many of the QRs apply to products where imports among the unrestrictive member states are small, in some cases, minute. France restricts imports of tomatoes, cabbage lettuces, other lettuces, endives and other salad vegetables during the EC growing season even though Community preference under the CAP (here the reference price system) means that imports are minimal (in each case less than one million ecus in 1987). Not content, like most member states, to restrict imports of potatoes in their traditional format, Germany restricts their import as frozen, frozen homogenised (sic), preserved as flour, meal or flakes, and preserved 'other'. Presumably these gestures are important to the farm lobby.

TABLE 6

MAJOR NATIONAL IMPORT RESTRICTIONS ON HORTICULTURAL AND FISHERY PRODUCTS

Fishery Products(a)

Product Nimexe no.	Member state	Exporting countries restricted(b)	 unrestricted(c)
Honey 0409 0000	France	Mexico Argentina	Class 1(d)
Tomatoes 1/11–14/15 0702 0010	Benelux Greece	Morocco Morocco	
Beans (Vigna Phas)	France	Egypt	Morocco Burkina Faso Senegal Kenya
	Greece	Egypt Mor., Burkina Faso Senegal, Kenya	
New potatoes(e)	All except UK	Morocco(f) Cyprus, Egypt	
Table grapes	BLEU	Chile	

(not Emperor)	France	Chile	
0806 1015	Greece	Chile	
Table grapes	BLEU	Cyprus	
1/11–14/7	France	Cyprus	
0806 1019	Greece	Cyprus	
Melons	France	Brazil	
0807 1090	Greece	Israel	
Pineapples	France	Kenya	Côte d'Ivoire
0804 3000		Costa Rica	
Tuna	France	Mauritius	Côte d'Ivoire
preserved		Thailand	Senegal
1604 1310		Fiji	
Black skipjack	France	Thailand	Cotê d'Ivoire
preserved			
1604 1410/2070			
Orange Juice	France	Brazil	Morocco
frozen, unfrozen		Cuba, Israel	
2009 1199, 1999	Italy	Morocco, Brazil	
		Cuba, Israel	

(a) Headings where EC imported at least 10 mn. ecu in 1988, excluding QRs of Spain and Portugal.
(b) Country exported at least 2.5 mn ecu to the EC in 1987, and imports by the restricting country were 'significantly' below what might be predicted. See text.
(c) Imports were not 'significantly' below what might be predicted.
(d) Formally the QR only applies to Class 2 countries (LDCs). Class 1 countries in the EC 'geonomenclature' are the developed countries.
(e) Countries restricted based on exports to UK and from Morocco to France in the period 1/1–15/5.
(f) France does not appear to restrict imports from Morocco in the period 1/1 to 15/5.

Sources: Commission of the European Communities, 1990, COM (90) 194 final, 30 April; Eurostat, 1987, *External Trade – Statistical Yearbook 1987*, Luxembourg: EC.

Table 6 lists the identifiable QRs where total EC imports from the LDCs exceeded 10 mn ecus in 1987. The table identifies the significant exporting countries and whether they are restricted by the QR or not.[7]

From the list of products in Table 6 it is clear that the French QRs are primarily designed to protect the interests of ex-French colonies in Africa, although the interests of Guadeloupe in the case of melons and French beekeepers are also apparent. Still it seems almost due to chance that Kenya is treated on par with Senegal as far as beans are concerned, but not Egypt on par with Morocco. Greece, Italy and Belgium and Luxembourg (BLEU for Belgo-Luxembourg Economic Union) QRs tend to be applied more comprehensively. They are apparently designed to protect producers in those member states. The BLEU QRs are listed as Benelux QRs but a look at the data suggests that they are not enforced on imports into the Netherlands (which implies that Belgium finds that they are worth imposing despite opportunities for evasion through transhipment through the Netherlands).

The implications of removing these QRs on Africa will vary from country to country. On balance Morocco, Côte d'Ivoire and Senegal probably benefit more from their privileged access to the French market than they lost from restricted access to other EC markets. Egypt will gain market share in potatoes and beans. The essential arbitrariness of managed trade is well illustrated by the case of Kenya, which will lose its privileged access to France for its bean exports, while gaining access to the French pineapple market at Côte d'Ivoire's expense.

Bananas: At present somewhat less than half the EC's supply of bananas comes from the ACP states and EC overseas territories (primarily the Canary Islands, Guadeloupe and Martinique), while the rest consists of 'dollar' bananas almost entirely from Central and South America. The former enters the EC under special arrangements designed to preserve traditional markets. Thus Britain provides a guaranteed market for unlimited quantities of bananas from the English-speaking Caribbean (at least up to the total British consumption). France and Italy provide similar guarantees for the French overseas departments, Cameroon and the Côte d'Ivoire, and for Somalia respectively. Because it depends on the insulation of certain Member State markets from intra-EC trade, the privileged position of the ACP and EC suppliers (in EC parlance the 'traditional' suppliers) is not compatible with the SEM.

The current 20 per cent preference margin would not be adequate to sustain ACP or EC exports in a free market. Most of the protected producers are small scale and relatively inefficient and, even with major restructuring of the industry, their costs would remain considerably higher than those of the large plantations of Central America, Colombia and Ecuador, although this is less true of African producers. On the other hand, the present tariff on dollar bananas is bound under the GATT, and any attempt to negotiate a rise in the tariff would be resisted both in and outside the EC.

For the African producers, bananas are important in export earnings. In 1988 the value of banana exports of Côte d'Ivoire, Somalia and Cameroon were respectively ecu 47, 25 and 19 mn. For Somalia bananas are the second most important export product. They contributed 57 per cent of export earnings in 1988. For Côte d'Ivoire and Cameroon they made up 2.9 and 1.7 per cent of merchandise exports respectively. Among the EC/ACP bananas those from Africa are most price-competitive. In 1988 the cif price of EC (Canary Island, Martinique and Guadeloupe) and Caribbean bananas ranged between ecu 64 and 71 per kg., African bananas between ecu 53 and 63 per kg. while dollar bananas sold at between ecu 40 and 45 per kg.

Principal Options of Various Alternatives being Canvassed

- a free market in the EC though with a tariff on dollar bananas and the elimination of the present tariff-free quota in Germany. This would go with substantial aid payments to the ACP countries and EC regions in the form of structural funds for diversification and direct income or balance of trade support,
- a free market with a deficiency payments scheme for ACP and EC bananas,
- a quota system for dollar bananas with various forms of aid to preferential producers (which would not be related to the price or quantity of bananas they sold on the EC market),

or some combination of these options.

A combination of quotas on Latin American bananas and deficiency payments to the EC/ACP producers could preserve their export earnings but would be a high cost to the Community budget. Such a scheme may be proposed as a transitional measure but, in the medium-term, the EC will probably favour a programme which gives the high cost producers an incentive to diversify into other activities, though in the case of the Windward Islands the only alternative appears to be tourism. The outlook for the African producers, being generally the most efficient of the EC/ACP producers and with fewer topographical disadvantages, is not too unfavourable. Indeed at least one of the large multinational banana producer/trading companies is expanding plantations in Cameroon, even before a decision on the market structure has been taken. If the Community institutes a regime which gives African producers a breathing space in which to invest in the best plantation practices and in transport facilities, it is likely that the most efficient African producers could compete with Latin America.

IV. SECTORAL ISSUES: (2) HARMONISING INDIRECT TAXES

The original Commission proposal was that all member state Value Added Tax (VAT) and excise tax rates should lie within agreed bands and that excise taxes would be limited to alcoholic drinks, tobacco and mineral oils. There has been considerable difficulty in reaching the necessary unanimous Council agreement on VAT, although the principle of gradual approximation has been accepted. These are relatively unimportant issues as regards the developing countries. On the other hand, the abolition of excise duties on coffee, tea and cocoa is significant. The EC has made the elimination of excise taxes on tropical beverages a part of its offer to the tropical products negotiating group in the Uruguay Round. Still the original stimulus came from the concern to harmonise indirect taxation as part of the 1992 programme.

In certain member states these taxes are substantial, reaching over 50 per cent on tea in Germany, thus there will be important consequences for LDCs' exports, even though demand tends to be rather insensitive to price. LDC exports of coffee to the EC are enormous. Other than mineral oil they constitute the largest single commodity import at almost four billion ecus (1988 data) of which 1 bn ecu was supplied by ACP states.

Table 7 shows the estimated effects of (i) harmonising overall consumer taxes on coffee at five per cent on increase in the volume of LDC and African coffee exports, (ii) the impact of that on the world price of coffee and its effects of export earnings and (iii) the estimated effects of 1992-induced higher EC incomes on the demand for coffee and, again, its world price. The last two of these effects have already been 'counted' in the first section of this chapter. However, putting all the Project 1992-related coffee effects together in one table helps to give relative orders of magnitude to the different effects.

The net increase in world imports of coffee from both the tax harmonisation and the trade creation effect of 1992 is estimated at 8.6 per cent in value terms and 0.9 per cent in volume. This implies a substantial once-and-for-all impact on the exports of coffee-producing countries, some of which have a high degree of export dependence on coffee. At the same time the monthly average absolute percentage deviation from trend of coffee prices over the period 1980 to 1989 was 12.2 per cent, which does not detract from the significance of the SEM gain to the exporting countries but does put it into perspective [*UNCTAD, 1990: 378*].

The reduction in coffee prices associated with the elimination of excise duties on coffee, together with the effect of increased incomes in the EC (trade expansion), will not only lead to an increase in the volume of coffee imports but also to a rise in the quality of imports. There are some econometric estimates of the price and income elasticities of demand for coffee but none takes into account quality differences. In the past it appears that increased incomes have led to increased consumption of milks at the expense of robustas, with Brazilian and other Arabicas holding a constant market share [*Neumann. 1990*]. If this trend continues, the Central American producers and Kenya, Rwanda and Tanzania will do rather better than under the constant market shares hypothesis at the expense of the Côte d'Ivoire, Uganda, Zaire, Cameroon and Indonesia.

The same tax regime for cocoa would lead to an increase in world prices of 1.8 per cent and EC import volumes of 1.4 per cent. It would generate additional imports of about 47 mn ecus. The principle beneficiaries would be Côte d'Ivoire, Nigeria, Cameroon, Ghana and Malaysia. A five per cent harmonised consumer tax rate on tea would increase prices by almost one per cent and imports by 0.2 per cent in volume, leading to a an increase in export earnings of 4.4 mn ecus. The countries gaining most in this case would be Kenya, India and Sri Lanka.

Tobacco is a special case. Duties on cigarettes in the most popular price category range from 0.12 ecus in Spain to 2.76 ecus in Denmark. In response to the outcry about the loss of revenue and health concerns in certain member states, the Commission has withdrawn its proposal that duties be aligned on the EC average. Instead excise rates will gradually be harmonised upwards with negative consequences for tobacco exporters in the Third World. If, for example, tax rates were aligned on the average of the four states with the highest rates (Germany, Denmark, Ireland and the UK), the EC average tax would more than double (rising from about 48 per cent to 105 per cent). This would lead to an average rise in prices in the EC of 10.3 per cent and a reduction in EC imports of between 4.1 per cent and a loss in LDC export earnings from the EC of 147 mn ecus (based on 1988 imports). This would be partially compensated by an increase in imports to rest of the world following the reduction in world prices. Indeed it is estimated that the net reduction in export earnings by the LDCs as a whole would amount to only 63.2 mn ecus, and Brazil, Zimbabwe, India and Malawi would bear the brunt of the shortfall.

Zimbabwe alone would face a loss in export earnings of 18 mn ecus or 14 of the value of tobacco exports to the EC. After taking into account the rise in exports to other countries in response to the fall in world tobacco prices, the net effect would be a fall in tobacco exports of somewhat less than 12 mn ecus. Of course, this assumes unchanged market shares. The trend towards lighter, low-tar and low-nicotine cigarettes has been speeded up by EC legislation (which is also a Project 1992-effect). If Zimbabwe tobacco growers can adjust to these changes in demand for different varieties, they may be able to increase their market share.

V. SECTORAL ISSUES: (3) APPROXIMATION OF TECHNICAL STANDARDS

The LDCs are naturally fearful that their exports to the EC will be adversely affected by the abundance of harmonised technical standards which are being adopted as part of the SEM programme. The new standards that are most likely to cause problems for the Third World

TABLE 7

COFFEE(a): EFFECTS OF THE ELIMINATION OF EXCISE TAXES AND HARMONISATION OF VAT AT 5 PER CENT IN EC, AND OF INCREASED EC GDP

(ecu mn and per cent) (based on 1987 data)

I. Effects of Tax Harmonisation	
	per cent
Current EC weighted average excise tax on coffee	18.2
Current EC weighted average VAT rate	6.7
Current EC weighted average consumer tax rate	26.2
Harmonised EC VAT rate	5.0
Reduction in EC average tax rate	16.8
Change in EC imports (vol.) (b)	2.1
Increase in world coffee prices(b)	6.3
Change in non-EC world imports (vol.)	−1.7
Increase in EC imports (mn ecu)	395.2
Increase in rest of world imports (mn ecu)	256.5
Increase in total exports (mn ecu)	651.6
Increase in total exports (per cent)	6.3
II. Effects of Increase in EC GDP	
Change in EC imports (vol.) (b)	2.4
Increase in world coffee prices(b)	1.3
Change in non-EC world imports (vol.)	−0.3
in EC imports (mn ecu)	167.3
Increase in rest of world imports (mn ecu)	51.4
Increase in total exports (mn ecu)	218.7
Increase in total exports (per cent)	2.1
III. Total	
Increase in EC imports (mn ecu)	562.5
Increase in rest of world imports (mn ecu)	307.9
in total exports (mn ecu)	870.4
of which Cameroon	9.5
Côte d'Ivoire	26.8
Ethiopia	15.0
Kenya	17.5
Uganda	22.3
Zaire	12.8
Africa	142.8
Increase in world price	7.7
Increase in total exports (volume %)	0.9
Increase in total exports (value %)	8.6

(a) 'Green' coffee
(b) See appendix for a discussion of the elasticity assumptions.

concern exports of plants, fish and meat and the various products of these. For the first and third of these the main directives which concern imports from third countries on plant health (phyto-sanitary regulations), animal diseases and 'human health relating to animal products' (sometimes known, bizarrely, as animal hygiene) have been in place for some years. For fish and fish products a new batch of regulations has been tabled, although they have not all been accepted by the Council of Ministers and the details of implementation are still to be decided. In addition to these animal health and hygiene and phyto-sanitary rules, a set of 'horizontal' rules concerning maximum levels of antibiotic and pesticide residues have been in operation for several years.

Where higher standards create problems for Third World countries, they can generally be met by appropriate investment programmes – in the agricultural and fishery sectors, usually in raising standards of hygiene through pollution controls or improved processing facilities. It is difficult to have a sense of the economic significance of these investments, but in certain cases they could be considerable.

In the case of plant health, each consignment cleared at the EC border will be issued with a 'plant passport' which will guarantee free circulation throughout the EC. There is also the possibility of negotiating the consent of third country suppliers for pre-export inspection, probably to be undertaken (or at least controlled) by the newly-formed EC Plant Health Inspectorate, which will also have the task of overseeing member state inspection of third country imports. Thus higher standards are going to be instituted *de facto*. These are most likely to impinge on LDC exporters of tropical timber, planting material and cut flowers.

In recent years Kenya has rapidly built up a major export trade in flowers, sending in the main carnations, roses and alstroemerias to the EC. With the advent of the 'plant passport' system and a Community inspectorate, these will undoubtedly be submitted to more thorough border inspections in future. Plant growers in certain member states have been complaining about the presence of tropical pests in their greenhouses – including thrips from Kenya. Such pests can be controlled without great expense, but harassment of exporters of flowers from LDCs may take place, not so much motivated by protectionism, but rather to establish the credibility of certain member state inspection services which are currently suspected by others of a lack of vigilance.

As regards animal health and hygiene (that is, fresh meat) most of the regulations are now in force. The principal issue is whether there will be a major tightening up in the stringency with which they are implemented. In the case of meat products, there is at least one potentially important new directive. For meat products to be allowed into the EC from third countries, the slaughterhouses and processing plants must be licensed by Commission inspectors. There is also a proposal to establish additional or tighter rules on veterinary inspection and health certification for each consignment, on wrapping and packaging, conditions of storage and transport, as well as on inspection on arrival in the EC, conditions of transport in the EC. The general intention is not only to ensure the quality of the products coming from third countries, but to assuage the suspicions of certain member states that certain other member states are relaxed in their interpretation of existing rules.

It seems that at least in one important case provision has not been taken to meet existing rules on meat products. Riddell writes of the largest producer of canned meat in Zimbabwe, Lemco:

> Past policy appears to have been content to dominate the domestic market for canned beef. . . . [T]here is little to indicate that [Lemco] aggressively sought to lower unit costs, at least to the extent of being able to penetrate the much larger European market or even to think much about expanding into the export field. A chain of factors have restricted such expansion. To export to the EEC requires EEC-registration of the canning factory, which would necessitate expanding and upgrading at a cost estimated at ZS 1.5 mn a few years ago but no decision has been made on going ahead with this programme [*Riddel, 1990: 363*].

The directive, which requires registration and has until now prevented Lemco from exporting to the EC, appears to be that first proposed in 1984 (although it was not adopted till early 1989). The new meat product proposal tightens up the requirements for exports to the EC and will make it more expensive to enable a processing plant to register.

Of all the new EC standards, probably those with the greatest potential impact on the LDCs are the standards concerning fish and fish products. Under the new regime the Commission will, 'for each third country, lay down conditions for the importation of fishery products' which may include establishing a list of processing plants and factory vessels which are authorised to export to the EC. How often inspections will take place will depend on the 'the guarantees a third country can offer in relation with the checks carried at the place of origin (sic)' [*Official Journal, 1990*] which clearly leaves the EC inspector a large measure of discretion. In principal the same requirements are being applied to both member states and third countries, but LDCs may suffer technological and economic disadvantages in, say, clearing their coastal waters, or fish farms, of industrial and human pollution.

Climatic conditions also tend to work against the developing country producers. Satisfying the new rules may necessitate considerable investment in sewage infrastructure or upgrading existing plant. The conditions for authorisation of plant and ships appear very demanding, and give ample scope for denial of authorisation. How the regulation is implemented will be critical. It could also be significant for LDC exporters that the United States authorities are studying the introduction of similar regulations. The 'copycat' adoption of tougher import standards by third countries is one of the potential systemic effects of the SEM.

Among the main exporters are Morocco, Tunisia, Mauritania, Senegal, Madagascar, and Mozambique. In Morocco, for example, even under the older regulations, in February 1988, only 12 of Morocco's 60 fish canneries were on the SC approved list, the rest failing to satisfy standards of sterilisation.

There is also a set of so-called 'horizontal' food law directives. These cover preservatives and other additives, frozen foods, labelling, rules for foods of particular nutritional uses, and so on. Some of these are already in effect with the rest due to be implemented by the end of 1992, but it is difficult to determine what difficulties they may pose for Third World exporters. Any difficulties are likely to be limited to a few suppliers, but these new rules could in some cases impose relatively higher costs on LDC exporters and could be of significance to the countries involved.

At present some member states have different permitted lists for certain additives and some have derogations from the existing labelling directive. It is worth pointing out that prior to the 1992 programme, there were some 218 individual barriers in the EC with which outside suppliers of manufactured foods had to contend. Of these, 64 were specific member state import restrictions, 68 were controls on labelling or packaging, 33 were bans on specific ingredients, 39 were rules on product description and 14 were instances of tax discrimination. By 1992 a single set of rules covering all member states should be in place.

Among manufactured goods other than foods, it appears that Togo and Senegal will be adversely affected by the new regulations limiting cadmium (and other trace elements) residues in fertilisers. This problem can only be addressed by investing in new and expensive plant to eliminate these elements, which is now the intention. For most manufactured products, however, the Project 1992 requirement is mutual recognition. Domestic producers are not subject to testing or certification procedures, and exporters from outside will only have to satisfy the requirements of one member state and any tests they are subjected to and certificates of conformity will be valid throughout the EC. However, two nagging concerns remain. In many cases outside producers will still be required to obtain those tests and certificates and, in the process, could come up against delays and bureaucratic harassment. Secondly, there is plenty of scope for bureaucratic and, perhaps, unintentional but effective, protectionism by customs officials who will have to determine whether a particular shipment is covered by a certificate issued by another member state.

VI. EFFECTS ON TRADE IN SERVICES AND CAPITAL FLOWS

A recent study [*GATT. 1989*] shows that Western Europe (not confined to the EC) accounts for about two-thirds of imports of shipment, travel, and 'other' services. But, while the overall share of LDC services exports in trade in services may be small, for a number of LDCs services exports are an important share of total exports (merchandise and services). This is true of Egypt (53 per cent up from 13 per cent in 1970), Kenya (40 from 33), Sudan (35 from 9) and Morocco (32 from 26).

Apart from the Asian NICs, where shipping is an important service export, the service exports of the LDCs are dominated by travel, and, in particular, tourism. Tourism is generally thought to have a high income elasticity of demand although there is a dearth of econometric work in this area. To the extent that the 1992-induced income gains in the EC are spent on tourism, certain countries in Africa could be major beneficiaries.

As regards foreign investment, the implications of 1992 for the LDCs, including Africa, are generally negative. To some extent direct foreign investment (DFI) diversion will follow trade diversion. As intra-EC trade expands at the cost of extra-EC trade, so investment both by EC-resident and non-resident companies will be redirected towards the Community. Even companies with no particular previous interest in the EC market will be attracted by the advantages of locating in the large newly-integrated market. This attraction will increase with the establishment of monetary union.

The LDCs, including Africa, are in any event becoming less attractive to multinational companies. The traditional advantages of low labour costs have diminished, both in the electronics (although not an African speciality) and the textile industries; and clothing and footwear are likely to move in the same direction. Weak commodity prices have deterred investment in primary product production or processing. Heavy indebtedness has raised worries about the availability of foreign exchange, the repatriation of profits and, ultimately, capital. Certainly steps have been taken in a number of African countries to attract DFI. These include easier rules on the availability of foreign exchange for fixed and working capital and on the repatriation of earnings, fiscal incentives and the opening of sectors previously reserved for nationals. The importance of raising the flow of inward DFI has been appreciated, but whether these incentives can make more than a marginal impact is questionable.

The SEM may further the existing trend against Africa, especially sub-Saharan Africa, in the international allocation of investment. In the years 1982 to 1984, Africa attracted 12.9 per cent of net US DFI; in the years 1986 to 1988 net US DFI in Africa was actually negative (US Department of Commerce, various years). The figures for Germany were 5.2 per cent and 1.3 per cent [*Deutsches Bundesbank, 1990*].

It is too soon to find, in the available data on DFI, clear evidence of a diversion of investment from the LDCs in favour of the EC. Foreign investment figures are subject to considerable uncertainty and data problems may give an impression of even greater volatility than is inherent in the flows themselves. However, there is no doubt that the actual flows fluctuate considerably from year to year, partly in response to changes in political and economic environment, but also because of the variability of profits and retained earnings and of the valuation effects of exchange rate changes.

Nevertheless there are hints of a Project 1992 effect in several of the US investments in the EC from about 1985, which can only partly be explained by investment in the new entrants, Spain and Portugal [*Davenport and Page, 1990*]. The higher level of investment faltered in 1988 although it is too early to determine whether that year was maverick or the start of a new pattern. In the German data there seems to be a trend in favour of increasing the EC share in overseas direct investment. To some extent, this can be attributed to increased investment in the two new member states. However, when the figures for Spain and Portugal are subtracted from those for the EC as a whole, as in the US case, there seems to be a step increase in 1985.

It has often been suggested that a single trading bloc implies that, if aid is tied to the procurement of goods and services, it should be tied to EC exports rather than to the exports of individual members. However it is not easy to quantify the gain-to-aid recipients from the freedom to shop around for their procurement. According to the Padoa-Schioppa report, 'studies of price differences between countries of the Community for products brought by government suggest that economies of the order of 25 percent are often foregone in not buying at the lowest costs offered on the competitive markets' [*Padoa-Schioppa et al., 1987: 35*]. The procurement study [*CEC. 1988b*], which was prepared as background to the Cecchini Report, suggests that savings of four per cent in construction and over seven per cent in manufactured goods are available to member state governments through a liberalisation of public procurement rules within the Community. One would expect the gains for the developing countries to be even higher, due both to a greater share of procurement by the recipient government in the donor country being generally required rather than that by member state procurement regulations, and to there being no significant extra costs such as transport, insurance or exchange rate cover, which a member state government would have to meet when procuring in another member state.

On the other hand, if they were unable to tie aid to their own exports, some donor states could become less committed to maintaining bilateral aid levels. Moreover, a formal agreement to end-tying by the member states, or to tie to procurement within the EC rather than in the donor country, does not eliminate opportunities for informal conditionality.

Eight EC countries are members and so report to the OECD Development Assistance Committee (DAC) on the extent to which their total bilateral development assistance is tied [*OECD, 1990*]. These, however, cover by far the greater part of total bilateral aid from Community member states. I assume that, for each donor country, the same proportion of aid to Sub-Saharan beneficiary countries as for the total was tied, and that gains of the order of 20 per cent (as an upper limit) to the recipient countries from being able to buy from the cheapest EC source (plus some additional competition among EC companies in supplying the goods or services). Then the value of aid to Sub-Saharan Africa (excluding French overseas territories) in 1988 would have been increased by US$1408 million (ecu 1,198 million) or by 14.3 per cent.

The potential gain from untying aid, or tying to EC procurement, is uncertain but clearly considerable. However, the extent to which it can be construed as a Project 1992 effect is debatable. So far, at least, there has been no formal effort to make it part of the 1992 programme. Moreover, it is not clear that the present tying by the member states does not infringe the Treaty of Rome. However, legalistic arguments are less important than actual cause and effect. If untying becomes *de facto* a Project 1992 effect, it could be more important than trade creation to Sub-Saharan Africa.

VII. CONCLUSIONS

This chapter has concentrated on the effects of the SEM on existing trade flows between Africa and the EC. On balance the effects are small, but positive overall, and vary widely from country to country. For Africa as a whole, trade creation will outweigh trade diversion, with the net effect being a boost to real exports which is equal to 4.3 per cent of exports to the Community. Terms-of-trade effects are estimated as positive and equivalent to a further 2.1 per cent of export to the Community.

Certain countries will gain or lose disproportionately from specific sectoral effects. Clothing producers will have to face stronger competition from MFA-controlled exports when member state sub-quotas are abolished, although that competitive threat would be much greater in the event of the phasing out of the MFA as a whole – a Uruguay Round rather than a 1992 effect. Tropical beverage exporters will benefit significantly from the elimination of excise taxes in the Community. The banana exporters, Cameroon, Côte d'Ivoire and Somalia (the last two fortuitously also export tropical beverages), will find that moves towards an SEM in bananas will confront them with tough competition from the dollar banana producers. Elsewhere, the elimination of member state QRs, and special access for traditional suppliers of horticultural and fishery products on the French market, will benefit certain African producers at the expense of others, the overall effect being minor.

New Community standards or the stricter implementation of existing standards will be most damaging to exports of fish, both fresh and preserved, and of preserved meat. To meet higher standards generally requires investment in pollution control, slaughter houses and processing plants. While investment funds are at a premium, it is important that precise information on what needs to be done to meet EC standards is made available to decision-makers so that investment priorities can be properly assessed. Anecdotal evidence points to a current inadequacy of such information, or the facilities for making it available. The threat of back-door protectionism or, simply, harassment, of LDC exports of these products by overzealous or ill-informed inspectorates and customs officials needs to be emphasised.

These are the principal effects of Project 1992 on African trade flows. They are essentially static. The SEM will have further, 'dynamic', implications for the rate and pattern of development in Africa. Most important is the bias against manufacturing exports. Trade diversion will make it more difficult for Africa to compete with EC domestic industry in chemicals, fertilisers, and textiles. Even the simple processing of primary products may require, to remain competitive, significant improvements in productivity. At present, there is little processing of cocoa beans into butter or powder and almost none into chocolate, or of coffee beans into soluble coffee or extracts. Few countries have gone beyond exporting raw cotton to exporting significant quantities of yarn or fabrics, from exporting tropical timber to veneer sheets or plywood or from hides and skins into shoes and leather goods.[8] Moving up the processing chain will be made more difficult by improved competitiveness in the Community itself, although the effect will be very different from sector to sector. But even in some of the most labour-intensive sectors, such as shoes, new forms of mechanisation are being developed which will allow economies of scale to be exploited. These effects can only be exacerbated by the diversion of DFI.

Diversion from primary product dependency into certain simple manufacturing processes will become more difficult because of certain sector-specific changes related to the SEM. The degree of effective protection given to African clothing producers by the MFA will be eroded by the establishment of a SEM in those goods. Tighter EC standards will make establishing or expanding the meat and fish products sector more expensive, while the risk of being found in contravention of those standards is increased.

Many of the problems associated with the SEM can be overcome, although at some cost. The SEM clearly presents opportunities for individual African countries – even in those sectors where the problems are most serious. Tighter standards give opportunities to those who can adjust to them rapidly. Project 1992 will expand the EC markets for raw materials and manufactures, and, although the overall balance between creation and diversion seems to be negative for African manufactures, this need not be the case for every country. In calculating the general trade effects on Africa and on individual countries, and in the specific estimates on coffee, the assumption has been that suppliers outside the EC will retain an unchanged share of extra-EC imports. However, market shares are not set in stone. For individual suppliers the SEM presents opportunities, but for Africa, as a whole, the once-and-for-all boost to exports may not be sufficient to compensate for adding to all Africa's present structural handicaps a new set of hurdles to diversification away from dependency on raw material exports.

NOTES

1. Baldwin has argued that the Commission studies do not take account of the medium-term investment effect and thus underestimate the impact of the SEM on innovation and investment [*Baldwin, 1989*]. He would nearly double the Cecchini effects on EC GDP growth.
2. The term 'trade diversion' is used to refer to the total displacement of imports from suppliers outside the EC by those within, regardless of whether that displacement is directly occasioned by the elimination of intra-EC barriers (trade diversion in the strict trade theory sense) or other Project 1992-related cost reductions in the EC. The term 'trade creation' is also used for the increase in extra-EC imports stimulated by the rise in EC output or income. These usages are strictly at variance with the traditional trade-theoretic meanings of extra-customs union trade diverted or intra-union trade stimulated solely by the price effects of removing barriers but have now become general usage in the context of Project 1992.
3. The analytical framework and quantitative methods follow Davenport and Page [*1991*].

4. For the taxonomy of the micro-economic effects of the SEM and the quantitative back-up to the Cecchini Report, see Cawley and Davenport [*1988*].
5. Several other developing countries are restricted through different mechanisms. In particular Turkey and the North African suppliers are limited through their Association and Co-operation Agreements with the Community.
6. Many of the restrictions apply to horticultural goods which operate under the 'import calendar' system where different trade regimes – EC as well as member states – apply to the same goods over different periods of the year.
7. The only case where QRs were imposed by so many member states that an EC import value criteria might miss an important set of QRs, was potatoes. The QRs on potatoes are discussed below. For any categories in all the exporting countries, only those with total exports to the EC of over five mn ecus are identified as 'restricted' or 'unrestricted'. The countries are identified as 'restricted' if their exports to the member state(s) in question are 15 per cent more or less than that 'predicted', where predicted imports are given by taking the value of non-restrictive member states and assuming that the restrictive states would have imported a value proportional to the share of those member state in total expenditure on food in the EC in 1987. Clearly the criterion takes limited account of different tastes in the member states (by simply allowing a 15 per cent margin) or, since the calculations are done in value terms, the fact that prices might be higher where imports are restricted.
8. On the issue of the lack of processing in the ACP states, see, for example, Davenport and Stevens [*1990*].

REFERENCES

Agarwal, J.P., Dippl, M. and R.J. Langhammer, 1985, *EC Trade Policies Towards Associated Developing Countries: Barriers to Success*, Kiel: Rieler Studien 192, University of Kiel.

Askari, H. and J.T. Cummings, 1977, 'Estimating Agricultural Supply Response with the Nerlove Model', *International Economic Review*, Vol. 18, No. 2.

Baldwin, R., 1989, 'The Growth Effects of 1992', *Economic Policy*, Cambridge, Oct.

Bond, M.E., 1983, 'An Econometric Study of Primary Commodity Exports from the Developing Country Regions to the World', Washington: Staff Papers, International Monetary Fund.

Cawley, R. and M. Davenport, 1988, 'Partial Equilibrium Calculations of the Impact of Internal Market Barriers in the European Community', in *Studies in the Economics of Integration, Research on the Cost of Non-Europe, Basic Findings*, Brussels: Commission of the European Communities, Vol. 2.

Cecchini, P., 1988, *The European Challenge 1992*, Aldershot: Wildwood Press.

Commission of the European Communities (CEC), 1988a, 'The Economics of 1992', *European Economy*, 35, March.

CEC, 1988b, 'The Cost of Non-Europe in Public Sector Procurement', in *Studies in the Economics of Integration, Research on the Cost of Non-Europe, Basic Findings*, Brussels: Commission of the European Communities, Vol. 5.

CEC, 1990, COM(90) 194 final, 30 April.

Davenport, M. and C. Stevens, 1990, 'The Outlook for Tropical Products', in C. Stevens and D. Faber (eds.), *The Uruguay Round and Europe 1992: Implications for Future ACP/EC Cooperation*, Maastricht: European Centre for Development Policy Management.

Davenport, M. and S. Page, 1991, *Europe: 1992 and the Developing World*, London: Overseas Development Institute (ODI).

Deutsches Bundesbank, 1990, *Statistical Supplement to Monthly Reports*, Frankfurt: Series 3, 4, April.

Erzan, R., Goto, J. and P. Holmes, 1989, 'Effects of Multifibre Arrangement on Developing Countries: an Empirical Investigation', in C.B. Hamilton (ed.), *Textiles Trade and the Developing Countries: Eliminating the Multifibre Arrangement in the 1990s*, Washington: World Bank.
Eurostat, 1987, *External Trade – Statistical Yearbook 1987*, Luxembourg: EC.
GATT, 1989, *International Trade, 1987–88*, Geneva, GATT, Vol. 2.
Islam, N. and A. Subramanian, 1989, 'Agricultural Exports of Developing Countries: Estimates of Income and Price Elasticities of Demand and Supply', *Journal of Agricultural Economics*, May.
Matthews, A., 1989, 'African Primary Product Exports to the European Community: Prospects Post 1992', paper prepared for the World Bank/HEDCO Seminar on Africa and Europe After 1992, Dublin, 27–30 Nov.
McQueen, M. and C. Stevens, 1989, 'Trade Preferences and Lomé IV: Non-traditional ACP Exports to the EC', *Development Policy Review*, Sept.
Neumann, M.R., 1990, 'Green Coffee in the Process of European Integration', speech given at the EUCA/CECA Coffee Congress, Berlin, 15 June.
ODI, 1990, 'Crisis in the Franc Zone', *Briefing Paper*, London: ODI, July.
OECD, DAC, 1990, *Development Co-operation*, Paris: OECD.
Official Journal, 1990, C 84/58, 2 April.
Padoa-Schioppa, T. *et al.*, 1987, *Efficiency Stability and Equity: A Strategy for the Evolution of the Economic System of The European Community*, Oxford: Oxford University Press.
Riddell, R.C., 1990, 'Cote d'Ivoire', in R.C. Riddel (ed.), *Manufacturing Africa: Performance and Prospects of Seven Countries in Sub-Saharan Africa*, London: ODI.
UNCTAD, 1990, *Handbook of International Trade and Development Statistics 1989*, New York: UN.
Valdes, A. and J. Zietz, 1980, 'Agricultural Protection in OECD Countries: its Cost to Less-Developed Countries', Washington: International Food Policy Research Institute, Research Report No. 21.
'Wass Report' (United Nations Advisory Group on Financial Flows for Africa), 1988, *Financing Africa's Recovery*, New York: UN.

TECHNICAL APPENDIX

(i) Trade creation: Income elasticities for the fivefold trade breakdown were averages, using LDC exports to the EC as weights, of detailed 2-digit NIMEXE and SITC headings [*Davenport and Page, 1990*]. The 1992-induced rise in EC GDP was assumed at five per cent.

(ii) Trade diversion: Diversion in manufactures was based on an average 'diversion elasticity' for LDC manufactured exports of 1.52, that is, the increased competitiveness of EC, associated with one per cent rise in EC GDP, leads to a 1.52 per cent reduction in manufactured imports from the LDCs. This figure is based on the estimates of Cawley and Davenport [*Cawley and Davenport, 1988*] of the trade diversion effects of Project 1992. Alternatives 'A' and 'B' were averaged.

(iii) Terms of trade effects: For price rises in world markets of primary products, the same income elasticities as in (i) were used. Price elasticities of import demand and export supply for primary products were taken from Matthews [*Matthews, 1989*] who derived them from Bond [*Bond, 1983*]. For the reduction in the price of EC exports of manufactures a figure of 1.6 per cent was taken on the basis of the 2-digit sectoral estimates in Cawley and Davenport [*Cawley and Davenport, 1988*] of the price reductions due to the 'direct effects' of 1992.

(iv) Tropical beverages and tobacco: The income elasticity of demand for coffee in the EC and world-wide was taken as 0.47 (Islam and Subramanian, 1989, the price elasticities of import demand as −0.27 (Islam and Subramanian) and of export supply for ACP suppliers as 0.46 and for other suppliers as 0.65 [*Askari and Cummings, 1977; Bond, 1983; Valdes and Zietz, 1980*]. On the basis of the same sources, for cocoa the price elasticity of demand was set at −0.58 and the supply elasticity at 0.8. For tobacco the elasticities were set at −0.4 and 0.4 respectively.

9

Trade Relations Between the European Community and Developing Countries

ROBERTO FUMAGALLI and ANTONELLA MORI

I. INTRODUCTION

During the past 30 years the European Community (EC) has been the most important trading area in the world: even excluding intra-EC trade, European exports have always accounted for more than 20 per cent of world exports (Table 1). In the same period the US has ranked second to the Ec, but during the 1970s it lost its importance to the growing strength of Japan in world trade. If intra-EC trade is included, the Community's share of world exports is clearly even higher, rising to 36.5 per cent in 1986 which is more than half the share of the total exports of all the industrialised countries – (Table 3).[1] Over the past 30 years, the most interesting event in international trade has probably been the phenomenal increase in the Newly Industrialising Countries' (NICs) exports: Taiwan, Hong Kong, Singapore and South Korea have doubled their share of world exports every ten years.

On the import side, too, the EC, Japan and the US have been important in world trade, except that there was a striking increase in US imports during the 1980s. The loss in US competitiveness and the appreciation of the US dollar made it the biggest importer in the world. Most EC trade is within the members of the Community itself. In 1987 almost 60 per cent of the trade flows of each member country was with one another.

Table 2 shows the development of European trade flows since the formation of the EC and that the extra-EC share of the total trade

This chapter is based on research carried out by the authors on behalf of ISPI-Osservatorio di Economia, Milan, Italy.

TABLE 1
STRUCTURE OF WORLD TRADE
(Excluding intra-EC trade, percentages based on values in US$)

Exports	1960	1970	1980	1987
EC (12)	23.1	21.5	18.7	20.4
USA	18.4	17.2	13.7	13.2
Japan	3.7	7.7	8.1	12.0
NICs-4 (a)	1.7	2.5	4.7	9.3
Others	53.1	51.1	54.8	57.1
Total	100.0	100.0	100.0	100.0
Imports	1960	1970	1980	1987
EC (12)	24.7	23.2	23.5	19.5
USA	2.5	15.0	14.4	20.2
Japan	4.3	7.1	8.4	7.4
NICs-4 (a)	2.5	3.3	5.2	7.9
Others	56.0	51.4	48.5	45.0
Total	100.0	100.0	100.0	100.0

(a) Taiwan, South Korea, Hong Kong and Singapore.
Source: CEC, *External Trade. Statistical Yearbook, 1988.*

flows has progressively diminished (trade diversion effect). During the last two decades the decreasing trend slowed down twice after the oil crises; however, once the shocks were absorbed, intra-EC trade again grew faster than extra-community. In 1987 the share of extra-EC exports went back to the lowest level previously reached immediately before the oil crisis of 1973. On the import side, the share of extra-community flows reached its minimum in 1987, equalling the export share for the first time in thirty years.

When market penetration figures for manufactures are used to measure the openness of different trading areas, the EC appears to be the most open trader, closely followed by the US. At the end of the 1980s, Japan was still as closed to imports as during the early 1970s. The high openness of the EC is partly due to its geographical and political proximity to the EFTA countries which are major importers and exporters of manufactures. The recent breakdown of the political barriers that isolated the East European countries could foreshadow a further opening of the Community's economies. Table 5 lists the market penetration values of 16 manufacturing sectors for the EC; it appears to be an open trading area. Not surprisingly the values for the non-EC industrialised countries' exports are on average higher than those for the LDCs, with the only significant exception being in the traditional sector, where the LDCs usually have a comparative advantage.

Table 3 shows that the growth of world trade in the last ten years

TABLE 2
TREND OF EXTRA-EC TRADE (a)
(Percentages)

	Exports	Imports
1965	50.8	55.1
1970	46.7	49.7
1980	43.8	51.2
1984	45.8	48.9
1985	45.1	47.1
1986	42.9	42.5
1987	41.4	41.4

(a) Share of extra-EC flows as percentages of total EC trade (intra plus extra-EC).
Source: Authors' calculations using Volimex and Eurostat data.

mainly reflects trade among industrialised countries: in 1979 nearly 48 per cent of world trade was among industrialised countries, whereas in 1986 this share reached 54 per cent. Nevertheless, the non-oil producing developing countries successfully entered some industrialised country markets taking advantage of their expansionary phase (Table 4). Between 1979 and 1986 about two-thirds of the LDCs' increased share in world trade derived from trade with industrialised countries. The flows among the LDCs also increased, but at a lower rate, mainly because of the reduction in trade by the oil-exporting countries after the oil price fall.

A geographical breakdown of LDCs' exports shows that EC imports of manufactures are strikingly low. South Asian and Latin American countries mainly export to the US, Europe and Japan being less important markets. The EC is the main importer of African manufactures. This flow is, however, less than three per cent of total manufactured imports of the EC. Thus the commercial relations between LDCs and industrialised countries seem to reflect geographical proximity: Latin America mainly exports to the US; Africa, and in particular, North African countries to the Community; the South East Asian countries to Japan and the US. The geographical distance of Asian NICs from the European market can help to explain why the NICs' aggressive competition has been less successful in Europe than in other markets.

II. IMPORTANCE OF EUROPEAN TRADE

EC, Non-EC Industrialised Countries and Less Developed Countries

Table 6 shows the share of European trade with the LDCs in total European flows: the figures clearly indicate that the LDCs have a

TABLE 3

TRADE BETWEEN DIFFERENT ZONES AS A PERCENTAGE OF WORLD EXPORTS

(Percentages based on values in US$)

1979	**Destination**					
	Developed Countries		Developing Countries		State Trading Countries	World
Origin	EC-12	Total	OPEC	Total		
Developed Countries	26.8	47.6	4.8	14.4	3.5	65.5
EC 12	18.9	27.4	2.4	5.8	1.9	35.2
Developing Countries	6.5	17.5	0.9	6.1	1.2	24.8
OPEC	3.7	9.5	0.2	0.3	0.3	12.8
State Trading Countries	1.7	2.8	0.3	1.7	5.2	9.7
World	34.9	67.9	6.0	22.2	9.9	100.0

1986	**Destination**					
	Developed Countries		Developing Countries		State Trading Countries	World
Origin	EC-12	Total	OPEC	Total		
Developed Countries	29.0	53.9	3.0	12.5	2.7	69.1
EC 12	21.1	30.3	1.6	5.0	1.2	36.5
Developing Countries	4.5	13.6	1.0	5.7	1.6	20.9
OPEC	1.5	3.6	0.2	1.9	0.2	5.7
State Trading Countries	1.4	2.6	0.2	1.8	5.6	10.0
World	34.9	70.1	4.2	20.0	9.9	100.0

Source: CEC, 'International Trade of the European Community', *European Economy*, 39, March 1989, p.15.

TABLE 4

MANUFACTURES EXPORTS FROM LDCs

(Percentages)

to / from	Years	World	Developed Countries				LDCs	State Trading Countries
			Total	EC	USA	Japan		
Developing Countries	1970	100.0	58.1	18.9	29.5	6.3	33.3	8.6
	1980	100.0	56.2	18.9	22.7	5.6	36.6	6.1
	1987	100.0	66.9	18.8	34.5	6.7	25.0	7.5
Africa	1970	100.0	37.9	23.8	2.1	1.2	45.8	16.2
	1980	100.0	66.6	55.9	3.3	0.5	24.5	6.1
	1987	100.0	64.6	52.3	6.7	0.5	25.5	9.2
Latin America	1970	100.0	54.1	15.4	31.2	1.9	44.2	1.4
	1980	100.0	46.2	15.7	21.8	3.3	51.4	2.2
	1987	100.0	67.9	11.8	49.6	2.5	28.2	3.5
South and South East Asia (a)	1970	100.0	65.6	15.4	34.3	6.4	29.0	5.4
	1980	100.0	62.2	19.0	28.1	6.9	33.4	3.4
	1987	100.0	69.7	16.9	36.9	8.3	23.3	6.5

(a) Hong Kong, South Korea, Singapore, Taiwan, Indonesia, Malaysia, Philippines and Thailand.

Source: UNCTAD, 'Trade in Manufacturers and Semi-Manufacturers of Developing Countries and Territories: 1989 Review', TD/B/C.2/228, 17 Aug. 1989, p.11.

TABLE 5

EUROPEAN COMMUNITY: MARKET PENETRATION OF MANUFACTURES IN 1985
(Percentages based on current value of extra-EC trade)

Market Penetration (a)	Total (%)	LDCs (%)	OECD non-EC (%)
Total Manufactures	12.5	3.6	8.9
Mineralliferous Ores	21.6	8.7	12.9
Non-Metallic Minerals	7.7	2.8	4.6
Chemical Products	12.5	2.7	9.8
Metal Products	3.9	0.6	3.3
Agricultural and Industrial Machinery	18.4	1.8	16.6
Office Machines	38.2	5.4	32.8
Electrical Goods	19.0	3.8	15.2
Motor Vehicles	7.5	0.5	7.0
Other Transport Equipment	19.6	9.3	10.3
Food, Beverages	5.7	3.4	2.3
Textiles, Clothing	17.7	9.4	8.3
Leather, Footwear	24.4	13.4	11.3
Wood, Furniture	17.4	4.7	12.7
Paper and Printing	13.5	0.8	12.7
Rubber, Plastic Products	5.1	1.1	4.0
Other Manufactures Products	5.5	3.0	2.5

(a) Market penetration is defined as the ratio between imports and apparent domestic consumption, equal to production plus imports minus exports.

Source: CEC, *Industry. Statistical Yearbook*, Luxembourg: Eurostat and Volimex.

TABLE 6

THE IMPORTANCE OF THE EC'S TRADE WITH THE LDCs
(Percentages)

a. Share of exports (imports) to (from) the LDCs as a percentage of total EC trade (intra plus extra-EC)

	All products		Excluding energy products	
	Exports	Imports	Exports	Imports
1965	20.8	25.4	20.8	18.5
1970	16.4	20.7	16.4	14.7
1980	20.1	25.4	20.4	13.9
1985	19.3	22.3	19.5	13.8
1987	16.0	16.8	15.5	12.3

b. Share of exports (imports) to (from) the LDCs as a percentage of total extra-EC trade

	All products		Excluding energy products	
	Exports	Imports	Exports	Imports
1965	41.0	46.0	40.4	54.3
1970	35.0	41.6	34.8	31.9
1980	45.8	49.6	45.6	32.5
1985	42.7	47.4	41.9	33.8
1987	38.8	40.5	37.0	32.3

Source: Volimex and Eurostat.

TABLE 7
GEOGRAPHICAL BREAKDOWN OF EC'S IMPORTS FROM THE LDCs

	1965	1970	1980	1985	1987
OPEC	31.0	34.8	52.5	35.7	24.3
Latin America	23.0	20.6	13.4	16.9	14.9
Asian NICs	4.7	5.7	8.6	7.8	13.4
Africa	15.0	15.0	6.4	10.3	10.0
Mediterranean Countries	6.0	5.6	6.2	6.7	7.1
Rest of LDCs	20.3	18.3	12.8	22.7	30.3
Total non-OPEC LDCs	69.0	65.2	47.5	64.3	75.7
Total LDCs	100.0	100.0	100.0	100.0	100.0

Source: Volimex.

decreasing proportion of the Community's trade. However, if oil is excluded from the flows, the picture is rather different, particularly after 1980, the share of LDCs on the import side decreases more slowly.

During the 1980s, EC exports to non-OPEC LDCs accounted for a fairly constant share of European exports towards non-European countries, a fact that strengthens the thesis that when LDCs' share of European exports fell from 20 to 16 per cent, it was completely due to the diminished purchasing power of the oil-exporting countries. Thus, non-oil-producing LDCs and non-European industrialised countries suffered equally from the trade diversion process caused by European integration. The shares in extra-EC trade of non-EC industrialised countries and LDCs remained unchanged over time.

The EC and Groups of LDCs

Tables 7 and 8 show European trade with developing countries divided by area of origin and destination: the tables give the proportion of each area to overall LDC imports from the EC and to overall LDC exports to the EC. As already mentioned, during the 1980s the non-oil-exporting developing countries maintained their relative importance in European imports. After 1980 not only the oil price but also the prices of other raw materials decreased relative to the prices of manufactured products, the main items in LDC imports.

The purchasing power of non-oil-producing developing countries increased differentially from country to country, depending on their product specialisation: the situation of the countries heavily dependent on raw materials exports was worst. The shares of Latin American countries, Mediterranean countries and African countries increased only slightly after 1980 (whose performances was negatively affected by the presence of some oil producing countries). This unfavourable pattern of terms of trade did not affect the Asian NICs, which specialised more in manufacturing production, and to a lesser extent, the group 'Rest of LDCs', which mostly consists of Asian countries, was also protected. Both groups increased their share of European imports between 1980 and 1987: the latter doubled its share, becoming in 1986 the developing world area with which the European Community has the closest relations. Although the Asian NICs increased their exports to the Community, they still have only a relatively small percentage of the total European trade, particularly on the import side.

The trade balances between these developing areas and the Community reveal lasting and deep differences: Asian NICs essentially trade manufactures with Europe and they are the only LDCs with a positive balance in manufactures trade since 1980. The group 'Rest of LDCs' has a more traditional commercial structure for developing countries, recording negative balances in manufactured products and surpluses in agricultural and energy raw materials. Since 1985 the lower energy trade surplus and the higher manufactured goods trade deficit of the 'Rest of LDCs' has turned the Community's trade balance with this group of countries, positive. The EC's trade balances with Latin America, Africa and OPEC had the same pattern. OPEC's surplus in 1987 was slightly more than one-tenth of that in 1980 (US $6 million against nearly 50), while in 1987 the trade balance with Africa was positive. Since the sectoral composition of exports by the latter three groups of developing countries is much more biased towards primary commodities than that of the 'Rest of LDCs'' exports, the consequences of unfavourable movements of the terms of trade had, and will have, bigger effects on the balances of the former Africa, Latin America and OPEC. From 1985 to 1987 European imports from Mediterranean countries were always smaller than exports. The performance of Asian NICs is very atypical: their positive balance with the EC – after shrinking between 1980 and 1985 – more than doubled in each of the following two years.

Table 9 shows the main LDC trading partners of EC in 1988: Brazil is the most important exporter to the EC among developing countries, with a trade balance much higher than that of the more advanced Asian NICs. On the export side the major market for the Community's products is still an OPEC country, Saudi Arabia.

TABLE 8

GEOGRAPHICAL BREAKDOWN OF EC'S EXPORTS TO THE LDCs

	1965	1970	1980	1985	1987
OPEC	17.0	18.1	37.9	29.1	20.2
Mediterranean Countries	20.1	12.5	13.1	13.4	12.7
Latin America	6.8	23.0	15.8	11.1	12.6
Africa	15.5	15.1	9.2	11.2	11.2
Asian NICs	11.6	8.3	7.3	7.7	9.9
Rest of LDCs	29.1	23.0	16.7	27.4	33.3
Total non-OPEC LDCs	83.0	81.9	62.1	70.9	79.8
Total LDCs	100.0	100.0	100.0	100.0	100.0

Source: Volimex.

III. THE STRUCTURE OF EUROPEAN TRADE

Exports

The structure of European exports has two distinctive characteristics: first of all, as in many other industrialised countries, it is mainly composed of manufactured products (Table 11); secondly, it is very

TABLE 9

MAIN LDC TRADE PARTNERS OF THE EC IN 1988

(Million of US$)

	Imports		Exports
1 Brazil	10562	1 Saudi Arabia	8968
2 Taiwan	9719	2 Hong Kong	6861
3 Hong Kong	8758	3 China	6771
4 South Korea	8622	4 India	6622
5 China	7677	5 Israel	5569
6 Saudi Arabia	6987	6 South Korea	5147
7 Libya	6077	7 Taiwan	5127
8 Algeria	5555	8 Singapore	4723
9 Singapore	3987	9 Egitto	4326
10 India	3920	10 Algeria	4288
11 Israel	3780	11 Brazil	3678
12 Iran	3740	12 Iran	3325
13 Malaysia	3547	13 Libya	3180
14 Thailand	3521	14 Morocco	3020
15 Nigeria	3413	15 Venezuela	2788
16 Iraq	3153	16 Iraq	2776
17 Argentina	3129	17 Mexico	2669
18 Mexico	2955	18 UAE	2593
19 Morocco	2630	19 Nigeria	2497
20 Chile	2535	20 Thailand	2433

Source: IMF, *Directions of Trade Statistics. Yearbook 1989*, 1989.

TABLE 10
STRUCTURE OF EC'S EXPORTS
(Share as percentage of total exports to each group of countries)

	World	Total LDCs	Medit.	Latin America	OPEC	Asian NICs	Africa	Rest LDCs
Year 1965								
Intermediate goods	24.4	24.2	24.6	29.5	24.0	21.8	18.3	24.3
Investment goods	38.7	47.2	38.9	50.0	43.8	48.3	45.5	51.1
Consumer goods	25.9	22.2	30.4	17.5	27.0	28.1	32.1	12.7
Total manufactures	89.1	93.6	93.9	97.0	94.8	98.2	95.9	88.1
Year 1970								
Intermediate goods	25.3	24.0	25.3	27.0	24.6	20.0	19.7	24.2
Investment goods	40.7	48.2	41.1	57.2	53.5	54.1	48.8	36.3
Consumer goods	24.2	21.5	25.1	12.9	18.1	24.1	26.4	26.5
Total manufactures	90.2	93.7	91.4	97.0	96.2	98.2	95.0	87.0
Year 1980								
Intermediate goods	24.0	21.5	22.9	24.0	20.6	21.6	19.7	20.8
Investment goods	38.5	49.1	41.2	54.4	52.3	56.4	47.6	40.4
Consumer goods	23.7	19.6	25.4	16.4	20.0	19.6	23.5	15.0
Total manufactures	86.2	90.1	89.5	94.8	92.9	97.6	90.7	76.2
Year 1985								
Intermediate goods	23.2	24.0	23.5	27.4	21.9	24.9	20.3	26.6
Investment goods	38.6	45.8	40.3	51.8	50.9	50.7	50.8	37.2
Consumer goods	23.1	19.3	26.9	16.4	21.6	21.9	22.2	12.5
Total manufactures	85.0	89.2	90.8	95.6	94.4	97.4	93.3	76.2
Year 1987								
Intermediate goods	22.3	23.7	22.0	25.6	21.8	25.9	20.9	25.1
Investment goods	42.5	47.1	41.4	54.8	49.5	48.2	51.7	43.1
Consumer goods	24.4	18.9	31.0	15.8	23.4	22.1	22.9	10.5
Total manufactures	89.3	89.7	94.4	96.2	94.7	96.2	95.4	78.6

Source: Volimex.

stable over time. In the period analysed the share of manufactured exports in total Community exports (including intra-EC trade) has been virtually unchanged, ranging between 85 and 90 per cent. Over the same period European exports of manufactured products to LDCs as a percentage of total European exports to these countries have been just as stable, and only a few percentage points higher.

Even the categories of manufactures exported remained stable over time and do not show big differences between the world and the LDCs (Table 10). The European Community was and still is primarily an exporter of investment goods:[2] about half its manufactured exports are goods of this kind. Intermediate goods products and consumer goods share the rest evenly. The LDCs as a whole show a different import pattern, purchasing from the Community a smaller share of consumer goods and a bigger one of investment goods. The composition of

TABLE 11
MAIN SECTORS OF EC'S EXPORTS TO LDCs
(Share as percentage of total exports to LDCs as a whole)

	1965	1970	1980	1987
Agricultural products	1.8	2.3	2.2	1.9
Energy products	3.2	3.2	6.2	3.4
Manufactures	93.6	93.7	90.1	89.7
Agricultural and industrial machinery	16.2	18.4	18.0	17.5
Chemical products	13.7	14.4	12.5	17.0
Electrical goods	11.0	9.2	10.0	12.4
Motor vehicles	8.7	9.5	8.5	6.0
Metalliferous ores	8.6	7.7	6.1	4.6
Foods, beverages	7.4	7.0	8.1	7.3
Textiles, clothing	6.6	4.4	n.a	3.3
Other transport equipment 4.7	4.8	5.7	6.5	
Metal products	4.7	4.2	4.9	n.a
Other manufactured products	3.1	5.2	3.4	3.5

Source: Volimex.

European exports to the LDCs does not differ notably from area to area except for the case of Mediterranean countries which buy a higher proportion of consumer goods, and a smaller one of investment goods. Both Mediterranean and OPEC countries are important export markets for European consumer goods, accounting for slightly less than 50 per cent of LDCs' consumer goods demand.

Imports

In 1965 nearly 30 per cent of total European imports were agricultural products and energy (Table 12); in 1987 those categories of goods accounted for about 18 per cent of the whole. The sharp decrease in the share of primary goods imports is almost completely due to a reduction of the percentage of agricultural imports which more than halved between 1965 and 1987. The other component of primary goods, energy, had a very similar share in these years (11.2 per cent in 1965 and 10.6 per cent in 1987).

The structure of EC imports from developing countries has undergone a similar change over the last two decades, but it has been longer and biased towards manufactured goods (Table 12). In 1965, 56 per cent of European imports consisted of primary commodities: manufactured goods, which were 39 per cent of the export flows, were most important in LDC exports, exceeding exports of energy goods (30.2 per cent). In 1987 energy goods still accounted for 30 per cent of total exports but manufactured goods were 53 per cent of the total: the developing

TABLE 12
STRUCTURE OF EC'S IMPORTS
(Share as percentage of total imports from each group of countries)

	World (a)	Total LDCs	Medit.	Latin America	OPEC	Asian NICs	Africa	Rest LDCs(b)
Year 1965								
Agricultural products	16.7	25.8	39.3	40.8	8.5	36.6	39.7	24.7
Energy products	11.2	30.2	18.2	14.3	81.5	0.4	1.4	2.3
Manufactures	70.4	38.9	42.2	44.8	9.9	62.9	58.9	73.0
Year 1970								
Agricultural products	12.1	21.6	36.7	36.0	6.1	24.0	31.7	21.6
Energy products	10.8	36.3	20.0	7.2	88.8	0.1	2.5	13.4
Manufactures	76.3	41.8	42.9	56.8	5.1	75.8	65.7	65.0
Year 1980								
Agricultural products	7.6	9.8	13.9	27.7	1.2	8.8	41.5	9.5
Energy products	23.2	57.8	46.5	26.3	95.8	0.6	9.3	3.1
Manufactures	68.3	31.6	39.0	45.7	2.8	90.3	44.3	87.4
Year 1985								
Agricultural products	7.2	11.7	13.2	28.6	1.5	7.5	31.9	7.7
Energy products	21.0	48.7	41.6	29.0	93.5	0.9	25.1	24.9
Manufactures	70.8	36.9	44.9	42.3	4.9	91.4	42.3	67.3
Year 1987								
Agricultural products	7.1	12.7	15.4	30.9	3.3	4.3	33.5	8.6
Energy products	10.6	30.0	25.2	16.3	87.3	0.1	16.9	11.0
Manufactures	81.2	52.9	59.2	52.6	9.3	95.5	49.2	80.4

(a) Including intra-EC trade.
(b) Figures for Rest of LDCs can differ from these of other tables due to differences xp(b) in the residual category.
Source: Volimex.

countries' exports to Europe repeat the pattern of overall European imports, showing an increase in the share of manufactures and a remarkable reduction in the share of agricultural products.

The modified structure of European imports is partly due to the shift of LDCs from primary commodity production to manufacturing. In order to show the development of LDCs' comparative advantages over the past 20 years, the Community's imports of manufactures from LDCs have been grouped into four categories of products on the basis of factor intensity: resource-intensive product, consumer products, engineering products and basic products. Food and beverages, metalliferous ores and non-metallic minerals are classified as resource-intensive products. Textiles and clothing, leather and footwear, wood and furniture, paper and printing, the whole category of highly labour-intensive goods, are classified as consumer products. The engineering products consist of machinery, electrical goods, transport equipment and office machines. Among the basic products are included all the capital-intensive processes: chemical and metal products, rubber and plastic products. Table 13 shows the shares of the four categories in total manufactures exports to the Community for each developing country area.

Asian NICs have undergone the most spectacular transformation: in 1965 nearly 40 per cent of their exports to the Community were agricultural products (Table 12), and manufactured products, the remaining 60 per cent, were almost one third resource-intensive products. In 1970 the situation had already changed and from strong primary commodity exporters these countries became specialised in highly labour-intensive consumer goods: 65 per cent of manufactures sold in Europe were in fact labour-intensive. In 1980 the share of primary products had shrunk so much that the export composition by main headings was identical to the European; more than 90 per cent of total exports were manufactured products. Meanwhile, the share of engineering goods rose from 7.4 per cent in 1970 to 27 per cent in 1980 and kept rising until 1987, becoming 43 per cent of total sales. In contrast, the share of consumer goods decreased from the 1970 maximum to 56 per cent in 1980 and 46 per cent in 1987. Between 1980 and 1985 the value – not the share – of European trade flows with Asian countries experienced a sharp slowing-down; Community imports decreased from about US $16 million to $11 million. Asian exports of highly labour-intensive products declined more in relative terms because they decreased more than the other export categories until 1985, and then in the following two years they increased less quickly than the others. Engineering products experienced an opposite trend: besides having shrunk less than all other types of exported products they began to grow in current values from 1985, before the other categories. In 1987 Asian exports of highly labour-intensive products were, in absolute value, still greater than exports of engineering goods, due to the fact that among the Asian NICs are Malaysia and Philippines, which are still more specialised in consumer goods productions.

The importance of the Asian NICs' performance stems not from their share in Community trade which is less than either the share of other trading partners or the share that they have in the US and Japanese markets, but from the hypothesis that the changes in comparative advantage of those countries and their export structure could be followed, even if only partially, by other developing countries with whom the European Community has more significant economic ties. Excluding OPEC countries, whose factor endowments could bias their development in completely different directions, the Mediterranean countries and the group 'Rest of LDCs' are interesting cases: between

TABLE 13

STRUCTURE OF EC'S MANUFACTURES IMPORTS

(Share as percentage of total manufactures imports from each group of countries)

	World	Total LDCs	Medit.	Latin America	OPEC	Asian NICs	Africa	Rest LDCs
Year 1965								
Resource intensive prod	37.0	66.1	70.9	89.2	78.1	27.9	83.9	36.2
Consumer products	22.0	27.5	20.8	6.5	18.0	60.2	14.2	53.1
Engineering products	27.0	3.5	3.1	0.7	2.3	6.0	0.6	8.1
Basic products	14.0	2.9	5.1	3.6	1.6	5.9	1.2	2.6
Year 1970								
Resource intensive prod	32.9	67.7	63.1	87.5	61.0	24.3	90.0	47.2
Consumer products	19.9	25.8	24.4	6.1	30.4	64.8	7.7	45.5
Engineering products	31.8	3.1	4.1	1.5	6.6	7.4	0.9	4.2
Basic products	15.5	3.5	8.3	4.9	2.1	3.4	1.4	3.0
Year 1980								
Resource intensive prod	25.1	35.2	32.3	71.0	45.2	11.7	82.7	18.8
Consumer products	22.5	42.0	44.2	15.9	32.1	55.7	12.5	55.5
Engineering products	34.7	16.2	8.9	5.8	17.3	26.7	2.5	19.8
Basic products	17.7	6.5	14.6	7.3	5.5	5.9	2.3	6.0
Year 1985								
Resource intensive prod	22.0	33.7	28.6	69.4	31.4	9.4	75.1	15.7
Consumer products	20.0	32.5	40.4	12.6	24.9	46.9	18.4	39.3
Engineering products	38.6	23.3	12.7	9.9	26.7	37.3	3.0	31.4
Basic products	19.4	10.5	18.3	8.2	17.0	6.4	3.5	13.6
Year 1987								
Resource intensive prod	18.7	23.7	20.5	63.1	19.2	5.5	64.7	11.7
Consumer products	20.9	39.5	49.0	17.2	38.9	46.0	27.7	44.9
Engineering products	41.4	26.6	13.1	11.4	22.7	42.7	4.3	30.9
Basic products	18.9	10.1	17.3	8.2	19.2	5.8	3.4	12.6

Source: Volimex.

1970 and 1980 both areas, like the Asian NICs, had sharply reduced the share of agricultural products in their exports to the Community.

In 1965 the share of manufactured products in total exports was smaller for Mediterranean countries than for all other developing areas (Table 13); then their share expanded steadily and in 1987 it was second only to manufactures' share in 'Rest of LDCs" exports, which has been since the 1960s more than 70 per cent of their exports to the EC. However, the great importance of energy exports for those countries, greater than for Asian NICs, limited the impact of this expansion of manufactures at least until 1985. None the less, during the 1970s 'Rest of LDCs' and the Mediterranean countries diversified into the production of consumer goods and reduced raw materials intensive products for the EC markets. This choice of specialisation was complementary to the one chosen by the Asian NICs which from 1980 reduced the share of consumer goods

TABLE 14

TREND OF THE EC MEMBERS' TRADE WITH DEVELOPING COUNTRIES
(Percentages)

	1965			1970			1980			1984			1987		
	Exp (a)	Imp (a)	Imp manuf (b)	Exp (a)	Imp (a)	Imp manuf (b)	Exp (a)	Imp (a)	Imp manuf (b)	Exp (a)	Imp (a)	Imp manuf (b)	Exp (a)	Imp (a)	Imp manuf (b)
Belgium-Lux	10.7	16.2	10.2	8.7	15.0	10.0	12.1	16.1	6.6	13.6	12.7	8.2	10.5	10.5	7.3
Denmark	11.4	14.2	7.3	11.0	10.4	3.6	11.6	12.5	6.8	15.3	12.7	7.4	11.6	10.3	6.9
France	26.3	30.4	14.8	20.7	21.8	8.9	24.4	28.3	9.7	25.3	23.5	10.3	18.6	16.1	10.6
Germany	17.4	26.4	13.0	12.6	16.7	9.5	15.9	21.0	11.0	18.8	24.4	13.2	14.0	18.0	11.3
Greece	9.5	11.8	6.4	8.0	11.9	7.1	29.6	28.3	6.2	23.1	23.5	4.9	12.0	18.4	7.7
Ireland	7.6	14.4	7.9	5.1	10.7	5.1	11.0	9.4	4.4	9.6	6.4	6.2	7.9	6.0	5.3
Italy	19.2	28.5	11.6	16.0	23.8	9.5	26.3	30.1	9.3	24.5	27.8	10.3	15.5	18.5	9.2
Netherlands	21.8	19.8	10.5	10.8	16.5	5.6	13.5	24.1	7.6	18.0	23.5	12.3	17.7	17.4	10.9
Portugal	33.0	27.1	12.4	30.8	25.7	13.8	16.7	28.5	7.3	14.1	32.3	9.2	7.8	17.8	6.2
Spain	21.4	21.7	10.7	23.2	26.0	10.1	31.8	45.3	10.7	28.6	43.0	11.5	18.8	23.3	9.4
United Kingdom	28.5	30.0	21.8	27.4	30.6	24.1	26.7	29.0	24.0	23.5	19.4	16.7	22.5	17.1	15.9
EC(12)	20.8	25.4	14.0	16.4	20.7	11.3	20.1	25.4	11.8	20.8	23.1	12.0	16.0	16.8	10.9

(a) Share of member's exports (imports) to LDCs of total members's exports (imports) to the world (intra plus extra-EC).
(b) Share of member's manufactures imports from LDCs of total member's manufactures imports from the world (intra plus extra-EC).
Source: Volimex.

TABLE 15
MARKET PENETRATION OF MANUFACTURES IMPORTS FROM LDCS
(Share as percentage of apparent consumption) (a)

Sectors	Years	France	Germany	Italy	UK	USA	Japan
Total	1975	1.5	2.5	2.2	2.5	2.0	1.8
Manufacturers	1980	2.6	3.7	3.9	2.8	3.0	2.2
(3)	1987	3.1	4.6	3.8	4.2	5.1	2.9
Textiles	1975	1.8	4.9	3.7	3.8	1.6	3.6
(321)	1980	3.6	8.7	5.5	5.3	2.5	4.5
	1987	4.9	9.2	5.4	10.1	4.8	4.3
Clothing	1975	3.4	18.6	1.8	13.8	7.8	6.2
(322)	1980	8.7	29.8	4.6	19.3	15.2	9.8
	1987	18.1	47.7	7.9	29.3	29.4	15.8
Iron and	1975	1.6	0.4	0.9	0.2	0.7	0.3
Steel	1980	1.3	0.9	1.4	0.4	1.3	0.9
(371)	1987	0.5	1.3	1.5	0.4	3.5	1.6
Electrical	1975	0.7	1.6	0.8	1.2	3.6	0.9
Goods	1980	1.8	3.5	2.0	2.6	6.0	1.0
(383)	1987	3.9	5.8	2.9	6.3	9.1	0.9
Radio, TV &	1975	1.2	2.6	1.4	2.2	5.6	1.2
Telecom	1980	2.8	6.2	4.2	3.9	8.0	1.3
(3832)	1987	6.2	9.6	7.2	9.4	9.5	1.1
Motor	1975	0.2	0.5	0.1	0.2	0.2	0.0
Vehicles	1980	0.4	0.5	1.1	0.3	1.3	0.1
(3843)	1987	0.5	0.7	2.6	0.7	2.4	0.1

(a) Numbers between brackets refer to ISIC categories. Figures for 1987 are estimates.
Source: UNCTAD, *Protectionism and Structural Adjustment,* TD/B/1240/Add.1, 1989.

in their exports to the Community; the path was eased by the less protectionist policy of the European Community in these sectors for those countries.

The group 'Rest of LDCs' seems to follow the Asian NICs model more closely: resource-intensive product exports fell in importance, although more slowly and about ten years later than the NICs, and allowed exports of consumer and engineering goods to increase, the latter expanding more quickly than the former after 1980. Moreover, the NICs during the period considered could no longer achieve the growth rate of previous years in capital-intensive production, primarily in chemical and metal products. The metal industry is a special case because it is considered a strategic sector by many countries: some LDCs began to develop this industry in the 1960s.

In the Mediterranean countries' exports, energy products were more important; the share of capital-intensive products considerably exceeded that of engineering products, particularly at the beginning of the 1980s.

Finally, the case of Latin America differs from the others because only after the mid-1980s did manufactures become important exports to the Community: Latin American countries, with some exceptions such as Brazil and Mexico, were, and continue to be, primarily exporters of agricultural raw materials and energy, at least to the EC. This specialisation emerges also from the structure of their manufactured exports: highly resource-intensive products are their principal exports, while consumer goods are the least important. The development process was different from that of other groups, passing from resource-intensive products to industrial goods without going through the stage of expansion of the consumer goods sector.

IV. THE TRADE PATTERN OF INDIVIDUAL EUROPEAN COUNTRIES

This section describes the commercial relations between LDCs and individual members of the Community, outlining the major differences in the sectoral and geographical composition of trade flows. As a consequence of historical linkages, trade and industrial policies, European countries have very different commercial relations with different groups of developing countries.

In general, LDCs experienced decreasing relative importance – compared to industrialised countries, with respect to all the Community members, both as markets and suppliers. The sharpest reduction in LDCs' importance occurred after each European country's entrance to the Community: the UK is the only significant exception: the reduction took place at the beginning of the 1980s, about ten years after its entrance.[3] This evolution has a twofold explanation: the effect of trade diversion and the greater dynamism of trade flows among industrialised countries, due to the widening of the gap between the industrial countries' growth rate and the LDCs'.

Over the past 20 years France, Germany, Italy and the UK have been the most important European trade partners of developing countries (Table 14). The UK, even if progressively losing in importance, is a member country with the highest share of manufactures imports from the LDCs in total imports of manufactures (in 1987 the UK had a share of 15.9 per cent followed by Germany with 11.3 per cent). Since the 1970s Germany has been the main partner for almost all the groups of LDCs.

Table 15 shows an alternative measure of countries' openness: the market penetration index (the ratio of manufactures imports from the

LDCs to apparent consumption) for the LDCs' manufactured exports increased between 1975 and 1987 in all cases – both countries and sectors – even if it remains very low for total manufactures. Only few sectors experienced aggressive competition from LDCs, textiles, clothing, radio, TV and telecommunications equipment. Germany is the European country with the highest index of market penetration; until 1980 it was greater than that of the US. In contrast, Ireland, Denmark and Belgium showed a low degree of openness and had little trade with developing countries. Finally, Spain and the Netherlands – and for imports only, Portugal and Greece – have small flows but a high degree of openness (Table 14).

Tables 16–19 show the geographical composition of trade flows between European countries and developing countries. In 1987, Germany was the most important trade partner for the LDCs as a whole and for Latin America, OPEC (only as exporter, because Italy was the main importer), Asian NICs and 'Rest of LDCs'. France was the most important partner for Mediterranean and African countries. In 1970 the picture of European trade relations with developing countries was completely different: the UK was by far the major partner of the LDCs as a whole and of Asian NICs and 'Rest of LDCs' (Tables 16 and 17).

In 1987 'Rest of LDCs' was the principal importer from the Community as a whole and from five member countries: its share of total exports to LDCs was 30 per cent for Belgium and Luxembourg, 40.8 per cent for Denmark, 39.3 per cent for Germany, 65.1 per cent for the Netherlands and 39.2 per cent for the UK (Table 18). OPEC, the second important LDC market for European exports, was a major importer from France (22.1 per cent), Ireland (29.6 per cent) and Italy (30.4 per cent). The Asian NIGs' share of European imports sharply increased for all countries even if it was still lower than that of other LDCs. Table 20 shows the current account balances with LDCs in 1970 and 1987: Spain and Italy had the highest trade deficit while the UK and France the highest surpluses.

France

In 1965 trade flows between France and developing countries were stronger than the Community average: 26.3 per cent of the country's exports went to LDCs and 30.4 per cent of imports came from LDCs. Nevertheless, the development of France's trade has been similar to that of the other European countries, experiencing a big contraction of LDCs' importance: in 1987 the LDCs' share of total exports was 18.6 per cent and in total imports it was 16.1 per cent.

TABLE 16

GEOGRAPHICAL BREAKDOWN OF THE EC'S EXPORTS
(Share as percentage of total EC exports to groups of LDCs)

1970	Medit. Countries	Latin America	OPEC	Asian NICs	Africa	Rest of LDCs	Total LDCs	World
Belgium-Lux	5.5	4.8	4.7	6.1	7.4	4.6	5.3	10.0
Denmark	1.4	1.9	1.6	2.1	2.8	1.7	1.9	2.8
France	25.3	13.1	24.0	9.2	30.6	15.2	19.4	15.3
Germany	20.8	31.4	23.3	26.9	15.1	18.3	22.8	29.5
Greece	1.3	0.0	0.4	0.0	0.1	0.1	0.3	0.6
Ireland	0.2	0.3	0.1	0.3	0.1	0.5	0.3	0.9
Italy	14.0	13.3	13.2	8.0	8.4	8.8	11.1	11.4
Netherlands	5.3	6.5	6.6	7.5	5.1	8.4	6.7	10.1
Portugal	0.6	0.5	0.2	0.3	7.3	0.9	1.5	0.8
Spain	3.6	7.1	1.6	0.5	1.8	1.0	2.9	2.1
United Kingdom	21.9	21.2	24.3	39.2	21.4	40.5	27.8	16.6
EC (12)	100.0	100.0	100.0	100.0	100.0	100.0	100.0	100.0
EC (12) $ mn	2368	4357	3427	1583	2873	4372	18979	116037
1987	**Medit. Countries**	**Latin America**	**OPEC**	**Asian NICs**	**Africa**	**Rest of LDCs**	**Total LDCs**	**World**
Belgium-Lux	10.1	3.8	4.5	6.3	6.2	5.1	5.7	8.8
Denmark	1.2	1.3	1.7	3.0	1.3	2.3	1.9	2.6
France	22.8	25.3	19.2	16.0	30.6	7.6	17.5	15.1
Germany	20.4	29.5	22.5	29.7	22.2	31.7	26.9	30.8
Greece	1.8	0.0	0.9	0.1	0.2	0.2	0.5	0.7
Ireland	1.1	1.1	1.2	0.8	0.7	0.4	0.8	1.7
Italy	17.1	13.1	18.0	11.9	11.0	6.2	11.9	12.3
Netherlands	5.2	5.5	6.3	4.6	5.9	21.1	10.8	9.8
Portugal	0.5	0.4	0.4	0.4	1.5	0.3	0.5	1.0
Spain	7.3	7.7	4.4	1.9	3.7	2.5	4.2	3.6
United Kingdom	12.6	12.3	20.8	25.4	16.6	22.7	19.3	13.8
EC (12)	100.0	100.0	100.0	100.0	100.0	100.0	100.0	100.0
EC (12) $ mn	19310	19220	30645	15074	17092	50631	151972	947098

Source: Volimex.

Until the mid-1980s, France had a negative trade balance with the LDCs as a whole but a positive balances with many groups of developing countries; the country has always been an important importer of energy and an exporter of manufactures (Table 20). Over the past few years the French trade balance improved with the LDCs as a whole and deteriorated with the Asian NICs and 'Rest of LDCs', the most important LDC exporter of manufactures to France.

Since 1965 Africa and OPEC have been the main buyers of French goods, but with a decreasing share over time. In 1965 those two groups were also the main LDC exporters to France, but Africa's loss of importance was so sharp that during the 1980s, first Latin

TABLE 17

GEOGRAPHICAL BREAKDOWN OF THE EC'S IMPORTS
(Share as percentage of total EC imports from groups of LDCs)

1970	Medit. Countries	Latin America	OPEC	Asian NICs	Africa	Rest of LDCs	Total LDCs	World
Belgium-Lux	5.8	7.1	5.1	3.0	14.9	3.6	6.6	9.1
Denmark	1.6	2.5	1.9	2.4	1.1	1.3	1.8	3.5
France	23.8	10.1	18.9	7.5	21.4	13.1	16.0	15.2
Germany	18.5	27.4	18.3	28.9	16.2	12.4	19.4	24.0
Greece	2.9	1.3	0.6	0.5	1.0	0.5	0.9	1.6
Ireland	1.1	0.5	0.6	0.6	0.4	0.9	0.7	1.3
Italy	13.9	16.0	18.1	9.3	11.7	6.6	13.8	12.0
Netherlands	10.0	8.5	11.8	7.6	5.3	5.2	8.6	10.8
Portugal	0.7	0.6	0.9	0.4	5.9	1.3	1.6	1.3
Spain	5.4	8.6	5.1	3.5	3.2	1.3	4.8	3.8
United Kingdom	16.4	17.6	18.7	36.3	19.1	53.7	25.8	17.4
Ec (12)	100.0	100.0	100.0	100.0	100.0	100.0	100.0	100.0
EC (12) $ mn	1436	5288	8958	1473	3854	4695	25705	124325
1987	**Medit. Countries**	**Latin America**	**OPEC**	**Asian NICs**	**Africa**	**Rest of LDCs**	**Total LDCs**	**World**
Belgium-Lux	7.9	5.9	5.6	3.4	12.8	2.9	5.4	8.7
Denmark	1.0	1.7	1.0	2.1	0.5	2.4	1.6	2.7
France	23.9	15.1	17.6	13.8	21.9	12.2	16.0	16.6
Germany	16.8	26.4	13.7	31.0	19.3	36.7	25.7	24.0
Greece	2.7	0.8	3.1	1.4	1.4	0.4	1.5	1.4
Ireland	0.5	0.4	0.1	0.9	0.8	0.6	0.5	1.4
Italy	20.8	13.9	26.1	7.4	13.5	6.6	14.2	12.9
Netherlands	5.6	8.9	12.5	8.3	7.7	10.8	9.9	9.5
Portugal	2.7	1.8	2.1	0.5	2.5	0.6	1.5	1.4
Spain	5.9	12.8	11.8	4.0	6.4	2.6	7.2	5.2
United Kingdom	12.2	12.3	6.2	27.1	13.2	24.2	16.5	16.2
EC (12)	100.0	100.0	100.0	100.0	100.0	100.0	100.0	100.0
EC (12) $ mn	11311	23647	38612	21348	15993	48239	159149	948362

Source: Volimex.

America, and later 'Rest of LDCs' overtook it (see also Table 22). France has always been the principal trade partner among the EC members for Africa and the Mediterranean countries, a relationship which has deep roots in the colonial past of the country.[4] Some countries continue to use the French language and follow an exchange rate policy tied to the French franc.[5] Over the past two decades the Asian NICs have been the most competitive developing countries in French markets, although they have only a small share of the total French imports.

Table 21 shows the principal products imported by France: the share of textiles and clothing increased considerably and Asian NICs are no

TABLE 18

GEOGRAPHICAL BREAKDOWN OF THE EC'S EXPORTS TO LDCs
(Share as percentage of total EC members' exports to groups of LDCs)

1970	Medit. Countries	Latin America	OPEC	Asian NICs	Africa	Rest of LDCs	Total LDCs	World ($ mn.)
Belgium-Lux	12.9	20.6	15.9	9.6	21.1	19.8	100.0	1009
Denmark	9.4	22.6	15.0	9.4	22.5	21.0	100.0	361
France	16.3	15.5	22.3	3.9	23.9	18.0	100.0	3678
Germany	11.4	31.7	18.5	9.8	10.0	18.5	100.0	4320
Greece	59.1	3.9	26.9	0.4	4.0	5.6	100.0	51
Ireland	10.9	22.3	8.6	9.5	2.8	45.8	100.0	51
Italy	15.6	27.3	21.4	6.0	11.4	18.3	100.0	2115
Netherlands	10.0	22.3	17.8	9.4	11.5	29.1	100.0	1268
Portugal	4.9	7.3	1.8	1.4	71.9	12.8	100.0	293
Spain	15.6	55.8	9.9	1.4	9.3	7.9	100.0	5279
United Kingdom	9.8	17.5	15.8	11.7	11.6	33.5	100.0	554
EC (12)	12.5	23.0	18.1	8.3	15.1	23.0	100.0	18979
1987	**Medit. Countries**	**Latin America**	**OPEC**	**Asian NICs**	**Africa**	**Rest of LDCs**	**Total LDCs**	**World ($ mn)**
Belgiun-Lux	22.4	8.4	16.0	10.9	12.3	30.0	100.0	8690
Denmark	8.2	9.0	18.6	15.6	7.9	40.8	100.0	2870
France	16.5	18.2	22.1	9.0	19.7	14.4	100.0	26636
Germany	9.6	13.9	16.9	11.0	9.3	39.3	100.0	40820
Greece	45.3	1.2	36.6	2.5	4.2	10.3	100.0	779
Ireland	16.8	16.4	29.6	9.6	9.7	18.0	100.0	1262
Italy	18.2	13.9	30.4	9.9	10.3	17.3	100.0	18099
Netherlands	6.1	6.5	11.8	4.3	6.2	65.1	100.0	16386
Portugal	12.7	9.5	17.3	7.8	35.0	17.7	100.0	715
Spain	22.0	23.1	20.8	4.4	10.0	19.7	100.0	29317
United Kingdom	8.3	8.1	21.8	13.1	9.7	39.2	100.0	6399
EC (12)	12.7	12.6	20.2	9.9	11.2	33.3	100.0	151972

Source: Volimex.

longer the major suppliers. They exported more advanced products such as office machines and electrical goods.

Germany

Germany's trade with LDCs has a very balanced geographical and sectoral structure, similar to the one described in the previous section for the Community as a whole. Over the past 30 years exports to LDCs as a share of total German exports declined slightly, remaining always lower than the shares of the other major European countries.

Until 1987 Germany had a negative balance with the LDCs as a whole, although not with all groups. Recently the main LDC markets for German exports have been the 'Rest of LDCs' (39.3 per cent of total LDCs) and OPEC (16.9 per cent of total LDCs) (see Table 24). At the beginning of the

TABLE 19

GEOGRAPHICAL BREAKDOWN OF THE EC'S IMPORTS FROM LDCS

(Share as percentage of total EC members' imports from groups of LDCs)

1970	Medit. Countries	Latin America	OPEC	Asian NICs	Africa	Rest of LDCs	Total LDCs	World ($ mn)
Belgium-Lux	4.9	22.0	27.0	2.6	33.6	9.9	100.0	1706
Denmark	5.0	28.5	36.4	7.6	9.1	13.4	100.0	456
France	8.3	12.9	41.2	2.7	20.0	14.9	100.0	4119
Germany	5.3	29.1	32.8	8.5	12.5	11.7	100.0	4986
Greece	18.2	30.0	23.6	3.0	16.0	9.1	100.0	232
Ireland	9.3	15.6	34.0	5.4	9.6	26.2	100.0	168
Italy	5.6	23.7	45.4	3.8	12.7	8.7	100.0	3559
Netherlands	6.5	20.3	47.8	5.1	9.2	11.1	100.0	2209
Portugal	2.4	7.2	19.1	1.5	55.4	14.4	100.0	408
Spain	6.3	37.0	37.4	4.2	9.9	5.1	100.0	6638
United Kingdom	3.5	14.1	25.2	8.1	11.1	38.0	100.0	1224
EC (12)	5.6	20.6	34.8	5.7	15.0	18.3	100.0	25705
1987	**Medit. Countries**	**Latin America**	**OPEC**	**Asian NICs**	**Africa**	**Rest of LDCs**	**Total LDCs**	**World ($ mn)**
Belgium-Lux	10.3	16.2	25.2	8.4	23.8	16.2	100.0	8638
Denmark	4.2	15.2	15.4	17.5	2.9	44.8	100.0	2609
France	10.7	14.0	26.8	11.6	13.8	23.1	100.0	25400
Germany	4.7	15.3	13.0	16.2	7.5	43.4	100.0	40857
Greece	12.8	7.8	50.2	12.6	9.1	7.5	100.0	2373
Ireland	7.4	12.8	3.5	24.3	15.6	36.5	100.0	812
Italy	10.4	14.5	44.5	7.0	9.5	14.1	100.0	22646
Netherlands	4.0	13.4	30.6	11.2	7.8	33.0	100.0	15765
Portugal	12.8	18.0	34.4	4.8	16.9	13.0	100.0	2388
Spain	5.9	26.6	40.1	7.5	9.0	11.0	100.0	26255
United Kingdom	5.3	11.1	9.1	22.1	8.0	44.4	100.0	11407
EC (12)	7.1	14.9	24.3	13.4	10.0	30.3	100.0	159149

Source: Volimex.

1970s, Germany's trade relations with LDCs were very different: the Latin American countries were its major LDC importers accounting for 31.7 per cent (in 1987 this percentage decreased to 13.9 per cent). German imports from LDCs clearly showed a decreasing trend: in 1965 26.4 per cent of total imports came from LDCs while in 1987 this figure was only 18 per cent. The largest drop of imports occurred in the second half of the 1960s.

OPEC, Latin America and Africa steadily lost their importance as exporters to Germany while the Asian NICs nearly doubled their share (of total imports from LDCs), overtaking the OPEC countries. In 1987 Germany's imports came mainly from 'Rest of LDCs' (43.4 per cent) and Asian NICs (16.2 per cent). On the energy import side Germany is an atypical case compared to the other European countries because

TABLE 20
BILATERAL TRADE BALANCES
(Million of US$)

1970	Medit. Countries	Latin America	OPEC	Asian NICs	Africa	Rest of LDCs	Total LDCs	World
Belgium-Lux	47	−166	−300	52	−360	31	−697	247
Denmark	11	−48	−112	−1	40	15	−95	−1099
France	259	37	−875	34	55	48	−442	−1184
Germany	228	−80	−837	−1	−192	216	−665	4375
Greece	−12	−68	−41	−7	−35	−18	−181	−1316
Ireland	−10	−15	−53	−4	−15	−21	−117	−571
Italy	130	−266	−1164	−10	−210	76	−1444	−1729
Netherlands	−17	−166	−831	7	−57	123	−941	−1627
Portugal	4	−8	−73	−2	−16	−21	−116	−641
Spain	9	−143	−403	−44	−70	−19	−669	−2328
United Kingdom	283	−8	−843	85	−122	−753	−1358	−2416
EC (12)	932	−931	−5531	109	981	−323	−6725	−8289
1987	**Medit. Countries**	**Latin America**	**OPEC**	**Asian NICs**	**Africa**	**Rest of LDCs**	**Total LDCs**	**World**
Belgium-Lux	1056	−667	−782	224	−987	1208	52	346
Denmark	126	−137	133	−11	150	1	261	−638
France	1694	1297	−919	−539	1730	−2027	1236	−14482
Germany	2031	−575	1583	−2137	717	−1657	−37	64155
Greece	50	−176	−905	−279	−184	−99	−1594	−6419
Ireland	152	103	345	−77	−4	−69	450	2357
Italy	942	−771	−4584	212	−279	−67	−4547	−5628
Netherlands	376	−1042	−2891	−1067	−218	5463	621	1808
Portugal	−216	363	−697	−60	−154	−183	−1673	−4271
Spain	741	−1552	−3238	−577	−389	6	−5008	−14912
United Kingdom	1048	−543	3988	−1964	717	−184	3062	−23581
EC (12)	7999	−4427	−7967	−6274	1100	2392	−7177	−1264

Source: Volimex.

its dependence on imports from the LDCs started to fall earlier and the fall was deeper (Table 23): in 1965, 68.7 per cent of energy imports came from LDCs, in 1987 this share was 40.4 per cent. Over the same period of time its dependence on OPEC decreased even more.

Italy

Trade relations between Italy and the LDCs showed a trend similar to that of the Community's overall trend but with high peaks in the early 1980s. In 1965, 19.2 per cent of total Italian exports and 20.1 per cent of manufactures exports went to LDCs. After having reached the highest point (26.3 per cent) in 1980, LDCs' share of total exports started to decrease. Italy has always had a negative trade balance with the LDCs as a whole; in 1987 the balances were positive only with the Mediterranean countries and Asian NICs.

The main exporters to Italy were traditionally OPEC and Latin America. The relative importance of the latter, however, decreased considerably over time: in 1970 23.7 per cent of total Italian imports from LDCs came from Latin America and by 1987 this share had fallen to 14.5 per cent. Since the 1960s, OPEC has been also the main buyer of Italian goods among developing countries, followed by Latin America until the 1970s and then by the Mediterranean countries.

Figures for agricultural imports of Italy are quite interesting: in 1987 only 25 per cent of total agricultural imports came from developing countries while in 1965 this share had been nearly 43 per cent. Part of the explanation lies in the functioning of the Common Agricultural Policy (CAP) which protected European agriculture. The contraction of agricultural imports had a negative impact, mainly on Latin American countries: in 1965 more than one-fifth of Italian agricultural imports came from Latin America, while in 1987 these accounted to less than one-tenth. Primary commodities were always an important category in Italian imports: in 1987 more than 60 per cent of imports from LDCs were primary goods – agricultural goods (12 per cent) and energy (49.5 per cent). In 1987 the main imports among manufactures were textiles and clothing (Table 25) of which Italy became a net importer from the early 1970s. Even for Italy past colonial history is still very important: Libya is the main exporter among OPEC countries (Table 26).

The United Kingdom

Since 1965 the UK has had the biggest share of manufactures imports from LDCs within the Community. However, this share was lower in 1987 (16 per cent) than in 1965 (21.8 per cent) after increasing until the early 1980s. On the import side, the LDCs' share shrank constantly, but it remained the highest in the EC. In the early 1980s, before any other major European country, the UK was already a net exporter to the LDCs. In 1987 the UK had a negative trade balance only with Latin America, Asian NICs and 'Rest of LDCs'.

The British colonial empire which included some Asian, African, Caribbean and Mediterranean countries explains the dominant role played by the UK until the 1970s, when Germany imposed its economic superiority. In 1970 the UK was still the principal trade partner for all LDCs and for OPEC, Asian NICs and 'Rest of LDCs'. The latter group, which includes Asian countries other than the NICs, like India and China, has always been the main trading partner of the UK for both imports and exports.

Over the last 20 years the geographical composition of the British trade

TABLE 21
TEN PRINCIPAL SECTORS IN FRANCE'S IMPORTS FROM LDCs IN 1987
(Percentages)

Sectors	1970	1987
Energy products	40.6	29.7
Agricultural products	27.9	13.2
Textiles and clothing	1.6	10.7
Food and beverages	10.9	8.3
Electrical goods	0.1	7.0
Metalliferous ores	12.7	4.5
Office machines	0.2	4.4
Leather, Footwear	0.9	3.7
Chemical products	1.2	3.1
Other manufactured products	0.7	3.0
Total	100.0	100.0

Source: Volimex.

TABLE 22
FRANCE'S MAIN TRADING PARTNERS AMONG LDCs IN 1988
(Million of US$)

	Imports		Exports
Brazil	1597	Algeria	1563
Saudi Arabia	1576	Morocco	1277
Taiwan	1531	Saudi Arabia	1089
China	1427	Reunion	1034
South Korea	1426	Hong Kong	1027
Algeria	1248	South Korea	923
Morocco	1212	China	915
		Egitto	907
		Tunisia	906

Source: IMF, *Directions of Trade Statistics. Yearbook 1989,* 1989.

has undergone some important changes: Latin America lost its share in British exports and OPEC in British imports, the latter due to the higher energy self-sufficiency and to the diversification of suppliers. Meanwhile, the Asian NICs' share of British imports from LDCs increased by a factor of three. The sectoral composition of the UK's imports from LDCs reveals that the sectors which expanded more were the ones in which Asian NICs were the main exporters. In 1988 the top three LDC exporters to the UK were Hong Kong, Taiwan and South Korea (Tables 27 and 28).

Spain

The country had strong and increasing trade with LDCs until the early 1980s; after its entry into the EC, the LDCs' share of total Spanish

TABLE 23
TEN PRINCIPAL SECTORS IN GERMANY'S IMPORTS FROM LDCs IN 1987
(Percentages)

Sectors	1970	1987
Energy products	32.1	22.1
Textiles and clothing	6.4	14.4
Agricultural products	24.9	12.5
Metalliferous ores	17.6	6.6
Electrical goods	0.5	6.1
Food and beverages	11.4	5.3
Leather, Footwear	0.9	3.7
Office machines	0.2	3.0
Chemical products	1.0	2.5
Other manufactured products	2.1	2.3
Total	100.0	100.0

Source: Volimex.

TABLE 24
GERMANY'S MAIN TRADING PARTNERS AMONG LDCs IN 1988
(Million of US$)

	Imports		Exports
Brazil	2810	China	2786
Taiwan	2807	South Korea	1844
Hong Kong	2609	India	1668
South Korea	2573	Iran	1644
China	2463	Hong Kong	1617
Libya	1519	Brazil	1538
Singapore	1041	Saudi Arabia	1525
India	1040	Singapore	1428
		Israel	1323
		Egypt	1118

Source: IMF, *Directions of Trade Statistics. Yearbook 1989*, 1989.

trade dropped sharply (trade diversion effect). Between 1984 and 1987 the share of Spanish exports which went to LDCs decreased from 28.6 to 18.8 per cent, and that of imports from LDCs, from 43 to 23.3 per cent. Not only did the relative shares shrink, but also the absolute value of trade flows, in contrast with a considerable expansion of total Spanish trade.

Spain was, and still is, a net importer from the LDCs: Spain had positive trade balances only with the Mediterranean countries and 'Rest of LDCs'. In 1987 Spain's trade deficit with LDCs was the highest in the Community. Latin America is the principal importer from Spain and OPEC the principal exporter to it. Unlike the other EC countries, Spain has maintained the sectoral composition of its imports almost unchanged (see Table 29). In 1987 nearly 46 per cent of agricultural imports, 72.5 per

TABLE 25
TEN PRINCIPAL SECTORS IN ITALY'S IMPORTS FROM LDCs IN 1987
(Percentages)

Sectors	1970	1987
Energy products	47.0	48.6
Agricultural products	24.7	12.0
Textiles and clothing	3.0	6.8
Metalliferous ores	14.2	5.7
Leather, Footwear	1.3	4.2
Electrical goods	0.3	3.7
Chemical products	0.8	3.7
Food and beverages	6.6	3.3
Other manufactured products	0.4	1.9
Office machines	0.1	1.8
Total	100.0	100.0

Source: Volimex.

TABLE 26
ITALY'S MAIN TRADING PARTNERS AMONG LDCs IN 1988
(Million of US$)

	Imports		Exports
Libya	2547	Saudi Arabia	1451
Brazil	1665	China	1302
Algeria	1601	Libya1256	
China	1428	Hong Kong	1080
Saudi Arabia	1049	Israel	817
Egypt	1010	Algeria	809
Iraq	1003	Egypt	768
Taiwan	955	Taiwan	591

Source: IMF, *Directions of Trade Statistics. Yearbook 1989*, 1989.

cent of energy imports and 9.5 per cent of manufactured imports came from the LDCs. From the geographical composition side Spain has some peculiar features: in 1987 Latin America and OPEC exported mainly energy; Mediterranean countries, Asian NICs and 'Rest of LDCs', manufactures; while African countries exported agricultural products.

Other EC countries: Greece and Portugal

Greece and Portugal show different patterns of trade with the LDCs, although both were new entrants in the EC with a low level of development compared to the other members. Over the last twenty years Portugal's trade relations with LDCs (in relative terms) have declined, while that of Greece have increased.

An explanation for the difference in performance is given by the different geographical orientation of their trade flows. In 1970, 72 per cent of Portugal's exports to LDCs went to Africa,[6] while the most important markets for Greece were the Mediterranean countries (59 per cent) and the OPEC (27 per cent). The deep crisis in Africa over the last two decades reduced its purchasing power so much that between 1970 and 1987, although total Portuguese exports to the rest of the world increased tenfold, the value of its exports to African LDCs remained almost unchanged. The increase in Portugal's exports to other developing countries was not enough to compensate for the drop in Africa and thus in 1987, LDCs accounted for only 7.8 per cent of total Portuguese exports compared to 33 per cent in 1965. Over the same period of time, Greece, with more diversified export markets, expanded its trade with LDCs, reaching a historical high after the oil shocks, when OPEC's imports exploded.

Besides the different geographical pattern of exports of Portugal and Greece, the different product composition also played an important role. At the end of 1960s Portugal exported mainly traditional consumer goods to the LDCs (that is, textile and clothing), specialising in sectors that many developing countries fostered over the following two decades, while Greece exported metalliferous ores, non-metallic minerals, chemical and food products.

V. CONCLUSIONS

The European Community is the most important trading area in the world. Its foundation spurred the growth of trade flows among member countries, a growth that, in part, restrained the development of commercial relations between the EC and extra-Community countries. The LDCs as a whole were a less important trade partner at the end of the 1980s than in the mid-1960s. In the 1980s, nevertheless, the EC's exports to the non-oil-producing LDCs were an almost constant share of total extra-EC exports: the sharp reduction of the LDCs' importance was due almost completely to the decreased purchasing power of oil-exporting countries. Non-oil-exporting developing countries and non-EC industrial countries suffered the same process of trade diversion, as a consequence of the expanded trade within the Community's borders. During the 1980s the share of European imports from non-oil-producing LDCs increased slightly, showing that some developing countries succeeded in penetrating industrialised countries' markets. European countries appear to be more open to manufactured imports from the LDCs than Japan and, until recently, the US.

Over the past two decades, the composition by product categories, of LDCs exports' to the EC underwent important changes: primary

TABLE 27

TEN PRINCIPAL SECTORS IN UK'S IMPORTS FROM LDCs IN 1987
(Percentages)

Sectors	1970	1978
Other manufactured products	14.2	14.0
Textiles and clothing	4.9	12.1
Electrical goods	0.6	9.9
Other transport equipments	0.2	9.6
Agricultural products	12.9	8.5
Food and beverages	19.9	8.3
Energy products	26.5	7.3
Metalliferous ores	13.7	5.0
Agricultural and industrial machinery	0.5	4.3
Office machines	0.2	3.8
Total	100.0	100.0

Source: Volimex.

TABLE 28

UK'S MAIN TRADING PARTNERS AMONG LDCs IN 1988
(Million of US$)

	Imports		Exports
Hong Kong	3161	Saudi Arabia	3044
Taiwan	2039	India	1982
South Korea	2011	Hong Kong	1841
Brazil	1318	Singapore	1127
Saudi Arabia	1155	Israel	869
India	1031	United Arab Emirates	807
Singapore	1030		
China	786		

Source: IMF, *Directions of Trade Statistics. Yearbook 1989*, 1989.

TABLE 29

TEN PRINCIPAL SECTORS IN SPAIN'S IMPORTS FROM LDCs IN 1987
(Percentages)

Sectors	1970	1987
Energy products	41.3	51.8
Agricultural products	30.7	16.8
Metalliferous ores	11.0	5.2
Food and beverages	11.2	4.2
Electrical goods	0.2	3.9
Office machines	0.1	2.9
Chemical products	1.9	2.7
Textiles and clothing	0.4	2.7
Other manufactured products	0.2	1.7
Leather, Footwear	0.3	1.7
Total	100.0	100.0

Source: Volimex.

TABLE 30
SPAIN'S MAIN TRADING PARTNERS AMONG LDCs IN 1988
(Million of US$)

Imports		Exports	
Mexico	1105	Morocco	493
Brazil	939	Saudi Arabia	449
Nigeria	938	Algeria	362
Taiwan	587		
South Korea	556		
Iran	485		

Source: IMF, *Directions of Trade Statistics. Yearbook 1989*, 1989.

goods, in particular agricultural ones, lost in importance relative to manufactures. The composition of manufactures exports from the LDCs suggests that their main comparative advantage is still exclusively in natural-resources-intensive and unskilled-labour-intensive products.

The heritage of the colonial past emerges clearly from the geographical pattern of trade relations between individual EC members and LDCs: excluding trade with oil-exporting countries, France has its strongest trade links with Africa; the UK with Asia (particularly with the area called 'Rest of LDCs') and Spain with Latin America. Germany, the main European trade partner of LDCs as a whole, has a more balanced geographical composition of trade, reflecting its competitiveness more than historical linkages.

NOTES

1. In this work the European Community always means the present 12 Member States. Trade of the EC and of its Members with the World includes intra-EC trade, unless specified otherwise. The study is mostly based on Volimex, which is an official source of the EC (DG II). Volimex has been preferred because it adopts a wider classification of manufactures (under NACE-CLIO R44 nomenclature) than the SITC nomenclature more commonly used. Under SITC manufactures include categories 5–8 (sometimes except 68) thus omitting the group processed agrifood products (namely food, beverages and tobacco products) which come under the 'agricultural products' heading.
2. Under the NACE-CLIO R44 nomenclature (see Appendix) the groups are defined as:

   - intermediate goods: 13+15+17
   - investment goods: 19+21+23+25+27+29
   - consumer goods: 31+33+35+37+39+41+43+45+47+49+51

3. Although in this chapter the European Community always means the present twelve member states, it must be remembered that the present members joined the Community in different years, Belgium, Germany, France, Italy, Luxembourg and the Netherlands founded the Community in 1958; Denmark, Ireland and the UK joined in 1973, Greece in 1981 and Portugal and Spain in 1986.

4. Until the 1960s France controlled Indo-China (Laos, Vietnam and Cambodia) and nearly a third of Africa. Among French ex-colonies, Algeria, Morocco, Reunion and Tunisia, are the main commercial partners.
5. In France's African ex-colonies, French is still the main language. In addition in Africa most of these countries form a monetary zone pegging to the French Franc: Benin, Burkina Faso, Cameroon, Central African Republic, Chad, Comores, Ivory Coast, Equatorial Guinea, Gabon, Mali, Niger, Senegal and Togo.
6. Until the mid-1970s Portugal had three colonies in Africa: Angola, Mozambique and Guinea Bissau. The Beira port in Mozambique was one of the most active in southern Africa.

REFERENCES

Chamberlain, M.E., 1985, *Decolonization: The Fall of the European Empires*, Oxford: Basil Blackwell.

Commission of the European Community (CEC), 1986, *EC/Developing Countries Trade. Industrial Products Analysis 1970–84* (Theme 6, Serie D), Luxembourg: Eurostat.

CEC, 1986a, 'ACP-EEC Trade: the Kiel Study', *Courier EC-ACP*, 98, July/Aug.

CEC, 1988, *External Trade. Statistical Yearbook*, Luxembourg: Eurostat.

CEC, 1988a, *Industry. Statistical Yearbook*, Luxembourg: Eurostat.

CEC, 1989, 'International Trade of the European Community', *European Economy*, 39, March.

CEC, 1990, *External Trade, Monthly Statistics*, Luxembourg: Eurostat, 1.

Cline, W.R., 1985, *Exports of Manufactures from Developing Countries*, Washington, DC: The Brookings Institution.

Davenport, M., 1986, *Trade Policy, Protectionism and the Third World*, London: Croom Helm.

Havrylyshin, O. and I.Alikhani, 1990, 'Changing Trade Among Developing Countries', *Economic Impact*, 69, Jan/March.

IMF, 1989, *Directions of Trade Statistics. Yearbook 1989*.

Mennes, L.B.M. and J. Kol (eds.), 1988, *European Trade Policies and the Developing World*, New York: Croom Helm.

Sideri, S., 1990, *La Communità Europea nell'interdipendenza mondiale*, Milan: Unicopli.

UNCTAD, 1989a, *Trade in Manufactures and Semi Manufactures of Developing Countries and Territories. 1989 Review*. TD/B/C.2/228, 17 Aug.

UNCTAD, 1989b, *Protectionism and Structural Adjustment*, TD/B/1240/Add.1, 14 Dec.

Waelbroeck, J. and J. Kol, 1987, *Export Opportunities for the South in the Evolving Pattern of World Trade*, Brussels: CEPS Papers 33.

Yeats, A.J., 1989, 'Developing Countries' Exports of Manufactures: Past and Future Implications of Shifting Patterns of Comparative Advantage', *The Developing Economies*, XXVII, 2, June.

APPENDIX

Geographical Analysis

European Community:	the Community of 12.
Mediterranean Countries:	Gibraltar, Malta, Cyprus, Israel, Gaza Strip, Morocco, Tunisia, Egypt, Spanish Sahara, Syria, Lebanon, Jordan.

Latin America:	Central and South America including the Caribbean.
OPEC:	Member Countries of OPEC excluding Venezuela and Ecuador.
Asian NICs:	Singapore, Taiwan, Philippines, South Korea, Hong Kong, Malaysia.
Africa:	All African countries except South Africa, North African Mediterranean countries and members of OPEC.
Rest of LDCs	All other non OECD countries except the former CMEA countries, South Africa and LDCs already included above. Many Asian countries including China, India, Pakistan and Thailand are listed in this group.

Product Analysis

The classification of goods presented in the tables is derived from the NACE-CLIO R44 for products and branches. The following table shows the definition of product classification used in the tables in terms of the NACE-CLIO R44 codes:

NACE-CLIO R44 codes

Agricultural products	01
Energy products	03+05+07+09+11
Total manufactures	13–51
Metalliferous ores	13
Non-metallic minerals	15
Chemical products	17
Metal products	19
Agricultural and industrial machinery	21
Office Machines	23
Electrical Goods	25
Motor Vehicles	27
Other transport equipment	29
Food, beverages	31+33+35+37+39

List of Contributors

Michael Davenport, Research Associate, Overseas Development Institute, London, UK.

Esperanza Duran, Consultant, UNCTAD and SELA, Geneva, Switzerland.

Roberto Funagalli, Researcher, Università Commerciale 'Lugiog Bocconi', Milan, Italy.

Antonella Mori, Researcher, Università Commerciale 'Luigi Bocconi', Milan, Italy.

Sheila Page, Research Fellow, Overseas Development Institute, London, UK.

Gianni Paramithiotti, Lecturer, Università Commerciale 'Luigi Bocconi', Milan, Italy.

Alessandro Pio, Lecturer, Università Commerciale 'Luigi Bocconi', Milan, Italy.

Jayshree Sengupta, Consultant, Brussels, Belgium.

Sandro Sideri, Professor, Institute of Social Studies, The Hague, The Netherlands.

Arianna Vannini, Researcher, Università Commericale 'Luigi Bocconi', Milan, Italy.

For Product Safety Concerns and Information please contact our EU representative GPSR@taylorandfrancis.com Taylor & Francis Verlag GmbH, Kaufingerstraße 24, 80331 München, Germany